Bite the Hand That Feeds You

Bite the Hand That Feeds You

Essays and Provocations

HENRY FAIRLIE

Edited and with an introduction by Jeremy McCarter

Foreword by Leon Wieseltier

A NEW REPUBLIC BOOK

Yale University Press   New Haven and London

Published with assistance from the Louis Stern Memorial Fund.

Set in type by Keystone Typesetting, Inc.
Printed in the United States of America.

Library of Congress Cataloging-in-Publication Data
Fairlie, Henry, 1924–1990.
Bite the hand that feeds you : essays and provocations / Henry Fairlie ;
edited by Jeremy McCarter.
p. cm.
Includes index.
ISBN 978-0-300-12383-8 (cloth : alk. paper)
I. McCarter, Jeremy, 1976– II. Title.
PN5123.F27A25 2009
814'.54—dc22   2008049888

A catalogue record for this book is available from the British Library.

This paper meets the requirements of ANSI/NISO Z39.48–1992
(Permanence of Paper).

10 9 8 7 6 5 4 3 2

CONTENTS

THE HARLOT'S PREROGATIVE
Writers and the Press

FOREWORD

Henry Fairlie was the most independent spirit I have so far
encountered in the highlands of journalism, which is of course a
profession made up entirely of independent spirits. He carried
his aversion to gangs and parties to extraordinary lengths, preferring friendlessness to clubbability, and regarding his alien-
ation of others, especially his admirers, as somehow a mark of
his probity. He regularly confirmed my belief that the surest sign
of intellectual integrity is the willingness to offend one's own
congregation, though as the years wore on it was no longer clear
who precisely belonged to Fairlie's congregation. He was not a
"contrarian"—his perversity was less calculated, more driven by
principle. He was an essentially solitary man, though he had a
talent for vivacity; and his provocations were never designed to
draw attention (or money) to himself. The objective of his out-
rages was not an invitation to dinner. Even when he was praising, he was impolite. For this reason, the salons and the press
rooms in various capitals received Fairlie warily: he came with a
rumor of trouble. He had an allergy to obligations. His indifference to conventional human attachments could make him
sloppy or hard, but also more open and more lucid. In the cen-
ters of power, Fairlie exemplified the temperament of the pe-
riphery. He was not an insider, but an outsider up close. The
concept of "the Establishment," after all, could have been coined
only from such a paradoxical standpoint: near enough to know
its ways, far enough to find them strange.

The writings of Henry Fairlie belong to that period in recent antiquity when journalism existed in some relation to literature. He was not a reporter, though he relished the labor of description; he was not a pundit, though he was overflowing in his opinions. He was professional, in that he could be counted upon, eventually, for "copy"; and he was unprofessional, in that his copy could be wild. As a journalist he behaved like a writer, as a writer he behaved like a journalist. His literary cultivation was vast—even in his most reduced circumstances, when he was living in a small room in the back offices of *The New Republic*, he kept the complete Dickens on his window, where in the winter the bindings stiffened from the cold of the glass and the pages softened from the heat of the radiator; and many of his essays would have been perfectly in place in *Household Words*. He was confident of the enlightening effects of his own experience; but his journalism, while intensely personal, was almost never about himself. Though he was usually trustworthy, he was never objective. Instead he made partiality into an art. He was well-named, because he was always animated by an interest in fairness; and he was ill-named, because he was never fairly anything. What Fairlie brought to journalism, in England and in America, was his intelligent vehemence, the generous gift of his subjectivity. He did not "do" voice, he had one, the only one of its kind. In millions of words it gave evidence of the intellectual advantages that ill-fittingness may confer.

While it is common that literary sensibilities turn to political commentary, it is exceedingly rare that they know much about, or have much respect for, the unglamorous particulars of politics. In this way, too, Fairlie stood out. He adored politics, and saw even policy as a human expression. He was fascinated by the baroque entanglement of political ideas and political personalities. Like Tocqueville and Bagehot and Bryce, he was peculiarly enlivened by the observation of institutions, and in the machinery of government he found occasions for an inquiry into ideals and desires. Fairlie was a conservative who demanded large things of government, genuine betterments; who believed that the enemy of tradition is not modernity, but cruelty and stupidity. A child of the most historical century, his sense of the stakes never deserted him: nothing repelled him more than presidents or prime ministers who failed to transcend politics for history. His political writing was frequently savage, because he never became accustomed to historical disappointment—he was never too knowing for anger. People who were in a position to relieve some suffering but did not do so—they were Fairlie's villains.

In his time he was one of the most distinguished practitioners of ridicule as an instrument of criticism. Even when he was vicious, he was in the service of an argument. The bruising flamboyance of Fairlie's portraiture, when it was not just the wicked play of his perceptions, was a method for the demystification of status and reputation. Was there ever a less snobbish student of snobbery? He revered the offices, not the people who coveted and occupied them. Whatever his political worldview, and I cannot say that I exactly grasped it, Fairlie was an egalitarian in his bones. He was a loner who could talk to anybody. Over and over again he fell in love with ordinary life, and his most withering political writing was usually a protest against the traduction of ordinary life by power.

While he was not quite a man of the people, he was a man for the people—and he took pains to go beyond an editorialist's sentimentality in his attitude toward them, whoever they are. He set out to know them. While the legends of journalism were being ushered into the hideaways of the Capitol to have their importance proved to them on background, Fairlie was earnestly chatting about the issues of the day with interns and receptionists and bartenders (the ones who were foolish enough to let him open a tab). He hated the idea that he belonged to an elite.

His attraction to the demos was virtually erotic. The capital never obscured the country, for him.

His journeys into America were his deepest exhilarations—he saw equality, or the promise of equality, everywhere he went, and he determined to make himself equal to it. For Fairlie, America was a paradise of possibility. His curiosity, which was boundless, found its counterpart, its most perfect object, in the boundlessness of American reality. He loved this country with the ardor, and the disputatiousness, of a convert. Conversations with Fairlie were refreshments of one's patriotism. In the years when Americans were falling all over the fatuities of Alistair Cooke, it was Fairlie who was the great English explainer of America. He was Bryce's true heir—Fairlie's purview, too, extended from the character of party organizations to "the pleasantness of American life"—except that he was the better writer. He had a way of analyzing the American subject into lyricism. At the conclusion of his ferocity, there was joy.

He wrote, and wrote, and wrote. In the years when I knew him, it was what he lived for. Every morning I measured his productivity of the night before with a glance at the bottle of bourbon that I kept on my desk. When he was not producing essays and reviews, he was composing long epistles to various editors at my magazine, helpful accounts of our many errors. His annual Christmas poem was a riotous moment of reckoning for us all, and its clever quatrains spared no one: he was, as I say, a democrat. Occasionally he would leave a silly poem on my typewriter, and I would respond with a silly poem of my own, and in these duels of doggerel he invariably prevailed. And sometimes there would be just a brief intoxicated effusion, such as this one from New Year's Day in 1988: "Dear Leon, Re Friday: I wear a tie even when I fuck. What do you think held the Empire together? Henry." In editorial meetings he sometimes looked bored or distracted, until suddenly he intervened with an uncannily penetrating remark. (Nothing jarred him back to the discussion more immediately than the sound of an ideological piety from the other end of the table.) He was sly in his attention: he did not want you to know how much he was noticing. A young researcher in our office once reported to me something that Henry had observed about me in the early hours of the morning, and I still recall it, with surprise and with gratitude, as the most unexpectedly acute remark about my particular formation that I have ever heard.

Late one night Henry slipped on the marble floor in the lobby of our building and broke some bones, and in the hospital his physical being quickly crumbled, away from all the drink, away from all the discourse. He was the first person whose dying I witnessed, and as I watched him decline beneath the tubes and the pipes I muttered to a colleague who was devotedly attending him that this, too, the look of a man's end, was one of Henry's wise and emphatic lessons. His memorial service was held in Abraham Lincoln's church. As "Jerusalem" was sung, his brilliant and messy life seemed almost to assume a shape. I have still not stopped assigning him books for review, because in this long and turbulent hour of American re-creation there are so many illusions that he could best eviscerate, and so many attainments that he could best celebrate; but the dead never file.

Leon Wieseltier

Introduction

Even by the standards of a profession that likes to salute its own, the tributes to Henry Fairlie were unique. In the *Independent*, he was dubbed "a mythic figure" who had been, for a time, "the most influential journalist in the country." "His was a story of triumph and disaster," according to the *Daily Telegraph*. Sir Peregrine Worsthorne, the editor who had been a longtime friend, called him "quite simply the best political journalist, writing in English, in the last fifty years."

Political journalism was Fairlie's chief profession, and it is for a political column that he is best known: a 1955 article in which he coined the term "the Establishment." But in a career that spanned five decades, Fairlie was also a social critic, an observer of contemporary manners, and a memoirist, bringing to all his work, in a colleague's phrase, "sweep, colour, perspective, and drama." The combination made him extremely popular: between the Second World War and his death in 1990, his byline appeared in virtually every major newspaper and magazine in Great Britain and the United States.

Fairlie's reputation has declined since that burst of accolades, and not just in the ways endemic to departed journalists. In many respects, his path runs parallel to that of a contemporary with whom he occasionally sparred in print, Kenneth Tynan: precocious fame in the 1950s, early retreat from London journalistic prominence, self-imposed exile in America, untimely death (Tynan was 53, Fairlie 66), and posthumous revelations of messy indiscretions. The letters and memoirs of Fairlie's friends and acquaintances have demonstrated that even in the louche world of Fleet Street, where every vice found a champion, he distinguished himself: he drank; his finances were a crime against responsibility; his charm and darkly handsome looks availed him of endless affairs. If such charges have occluded Fairlie's reputation more than Tynan's, it's in part because of the relative availability of their work. While the basis for Tynan's preeminence as a critic lies secure in his many published collections, Fairlie's columns and essays—the short and mid-length pieces that best show his brilliance—gather dust.

Plenty about our world has changed in the twenty, forty, or fifty years since Fairlie wrote his stories. Yet when I encountered his work in the archives of the *New Republic*, it remained timely —urgently so. The longevity is due, in part, to his crisp, erudite style, a product of his extraordinarily broad reading in history and fiction. More crucially, Fairlie's work holds up because, at his best, he used little incidents to explore the eternal, fundamental qualities of our political and social life. The marvel of his work is not that he's still relevant in 2009 but that, as long as politicians slouch toward compromise, and America fumbles to fulfill its role in the world, and journalists crave media celebrity, he'll still be relevant twenty, forty, or fifty years from now.

Beyond the continuing potency of Fairlie's arguments about the life of British politics, the manners and morals of America, and the responsibilities and transgressions of journalists—the three sections of this book—his stories command our attention because of the glimpses they provide of their author. His behavior was often erratic and sometimes self-destructive, leading him to a level of penury hard to imagine for someone with his abilities today. Quiet and reserved when sober, he could be loud and combative when drunk. His relationships with his wife and three children were complicated, to put it mildly; his treatment of the editors and proprietors who signed his checks over the years bordered on the mutinous—one reason why he planned to call his memoir "Bite the Hand That Feeds You." Still: "The lower he sank in debauchery the higher he aimed in his work," wrote Worsthorne.

Because of his virtues and in spite of his flaws (though, at some junctures, it seemed like the other way around), Fairlie managed to survive for thirty-six years as a freelance journalist. Toward the end of that unlikely run, he developed a reputation in some quarters as a crank or a curmudgeon, but his *New Republic* colleagues got nearer the mark when they remembered him as "one of the last tribunes of a tougher, richer, grander time." They knew enough of his story to understand that here was an extraordinary, improbable man—brilliant and calamitously flawed—who was loved and reviled, and almost always forgiven.

ENGLAND

In 1937, Lord Beaverbrook, one of Britain's most powerful press barons, held a lavish dinner in Fleet Street for the staff of his *Sunday Express.* Some guests noticed that one of their colleagues had fallen ill. A cab was summoned, and the ailing man sent home. By the time it arrived, he was dead. Telling the story years later, Henry Fairlie would roar, "That's how I'd like to go!"

It might seem an indecorous way for Fairlie to remember the death of his father. Still the story captivates because of how well it distills essential qualities of both men: the Fleet Street career, the carousing, the passion for newsprint suggesting that ink in the veins may be hereditary.

Henry Jones Fairlie was born January 13, 1924, the fifth of seven children. Though his pride in his heritage led many to believe that he was raised in Scotland, in fact he spent his youth in London. His father, James, had come to work for

Beaverbrook after he "threw up his patrimony" (as Henry put it), abandoning his family's farm in the Scottish highlands to make a precocious rise through Fleet Street journalism.

Money was often scarce in Henry's youth, particularly after his father drank himself out of an editor's post in the middle of the Depression. Nevertheless, James and his wife, Marguerita (née Vernon, the daughter of a Presbyterian minister), sent the boy to the well-regarded Byron House and Highgate School. Henry's happiest and most instructive days, however, came on school breaks, which he spent at the family farms near Monikie, a small town outside Dundee. From watching the seasons pass there, he later wrote, "a deep conservatism, a belief that nothing very much changes, and then changes only slowly, was bred into me."

That conservatism, too, arrived only slowly. Ineligible for combat duty because of a lifelong heart problem, Fairlie spent most of the Second World War at Corpus Christi, Oxford. When not studying (and he was quite frequently not studying— after he managed second-class honors in Modern History, his tutor said he no longer had any confidence in the exam system), Fairlie threw himself into work for the Liberal Party. He was so drawn to the idea of remaking the world after the war that he got himself selected to be the perennial third-place party's standing candidate for the parliamentary seat of Southport, near Liverpool. He admitted that twenty-three struck him as "a provocatively early age" to run for office, and in this he was not alone. During a speech attacking the dairy policies of the prewar Conservative government, a woman called out, "All that you knew about milk before the war was from your mother's breasts!"

By the next general election in 1950, Fairlie's progress as a journalist had led him away from the campaign trail. He had joined the *Manchester Evening News* right after leaving Oxford, first as a beat reporter, then a leader writer, and had already shown himself to be a controversialist. He recalled that his editorials supporting the Jews in Palestine, even when Jewish militant organizations were blowing up British soldiers, sparked protests outside the paper's office. David Astor, sharp-eyed for fresh talent, brought him onboard the *Observer* in 1949. In part because of newsprint rationing, the paper made little use of him, miring him in his unhappiest year in journalism. But during this period he married Lisette Todd Phillips, the sister-in-law of a journalist he knew, and his professional life took a new turn when he got a recommendation from Astor that would set him on his way. Just twenty-six years old, Fairlie was hired by the *Times,* then widely regarded as the best newspaper in the world. His writing began to make him famous among the same people who had revered James Fairlie, and in the same pubs. The sin of the father, Henry wrote later, "has been visited upon his son."

As the chief author of the *Times*'s leaders on domestic politics—another post precociously attained—Fairlie wrote pieces that were more substantial than editorials in newspapers today. They ran longer and tended to involve direct observation of party conferences and House debates—virtually a political column without a byline. Although Fairlie revered Winston Churchill and increasingly sympathized with his conservative policies, his leaders gave him the chance to develop a crucial and distinctive part of his worldview: the sanctity of the political process, regardless of which side won or lost. "A Government which feels strong and an Opposition which is more coherent: these are the hopes held out by the conferences at Margate," reads a leader that ran after the party meetings in 1953. "They could be the foundations of an excellent parliamentary session, in which the national interest is pursued, according to their own lights, by both sides of the House of Commons."

Fairlie's editors entrusted their young charge with some daunting responsibilities, like rewriting the paper's monumental obituary of Churchill, drafts of which dated to the nineteenth century. (After the piece ran in 1965, the editor, Sir William Haley, sent Fairlie three copies of a specially printed Royal edition of that day's paper. "No one can possibly have a greater claim to these copies than yourself," he wrote.) Thanks to the force of his writing and the paper's influence, plenty of people outside the paper were beginning to know his name too. But Fairlie wanted the freedom to write what he wanted when he wanted. Out of some combination of principle and obstinacy (with a dash of self-sabotage), he decided to try his luck as a freelancer. Just after his thirtieth birthday, he quit the last full-time job he would ever have.

Amid imminent financial trouble—he already had two small mouths to feed—Fairlie's independence allowed him to help shape a new style in British journalism. Political columns at this time tended to be oracular, without the lively prose or individual insight that's now taken for granted. Alan Watkins, a distinguished political columnist in his own right, credits Hugh Massingham of the *Observer* with having brought to the politics of the 1940s and '50s the "wit and psychological insight" of a novelist, which he was. Fairlie admired Massingham, and, when the *Spectator* offered him its political commentary column, leapt at the chance to follow the master. "If Massingham in the *Observer* was the pioneer," wrote Watkins in his memoir *A Short Walk Down Fleet Street*, "it was Fairlie in *The Spectator* who carried the change through."

Fairlie chose as his nom de plume "Trimmer," after the seventeenth-century statesman Lord Halifax, who, in response to attacks on his seeming inconsistency, had written a pamphlet titled *The Character of a Trimmer*. Constant shifts of balance, or "trimming," Halifax had written, were the best way to keep a steady course between two extremes. Thus from one week to the next, even the politicians whom Fairlie admired, like future prime minister Harold Macmillan, would find themselves alternately lionized and belittled.

To colleagues as well as subjects, Fairlie could be "maddening," according to future *Spectator* editor Brian Inglis. "He had a remarkable attraction for girls, coupled with difficulty in arranging his schedule, so that they were forever ringing up to find where he was, and why he wasn't where he said he would be to meet them. His copy tended to arrive long after it was promised; he boasted that he had never missed a deadline, but our Wednesday evenings were plagued by his near-misses."

Aggravation notwithstanding, Fairlie was the magazine's "greatest asset at this time," Inglis wrote in his autobiography— the chief reason why the *Spectator* was beginning to rival the *New Statesman* as the journal to read first. His writing seems, quite literally, to have changed people's lives. While studying for the bar in these years, young Alan Watkins would read both magazines on the train, always starting with Fairlie's column. "On one occasion I remember thinking and asking myself the question: Now, who would you rather be?" he wrote in a memoir of his life as one of Britain's leading political columnists. "Would you rather be Mr. Justice Devlin (even then the most glamorous judge . . .)? Or would you rather be Henry Fairlie? And I answered it: Well I would rather be Mr. Fairlie."

Churchill's return to power in 1951 brought an era of relative consensus to British politics: stable Tory majorities in Parliament and an economy governed by "Butskellism," a fusion of the names of the Labour and Conservative chancellors who ran it. This consensus made Fairlie itchy. In 1954, he wrote an important essay for *Encounter* arguing that the political genius of Britain was not, as middle-class politicians would like to think, the ability to reach a compromise—it was the capacity for conflict, the willingness of MPs and journalists alike to do battle in defense of their beliefs. This was the context in which Fairlie wrote—and the nation's political class read—what turned out to be his most famous column.

In September 1955, just prior to the release of a White Paper confirming that Guy Burgess and Donald Maclean of the Foreign Office had defected to Moscow, Fairlie devoted a column to the network of social acquaintances who had rushed to defend the men's families from press scrutiny, a nexus that he dubbed "the Establishment."

> By the "Establishment" I do not mean only the centres of official power—though they are certainly part of it—but rather the whole matrix of official and social relations within which power is exercised. The exercise of power in Britain (more specifically, in England) cannot be understood unless it is recognised that it is exercised socially.

The column convulsed the letters page of the *Spectator* for months. Various grandees denounced Fairlie for implying that they were treacherous, but others rose to say that the Establishment did indeed exist and had wreaked far more havoc for far longer than anyone realized. Fairlie's detractors were not mollified when he wrote that he was glad that the Establishment existed because it kept even worse influences from operating— possibly because he couldn't resist adding that the strident response to his column by "all the right people" illustrated his point exactly.

By the time the debate ended, a new term had entered the political discourse. The phrase made the rounds of other magazines and newspapers and became the subject of a book-length collection of essays. The *Spectator* published "The Establishment Game," a board spread across two pages. Others had used the phrase before, as Fairlie well knew: in a 1968 essay for the *New Yorker*, he traced its lineage back to Emerson. Nonetheless, for introducing the term to the vocabulary of modern politics, the *Oxford English Dictionary* would name him its locus classicus.

"The Establishment" made Fairlie famous—it even got him tagged "the first of the Angry Young Men." Still he wished the term might disappear. He spent the rest of his life trying to explain what it did *not* mean. The Establishment is not a group of powerful people like C. Wright Mills's "power elite"; it is those who surround the power elite. "It is they who say to the power merchants that 'That is not good form.' It is they who query, 'We don't do that sort of thing, do we?'" Nor did he think the concept of the Establishment could be translated easily beyond England, though he watched many try. He was shocked to hear "the demure phrase which I had once put to paper" tossed around in the 1960s by the likes of Students for a Democratic Society and Charles Manson's followers, and he wrote that he came to feel "responsible for all the upheavals from America to Germany, since they were all rebellions against 'the Establishment.'"

As Fairlie's influence grew in the mid-1950s, so did his notoriety. He had been frequenting the pubs and restaurants of Fleet Street since his first days in London, when many an old hack wanted to buy a drink for the son of Jimmy Fairlie. Now the front bar at El Vino became a regular haunt—a popular, noisy, sometimes combative destination. "We were young then—grandly poor and irreverent," Fairlie recalled. "A group of hungry young journalists, intent largely on enjoying ourselves at the expense of our elders and betters." Their employers weren't the only unwitting backers of their fun: to finance his two-binge-a-day lifestyle, Fairlie spent the money he had and then some, often signing checks in his wife's name. When the bank cut her off, he told her to go to the branch and extract more in person. The manager refused her, so Fairlie went to the bank himself and brought him around: his charm was sadistic.

Fairlie's heavy-drinking set also included Kingsley Amis, then having his breakthrough success with *Lucky Jim*. The publication of Amis's letters in 2000 revealed Fairlie's affair with his wife, Hilly. Though Fairlie planned to run off with her and her children, this romance, like so many before and later, eventually came to naught—but not before Amis wrote a letter diagnosing with some acuity the mercurial streak that would cause Fairlie and his loved ones so much pain. A second marriage such as the one he and Hilly contemplated would demand "the utmost patience, resolution, calm, self-restraint etc.—qualities rather less noticeable in you than in others," he wrote.

Fairlie's boldness got him in more public forms of trouble, as well. On November 2, 1956, he was a panelist on an episode of *Any Questions?*, broadcast live on BBC radio. The host, Freddy Grisewood, began the program by warning the panelists not to mention the subject they plainly wanted to discuss: Britain's invasion of Egypt to reclaim the Suez Canal, which had begun a few days earlier. Doing so would violate the Fourteen-Day Rule, which in those years prohibited BBC guests from discussing an issue set to be debated in Parliament in the next two weeks. Fairlie immediately set out to break the rule, trying to smuggle Suez into the conversation by arguing that it was right that "three days ago, British forces went into Ruritania." As the crowd burst into laughter and applause, the BBC pulled the show off the air until Grisewood restored order.

Yet not for the first time, what should have been a triumph for Fairlie turned into a mishap. No sooner had the show ended than he was arrested. Having failed to turn up for an earlier bankruptcy proceeding, he had been found in contempt of court. Thanks to the listings in *Radio Times*, he had been easily traced by the authorities, who carted him away to Brixton. "At least I know where he is tonight," said his wife, trying to put the debacle in a positive light. He spent his several days in jail begging her for letters that left one side of the page blank. He needed a place to write.

Fairlie's proven ability to generate (or fall into) trouble boosted his profile so much that when he left the *Spectator* in 1956 for the larger audience and better pay of the *Daily Mail* (without informing his former colleagues, according to Inglis), his pieces ran with his photo and boldface author bios describing him at different points as a "controversial Right-Wing political commentator," "a top political writer of independent outlook," and "the most controversial political columnist in Britain."

This uncertainty about whether Fairlie was right-wing or independent reflected a tension increasingly apparent in his work. Like Churchill, he could best be described in these years as a Tory Democrat, an outlook he later described somewhat romantically as standing alongside "the Crown and People against the barons and capitalists." His politics led him to argue for a restoration of British leadership in the world (which he thought possible through the Commonwealth) and to demand respect for Christianity and other adhesives of English society in the face of the material prosperity that he saw coarsening postwar life.

Those imperatives didn't always line up with the Conservative platform, a split never more evident than during the 1959 general election. The Conservative Party slogan "You've never had it so good" struck Fairlie as craven and amoral. It led him to write—in a conservative paper—that he hoped his party would lose, and he predicted it would do so. When Macmillan and the Tories crushed the opposition, letters calling for his dismissal poured into the *Daily Mail*. As he recounted later, the proprietor, Lord Rothermere, didn't fire Fairlie, but he did send him to Africa for a three-month exile. Once again he made the most of his chances, interviewing Haile Selassie and landing some scoops about the rapid pace of decolonization already under way. He even covered Macmillan's famous "wind of change" speech, in which the prime minister told the South African Parliament that Britain would not support apartheid.

Fairlie's final break with the *Daily Mail* was even more ignominious, but this time it had nothing to do with politics. In May 1960, he received a cash advance to cover the Paris summit of Eisenhower, Khrushchev, Macmillan, and De Gaulle. He stopped in Fleet Street along the way and, as he usually did when "in funds," started buying rounds for friends. Soon they were off to an expensive dinner, also paid for by Fairlie. The next morning, he returned to the newsroom. He had spent his advance; he needed another. His byline continued to appear for a few weeks, but by the end of the summer of 1960, he was out of a job. For sixteen years, Fairlie did not write as regularly for any publication as he had for the *Daily Mail*.

Handsome and articulate, Fairlie continued to appear regularly on *What the Papers Say* and to make documentaries for Granada. He even did some work for his father's old employer, Lord Beaverbrook, conducting a series of long interviews with Harold Macmillan that elicited the prime minister's famous line, "If people want a sense of purpose, they should get it from their archbishops." But by the time he finished covering the 1964 general election, he wanted a change.

In 1965, Fairlie got the *Sunday Telegraph* to send him on his first trip to the United States, a country, he later recalled, about which he and his friends cared little. "What interested us about America was what it did, the exercise of its power, especially as it affected us, but otherwise we were not much interested in what

it was," he wrote. Whatever lingering disinterest he may have felt vanished when he reached Dulles Airport. Fairlie returned from his seven-month visit to inform his family that hereafter they would live in America.

Their grudging preparations gave him just enough time in Britain to appear on the television program *Three After Six,* where he suggested that his acquaintance Lady Antonia Fraser corrupted the young. She promptly brought a suit against the Independent Television Authority and Fairlie, seeking damages. Hounded by creditors, pursued for libel, and entranced by America, Fairlie left England early in 1966, telling his family it would be a three-year trip. They returned much sooner than that; he never did.

AMERICA

In the 1970s, Fairlie read the accounts of more than two hundred English visitors to America and wrote about his predecessors' experiences, one of several occasions when he completed a book-length manuscript that was never published. While proclaiming Lord Bryce, the author of the two-volume *American Commonwealth,* "the greatest of all English commentators on the society and politics of the United States," the twin poles of "Spectacle" (as he planned to call his book) were to be Dickens, who caught a cold, fought over his copyright, and had a generally miserable time in America, and Thackeray, who wrote letters home expressing joy at these new people and their customs. For Fairlie, the two novelists expressed the essential conundrum: "America keeps asking the traveller from the old world, who has come to ask questions of it, 'Who are you?'; and one either throws one's hat in the air with Thackeray at the sheer invigoration of the question, or sulks with Dickens."

In this, Fairlie proved to be a Thackeray man from the start.

He was no wide-eyed naïf when he landed on these shores. He was forty-one ("reassuringly, the same age as Columbus when he discovered America") and had reported from more than a dozen foreign countries. Still, the size and the customs and the manners and the ease delighted him. He was taken to a Washington supermarket, where he gaped; he was shown the view from Mt. Vernon—all that landscape rolling away to the horizon —and gaped some more. "So this is why you threw us out," he said to the friend who had brought him. "If I had gazed on all this land, I would have thrown us out."

Ostensibly he was here to cover civil rights. He had arrived on March 8, 1965, the day after the "Bloody Sunday" march from Selma to Montgomery. Starting toward Alabama by bus, he made so many stops that a trip that could have taken days stretched into months. This gave him a feel for the dimensions of the country and the opportunity to marvel at a free and stable society that could span a continent. "More than ever before," he wrote later, "the United States of America, by this example, is the last best hope of mankind; and for that reason alone no country more deserves our study and understanding." Alan Watkins has noted that Fairlie viewed politicians as "players in a great historical drama." Fairlie realized that in both day-to-day journalism and the sweep of history, America was the big story of his time. There was nowhere he'd rather have been.

When Fairlie brought his wife and two daughters to Washington in 1966, they settled in an elegant house in Georgetown. But neither his behavior nor his financial state had improved. In February 1967, while Lisette Fairlie was in England visiting their sixteen-year-old son, Simon, whom they had enrolled in boarding school, her husband called to say they'd been turned out of the house. He was putting Charlotte and Emma on a plane back to England. It was the functional end of the marriage.

As Fairlie's life grew more itinerant, his projects grew more sustained. In 1968, he finished his first book, *The Life of Politics*. It was, he wrote,

> an attempt, not made since the days of Bagehot, to describe how politics are *lived*—hence, the title of the book—by the politicians of a free country, and by the people of that country through their politicians. It is not an entirely flattering portrait of politicians, and yet it *is* a celebration of them; for the simple reason that what is being described is the public life of a free country and, however jaded we may sometimes feel when we watch the operations of politics, it is impossible in the end not to admire the at once sublime and ridiculous process by which free men contrive to govern themselves.

At its best, the book drew on his personal experiences with political figures. He devoted one section to "the patience of politics," a phrase that the Tory official R. A. Butler had used in an interview with him in 1959. Fairlie thought it expressed "more vividly than any other single phrase, the character of politics in a free country." For the politician, it demands "that he should never try to seize imaginary initiatives or seek speedy results; that he should wait calmly for his opportunity. . . . Above all, it demands that he should never, whatever the provocation, cease to trust in the right instincts of a free people." Yet there was an equal need for patience from the public, "to trust in the slow working of their institutions. . . . They must be patient of the politicians themselves; of their vanities and their peculiarities, which are usually only the vanities and peculiarities of themselves, but appearing larger than life; and of their weaknesses and faults, until these are seen to be pernicious." Not surprisingly, this reverent vision won welcome in Parliament.

Despite long and technical sections about the workings of British government, it also won favor on Capitol Hill, where the first two chapters were read into the *Congressional Record*.

Fairlie won an even broader readership around Washington with his next and best-known book, *The Kennedy Promise*. Published in 1973, it belongs to the first wave of revisionist accounts of the Camelot myth of John F. Kennedy's presidency. He criticized JFK for being too bent on action, too eager to keep the nation at a fever pitch. "An entire people was to be governed by keeping it in a constant state of expectation of the achievements which would be made possible, not merely by political action, but by the actions of a single ruler." Even more than *The Life of Politics,* the book bears the intellectual fingerprints of Michael Oakeshott, whom he called "the most formative conservative political thinker of his generation." The book's closing wish in particular has an Oakeshottian ring: Fairlie called for a return of "the conversation of politics, which pays attention to the actual world, historical and political, its untidiness and its intractability." The politics of expectation had to be rejected, he argued, in order to make politics once more "the art of the necessary," the pursuit of specific national aims through focused inspiration. No one had done this better, he thought, than Franklin D. Roosevelt.

Most reviewers found merit in Fairlie's critique of Kennedy's leadership but did not buy his conclusion that much of the tumult of the 1960s could be traced to it. Arthur Schlesinger, Jr., whose affection for the Kennedys won him no end of abuse from Fairlie over the years, called the book "in effect a dramatization of Oakeshottian philosophy"—not a bad thing in itself, but wedded to what Schlesinger deemed a "wrong-headed" idea about Kennedy, who was much less of an adventurer than Fairlie wanted to think. James Q. Wilson suggested this was because as a foreigner—specifically, from a country where the rhetorical

side of politics has a special importance—Fairlie had placed too much focus on Kennedy's words and not enough on his deeds, which told a more complicated story.

The most indelible reader response came in February 1973, when, on a trip to California, President Nixon made a gift of the book to the state's governor. Fairlie was glad to collect the royalty on the sale but derived little other satisfaction from the transaction: he was sure Ronald Reagan would learn the wrong lessons from it.

In the early 1970s, Fairlie left Washington for what turned out to be a pivotal trip to Boulder, Colorado. His participation in the World Affairs Conference, a freewheeling annual talkfest run by the irascible sociologist Howard Higman, led to a multiyear stay. There amid the Rockies he began thinking more and more of America, not Britain, as home—a shift that made him feel "a certain sense of treason or betrayal," he would later say. He never gave a definitive answer for why he didn't return to England after 1966, leaving his friends to find their own explanations among varying combinations of outstanding debts and angry husbands there, and freedom and new friends here. He came closest to explaining himself in an essay around this time for *Encounter*.

One thing Fairlie loved about America, he wrote, was being free of the "family-ness" of England, by which he meant "the immobility of the individuals and therefore of the society; everyone in his or her own place; everyone doing and saying and being what he or she has always done and said and been." From this distance it's not clear why Fairlie chose this, of the many metaphors at his disposal, to describe England's condition. Though he and his family sometimes fought or spent years in hurt or angry silence, his children remember that he was often a loving, attentive presence in their lives. (His daughter Charlotte, an undergraduate in Boulder during Fairlie's years there, recalls how he built a bird feeder for her and took her to museums in Washington.) He also had a good Tory's respect for the family as a social institution worth preserving. Still, "family" seems to have meant "stagnation" for Fairlie, and that meant "Britain." "Of course one misses it," he wrote of his homeland, "but I do not miss in it what is suffocating, and I have come more and more to believe that England is a country that is suffocated, more today than in the past, by its sense of its own family-ness."

Although he continued to write occasionally for British audiences after his years in Boulder, covering the 1980 presidential race for the *Spectator* (where he embarrassed himself by predicting that Carter would defeat the "slippered pantaloon" Reagan) and writing a weekly column for the *Times* (where he repeated his perennial complaint about rambunctious American children elbowing in on civilized adult life and the parents who let them do so), his professional focus turned more and more to covering the politics and culture of the United States for the people who lived there: in short, he would explain America to the Americans.

In 1974, he wrote a long essay for *Encounter* on the lessons of Watergate. The blame lay, he believed, with Nixon's defective view of politics as merely a business of "who gets what, when, how," and having no opponents, only enemies. The fault was a lack of political character, which is distinct from personal character.

> The character of a politician is to be found in the connection which he makes between the ideals and the realities of political life; in the nature of his relationships with political friends and of his dealings with political rivals; in the manner in which he returns to the people the trust which he invites them to bestow on him; in his sense of the dignity of his

office, and his reinforcement of it from day to day with his own dignity; above all, in his awareness that he is the focus, not only of power but of affections, not only of interests but of loyalties, not only of anxieties but of aspirations, not only of functions but of ideals.

Fairlie also continued developing a theme first sounded a few years earlier, when he lectured Senator J. William Fulbright (who had called him, because of Fairlie's support for the Vietnam war, "a British Gunga Din") on the proper understanding of American power—a still-ringing call:

> I have a belief, of which I cannot rid myself, that the Western tradition contains more understanding of what freedom is, a more strenuous will to maintain and extend it, more hope that it may one day be enjoyed by millions outside the West, than any other civilisation, either past or present. The West may be superior only in this, but it is ours, our tradition and our life, and I refuse to turn my back on it, and drop out. The survival of this tradition depends today on the power of America, and the exertion of that power. It will commit follies, and it will commit hapless crimes. But, while criticising and hoping to reduce the number of these, neither the Americans themselves nor the rest of the West have any right to condemn *facilely or maliciously* the exercise of power by the one nation which can preserve the Western idea of freedom for us and for the future. It is not "anti-Americanism" which is worrying—it is natural and healthy—but a form of anti-Americanism which sometimes suggests that the West itself has lost its will.

His capacity to celebrate—and castigate—his new country got a major boost in 1976, when editors at the *Washington Post* offered him a biweekly column. He told the editors he didn't want to write another column on politics but rather an essay on whatever caught his interest. "Paul Klee once said that drawing is 'taking a line for a walk,' and the essayist is really taking an idea (and his words) for a walk." In "Fairlie at Large," as the feature was called, he would range freely, trying to capture "something of the weave of life."

Sometimes he used the essays to revel in his enthusiasms, like space exploration, which he thought would give our doubting, self-absorbed civilization "not only the humility, but again the majesty that we need." More often, he tweaked Americans for being uptight and frequently unfree. The school cancellations that followed the first hint of snow in the Washington area were symptoms of "a refusal of discomfort and inconvenience [that] is one of the irreducible elements in what we slowly begin to understand as the American character." The impulse could be healthy, fueling innovation to benefit the greatest number, or detrimental, as in extreme cases it made people think they should be insulated from unhappiness. But the essay that, according to Fairlie, "outstripped all the others as a favourite from the moment it appeared" and that strangers would continue to bring up well into the 1980s was known as his "baths and showers" piece, about how the neuroses that afflict so many Americans might be quelled by a good soak in a proper tub.

"Fairlie at Large" lasted six years, a remarkably stable run for a writer who had long since earned a reputation for wearing out his welcome. The 1982 editorial change that finally brought the column to an end arrived at a terrible moment, mere weeks after Rupert Murdoch fired Harold Evans as editor of the *Times*, bringing an end to his column there as well. Fairlie went on freelancing for *Harper's, Vogue,* and others, but for the rest of his career most of his American studies would appear in the magazine that he'd figuratively—and, soon, literally—call home.

Shortly after Martin Peretz bought the *New Republic* in 1974, he installed as editor one of his former students from Harvard, Michael Kinsley. Over the next decade and a half, the magazine developed a reputation for brilliant heterodoxy. Fairlie, the conservative who wrote fondly of socialism and saved his sharpest jabs for Republicans, fit in perfectly. His colleagues recall that he had a formal, almost shy air around the office and often communicated with people just down the hall with letters dozens of pages long. But if someone made an argument that was specious or ill-informed at weekly editorial meetings, his counterattacks could be as ferocious as they were unpredictable, since no one could guess from which point on the political spectrum they might come.

The romantic Toryism that had made Fairlie so hard to pin down on Fleet Street made him a complete anomaly in Washington. His high expectations for what government should do and his wariness of the disruptive power of capitalism aligned him with Democrats; his belief in American force abroad and respect for social traditions sided him with Republicans. Washington in the Reagan era did not know what to make of this.

Partisans on both sides would, over the years, take plenty of fire from Fairlie. But as he demonstrated in an early series of essays on the political parties for the *New Republic,* the right wing would get the worst of it. As a self-described conservative, Fairlie alternated between bemusement and rage at Republicans who not only wanted to dismantle the government but seemed to hate politics itself. "The true conservative, with the politics of his country in his blood, delights in its skirmishes and battles, delights in difference, delights in his opponents; and he could never call his opponent a traitor," he wrote. Read today, during a time of upheaval in the conservative movement, his outsider's perspective makes his stories about the Republicans especially pertinent—and provocative. He offered them the advice that the great journalist Walter Bagehot had offered British conservatives a century earlier: "Try a little enjoyment."

By contrast, the Democratic Party, even when it erred—and Fairlie was prepared to say it erred often—remained "the normal governing party of the most powerful and most restless free nation in the world." At a time when fascism and communism were on the march, he argued, FDR and the Democratic Party had brought "gusto" to politics and proved that democracy works.

The Parties, a book-length collection of these essays, was not well reviewed. ("If the quality of the insights came close to matching the quality of the insults, it would be a helluva book," wrote David Broder.) One problem is that here, as in so many other cases, his work functions best at short and medium length. The gap between his books and his journalism is particularly wide in this case, since the best of the original essays had been so fine. Fairlie's columns for the *Daily Mail* and *Daily Express,* like so much short-form journalism, had sometimes lacked thoughtfulness; at the other extreme, his erudition had made some of his work for *Encounter* and "Fairlie at Large" too discursive. But at the *New Republic,* his work achieved a consistency of focus and an argumentative force to rival, and frequently surpass, anything he'd written since his Trimmer days.

Fairlie could be harshly critical of the United States, arguing in his 1976 book *The Spoiled Child of the Western World* that Americans were foolishly embracing the "aged and painted courtesan" of Europe at the expense of their own culture and letting their Gross National Product be consumed by their "Gross National Appetite." But in his best work for the *New*

Republic—some of his best anywhere, in fact—he deepened his effusive, all-consuming, deeply romantic embrace of America. For the July 4, 1983, issue he wrote what might be his masterpiece, a story billed on the magazine's cover as "My America!" Inside, he celebrated all the reasons he loved this country: the space, the freedom, the gadgets. The appeal wasn't just political or national, it was also personal: "If here history still invents itself, then here also, still, one may invent the future. But suppose that means that one may also invent oneself?"

In one way or another, he'd been exploring that question for almost twenty years. Now he decided to pursue it as completely as he knew how. In 1984, he made plans to spend fourteen weeks making a counter-clockwise tour of the country in a Chevy van and to write an account of his travels, to be called "Journey into America." The book was to be framed by Fairlie's insight that Americanization was not a force being directed outward from this country to the rest of the planet but a process still under way in the country itself—"an experience shared by the world with America." With his outsider's eyes, he saw how the process was "unceasing and never to be completed," continually working changes on the fabric of the country and the people who lived there, particularly its immigrants.

Yet on his return to Washington, this compendium of history, geography, anthropology, reportage, and autobiography thwarted him. Though Fairlie had agreed to submit 80,000 to 100,000 words to his editor at Harper & Row, the manuscript—still not complete—had swollen to 316,000 words. Not for the first time in Fairlie's life, Poe's self-defeating imp of the perverse struck. Contract be damned, he refused to make cuts. The publishers had little confidence Fairlie would be able to return the advance, even if they asked for it, and they canceled the deal. Thousands of manuscript pages remain today, in a series of incomplete drafts. Here and there, these include some gems: short passages in which Fairlie struck the intended balance of subject and tone, crystallizing a picture of American life and his place in it. One episode in Minnesota (included below) captures the volume's large themes and offers the chance to watch Fairlie encounter—and know he's encountering—someone who is, outward differences aside, a kindred spirit: a verse-spouting cowboy named Hooter.

A friend once told Fairlie that he was "half very domestic, half a gypsy." This was certainly true of his life in Washington, where he lived (with financial help from Peretz) in a modest apartment on P Street. But as he entered his sixties, his lifetime of booze and cigarettes began to catch up with him. Colleagues say that he began drinking more heavily during the 1980s, even as more and more bars shut their doors to him. Increasingly frail, he ceased to keep up payments on his apartment, and he was evicted.

In 1985, with nowhere else to go, he began sleeping in his office at the *New Republic*. Staffers who came to the magazine late at night or arrived early would hear him clicking away at his typewriter, with a lit cigarette and a scotch beside him. Though he wore a suit and tie every day—the only writer in the office to do so—at night he could be seen padding around in his socks. This went on for five years. James Fairlie's desire to be a journalist had led him to give up his farm for a modest home in London; in Washington, his son gave up even that.

THE PRESS

Even reduced to homelessness, Henry Fairlie was unbowed. "I bet you don't know anyone who lives in such a high-rent district as I do," he would say, a reference to the *New Republic*'s office near Dupont Circle. He slept, when he slept, on the couch next to his desk and used a shower elsewhere in the building. He continued to socialize at whichever bars still welcomed him, generally with nonjournalists. To finance his evenings, he augmented his *New Republic* wages by borrowing from friends like the artist Vint Lawrence, who said he was more than willing to part with the money to enjoy Fairlie's erudite conversation, and from Peretz. According to a story that circulated at the time, Peretz told associates he was taking Fairlie to lunch to ask him to stop selling review copies of books that came into the magazine. When they returned to the office, Peretz admitted the subject hadn't come up. "I lent him another $500," he said.

Even more than simple pride, Fairlie's ability to keep his chin up in these years was a function of how he viewed his profession. He didn't become a journalist because he expected the work to deliver fame or riches, and he didn't organize his life around attaining them. "Grub Street," Fairlie believed, "is where we come from and where we belong." It's a romantic view, one closer to the ink-stained world of *Pendennis* than the modern Washington of the pundit class. But it's not a slovenly one. All his life, Fairlie kept up a kind of two-front battle within Grub Street: he wanted journalists to think less of themselves and more of the work they performed in a free society. The claims he made for his craft and the charges he leveled against its errant practitioners—to say nothing of the way he lived his life—form a vision of political journalism barely in evidence today.

Fairlie thought journalists were called to play a role that was outside the political process but vital to it, supplying readers with the "moral information" needed to fulfill their duties as citizens. "If we do not understand what a political system is meant to do, we will not understand what it can do," he wrote in *The Life of Politics.* "We will expect the wrong things from it; and, in our anxiety to reform it, we will pull it out of joint in the wrong places for the wrong reasons." Both in print and conversation, according to friends, he could be damning of newspapers, magazines, and other journalists who fell short of this goal. He unleashed long attacks over the years on targets as diverse as the *Daily Mirror,* Nicholas Von Hoffman, the re-launched *Vanity Fair,* George Will (from whom he had expected much), and the American press corps generally. ("That most American journalists have yet to learn to write is an accepted fact of American journalism," he told an interviewer from *Newsweek* shortly after his arrival.) The much-celebrated Pentagon Papers, he believed, were hugely overrated, since—as he demonstrated by spending untold hours reading old clippings from the Kennedy era—the country knew everything that was happening in Vietnam as it was happening.

He saved some of his fiercest criticism for the Washington journalists who wanted to become television celebrities. Not only did it corrupt their work, it made them less free. "There's no real speaking the mind and causing a nuisance," he said in a 1989 interview. "Now they've all become terribly pompous, and see themselves as the fourth estate. They never disrupt a dinner party. It's not very much fun."

Fairlie's best-known feud pitted him against William F. Buckley. In a "Fairlie at Large" essay written in 1980, he compared Reagan supporters to H. L. Mencken's small-minded "booboisie." This drew a vituperative reply from Buckley in the pages of *National Review,* calling him undisciplined, a drunk, and a bad grammarian. When Buckley's collection *Right Reason* appeared in 1985, Fairlie reviewed it for the *New Republic,* arguing that its author was unconservative, overexposed, and not the aristocrat that many Americans took him to be—that he was, in fact, "the quintessential Common Man of our age." Neither writer was in top form in this exchange. Still, two weeks later, Buckley took out a full-page ad in the *New Republic,* paying $1,550 to reprint the complete text of his original indictment against Fairlie.

Fairlie's attacks rise above the usual journalistic sniping in part because of his willingness to make them even at considerable risk to himself. The best example of his fearlessness around power—his willingness to write anything about anybody, including his employers—came in 1977, when, in the midst of writing "Fairlie at Large" for the *Washington Post*, he wrote a two-part series attacking the paper in the *New Republic*. While he admired much of what owner Katharine Graham and editor Ben Bradlee had achieved (he wrote in the first part), "one puts down the *Washington Post* each day with a profound sense of dissatisfaction; and even of irritation that so much energy and even intelligence, so much cuteness, should have been expended to so little obvious purpose. . . . One feels not that it lacks credibility so much as that it lacks authority." In the second part, he criticized how the paper had broken its recent pressmen's strike. After the stories ran, Fairlie went to the *Post* to collect his mail, encountering Graham in the lobby. "That's bullshit, Henry, bullshit," he remembers her shouting. But she didn't cut off his column, or even threaten to do so. For all his specific criticisms of Graham over the years, Fairlie admired a proprietor who so clearly had "ink in her veins."

Fairlie's invective was harsh, but it occupied a vital place in the journalism he mastered on Fleet Street. After being criticized by readers for the toughness of a piece about the late-life diplomacy of George Kennan ("Old men can be very dangerous. They do not, as is thought by the vulgar, try to win their old battles. They try to lose them again," he'd written), Fairlie offered a defense that applies to much of his writing about politicians and journalists alike: "Of course my criticism of Kennan was *ad hominem;* if it had not been it would have been *ad nauseam.* Politics and politicians live by words—free government is wordy government —and we had better be in there pitching our words *ad hominem* against theirs."

The most valuable quality of Fairlie's work, however, isn't the attacks, entertaining as they are—it's the limit on the attacks. He believed that journalists could criticize individual politicians all they liked but had no right to diminish the political function. This was the cardinal sin of the profession, the one that fueled some of Fairlie's most forceful writing. After all he'd seen and heard in his long career, Fairlie believed that politics was "essentially good" and politicians "the most hopeful messengers of a society's will to improve." After Watergate, he chided journalists for writing as though "they're afraid to be caught believing in something." He could not excuse their cynicism. "There comes no word from them to suggest that democracy is the accumulation of the moral aspirations and decisions of vexed but hopeful individuals, and that their task is to reinforce the process with their own intellectual commitment," he wrote in "Press Against Politics," his fullest treatment of the theme.

Yet mounting a defense of Washington politics in the 1980s proved a challenge even to Fairlie. Jimmy Carter had brought his pollsters into the White House; Reagan consolidated the practice. To Fairlie, this was a subversion of democracy, a break in the tie between the people and their elected officials. More impressionistically, the number-crunching offended his romantic embrace of politics, draining some of the mystery from election nights. "I find it hard now to be interested in politics," he wrote in an uncharacteristically glum "Diarist" column for the *New Republic* in 1984. "I do not think that America and most of our Western societies engage any longer in political activity. In the age of the media and direct mailing, it is not only Ronald Reagan who has become a puppet."

It is around the figure of the "Great Communicator" that Fairlie saw money, media, and politics make their noxious convergence. Journalists gave Reagan an easy ride, Fairlie argued, not because of any political sympathy—which would at least show some conviction—but professional symbiosis:

> Anchormen read scripts; politicians read scripts. Anchormen talk in bites; politicians talk in bites. Anchormen speak over pictures; politicians speak over pictures. Anchormen don't have to say anything; politicians don't have to say anything. "Good Morning America" is a television program; "It's morning in America" is a politician's slogan. Politicians merge into Brokaw, Jennings, Rather, and they merge into the politicians they have chosen. They are all, in the end, great communicators, while saying as little as possible.

One of Fairlie's responses to this new Washington was to sound a theme that stretched back to his Fleet Street days, extolling the virtues of oratory, which, in its demands on both policy and personality, offered "the best test of political character." More surprisingly, he also started to change his view of JFK. Fairlie didn't abandon his wariness of the limitless call to action in Kennedy's inaugural address. "And yet—and yet—how we need something of that voice now," he wrote. The impulse to far-flung action that needed correcting after Kennedy's death had been over-corrected. Camelot seemed much less despicable than the conservatism that conquered Washington in the 1980s, a governing philosophy he criticized in words that could have been written this morning:

> The Reaganite conservative does not trust the political system, and so is always trying to circumvent it; he does not trust the instincts of Congress, but places profound faith in the wisdom of the executive if he is in charge; he does not trust the deep religious

instinct of a people, unless it is decked out in the tawdry costume of a minute of silent prayer in school. The only loyalty that eight years of Reaganite conservatism has inspired is of each to the country of his self.

Late in Reagan's second term, Fairlie started writing less about politics, turning more and more to history: tracing how different countries reacted to Lexington and Concord, reconsidering whether America should have entered the First World War. When he wrote about newly elected George H. W. Bush, he did so by comparing him to George Washington, whom he called "the greatest man who ever lived." Before Bush's election Fairlie had volunteered some memos for then-Senator Al Gore —a politician he never wrote about—suggesting he present himself in 1988 as a leader who could unify the country after the divisive Reagan years and counseling him not to be ruled by his advisors. Running beneath it all was Fairlie's concern about the growing fearfulness of the American people, which he saw manifest in the delay in returning to space after the *Challenger* explosion and the boom in product liability lawsuits. It reflected, he believed, "a loss of the American adventuring spirit, of the American gusto whose absence the world now laments, the gusto that, until the 1960s, blew like a fresh wind around the globe, showing what could be accomplished in so short a time by a nation that did not shrink from risk but found it a challenge."

So great was Fairlie's dissatisfaction with the "banality, crudities, and flagrant corruption" of the 1988 campaign that he began a downbeat sequel to his first book. In "The Death of Politics," he planned to trace how a series of changes since 1960, all inclining toward direct democracy, had turned America's leaders into puppets and disenfranchised its citizens. Fairlie didn't use the term "the Establishment," but his new argument echoed that earlier work. Once again, an unelected force was subverting democracy, but instead of "all the right people" being to blame, the culprits were Washington's "campaign staffs, consultants, pollsters, direct-mailers, PACs, and the media, all in league with each other: if not conspiring, at least working to each other's advantage against the democratic purpose of an election."

The inclusion of the media represents a shift from his anti-Establishment days. Then, he saw journalists stifled and bullied by the guardians of taste and by proprietors interested in maintaining the status quo; now, journalists played an actively destructive role. As soon as "the media" appeared in the 1960s, he wrote, it found itself "at the center of this coil of mischief" and in possession of a "stranglehold on the nominating and electoral process." The damage inflicted had been so grave, he argued, that by 1988 it was "becoming awkward to claim that elections remain free in America in any but a narrowly legal sense; it is the very activity of politics that is being drained of life." Nor was the damage limited to Washington. Fairlie reiterated his belief that politics is "the only conversation in a free society that encompasses all the others, and draws the society together in a common realization of itself, even if that does not always issue in some common endeavour of government."

It's hard to know where Fairlie planned to take this provocative argument. He drafted only three chapters of the manuscript and left no outline to suggest what would come next. It could be that, as he had so many times in the past, he simply lost interest in a long-term project before its completion. Or he may have put it aside temporarily for a work that, in these years, seized a great deal more of his attention.

In the fall of 1985, Fairlie's editor and friend Dorothy Wickenden offhandedly suggested that he try his hand at fiction. The idea apparently not having occurred to him before, he leapt into action.

"Dead Men," as he intended to call his novel, traces the couplings and uncouplings of a circle of friends—mainly middle-aged expats to America—in the weeks just before and after the 1980 election. The book's heroine was to be Jenny, a forty-something widow running a farm near the fictional town of Drover's Crossing, in the Blue Ridge Mountains. Fairlie had long objected to some aspects of feminism, believing that "the notion of what it can mean to be female and womanly is being narrowed and impoverished rather than widened and enriched." Jenny, a strong mother and community leader, presented something closer to what he regarded as a healthy balance. "What I feel the characters, especially Jenny, say in my novel is what I want to say to neo-conservatives like Midge Decter: that *mores* may have changed a little, but there's no evidence people are less *moral*," he wrote to one manuscript reader.

A more telling sign of Fairlie's authorship is the character John Simpson. This Scottish owner of a Washington bookstore quotes Oakeshott, wears tweeds, recalls his precocious stint on a Manchester newspaper, and reminisces about what he calls his "Britain's Lover" phase. Except for the profession, all these things echo Fairlie's life and experiences. But nowhere is the story more revealing of its author than in its peculiar but genuine romanticism. When a reader referred to one of the book's many, many trysts as a "roll in the hay," Fairlie made a sharp reply. "The fault of the promiscuous as well as the Puritans is that they think there can be sex without love. Bullshit!" wrote Fairlie to his reader. "All my characters say is that if there is no love, there is no sex. There is no 'roll in the hay.' The feelings continue. You form a love, if you hold someone even once, and it never dies, even if that person is never seen again."

Successive drafts of the novel grew better, smoother, less journalistic. Like so many projects of his late life, it also grew vastly overlong. He worked day and night trying to write it, then day and night trying to slim it down. Living at the office was ignoble, but some friends say it was a hidden blessing, as it let Fairlie escape the domestic responsibilities that always bedeviled him and devote more energy to work. Always industrious, Fairlie in these years seemed virtually a graphomaniac. A colleague recalls knocking on his door one afternoon and finding him asleep at his desk, with hands on typewriter keys. Awakened, he immediately picked up typing where he'd left off. A writer, then—first and last.

In 1989, on a trip to Washington, Peregrine Worsthorne paid his old friend a visit. Over lunch, they ordered lots of drinks, as was their custom, only Fairlie didn't touch his. That's when Worsthorne knew Henry was really ill.

One night in February 1990, Fairlie was returning to the office of the *New Republic* when he slipped and fell in the building's lobby. He was taken to George Washington University Hospital with a broken hip. The fall by itself shouldn't have been life-threatening for a sixty-six-year-old man, even one with his chaotic medical history. But over the next few days, his condition worsened. A theory passed around by his friends at the time is that the shock of being deprived the steady flow of alcohol and nicotine that had sustained him for decades proved more than his system could bear. He briefly felt well enough to work from his hospital bed, correcting proofs of an upcoming piece. But he suffered a stroke, then a heart attack. He died on February 25, 1990.

The memorial service at the New York Avenue Presbyterian Church in Washington was remarkably eclectic. Friends and family members read from *Ecclesiastes,* Thomas Jefferson's *Notes on the State of Virginia,* a Michael Oakeshott passage on friendship, "Musée des Beaux Arts" by W. H. Auden (his favorite poet), and excerpts from some of his best-loved stories, including "My America," "The Idiocy of Urban Life," and "Merry FAXmas." Having begun with "Onward, Christian Soldiers," the service ended with "The Battle Hymn of the Republic."

Fairlie's body was cremated, and, following another memorial service in Scotland, his ashes were interred in his family plot, near his parents, in a kirkyard at Kirkton of Monikie. After his death, Peretz gave Charlotte Fairlie the check owed to her father for his last story. She used it to pay for the cremation. She likes to say that his last bill, anyway, was paid.

Nineteen years after his death, Henry Fairlie is survived by two unlikely books—one in fact, one in legend.

In the summer of 1977, Fairlie wrote a series of essays for the *New Republic* that were soon collected in *The Seven Deadly Sins Today*. Each chapter offers a compelling, sometimes surprising, take on modern occasions of sin. Exercise, for instance, can be as slothful as indolence. The book is sharpest, though, on how society itself can sin. If there's avarice today, he argued, it's in part because "no other standard is today set against the pursuit of wealth and possessions" in modern America: "There is something seriously at fault with a society, something that will in the end destroy us, if poverty that is voluntarily chosen is nowhere celebrated as a good."

A work of moral philosophy may seem a strange project for someone like Fairlie, a self-described "reluctant unbeliever" whose personal conduct was very far from monkish. Yet something clicked. The essays were republished in paperback by the University of Notre Dame Press. More than three decades after its first appearance, *The Seven Deadly Sins Today* is the only book of Fairlie's still in print.

The other book is a mystery. "Bite the Hand That Feeds You" was to be Fairlie's memoir of his adventures as a freelancer, a story he envisioned as a tale not of triumph but of survival. According to various notes and outlines, he planned to intersperse his exploits with portraits of politicians, press barons, and other journalists that—Fairlie being Fairlie—couldn't help but be blistering. In early 1984, he drafted at least four chapters and sent them to his agent, Robert Ducas. Around this time, Ducas sent Mark Bonham-Carter, an editor at the London publishing house Collins, a manuscript written by Fairlie. According to Worsthorne, who spoke to Bonham-Carter, the text showed great promise but was already more than two hundred thousand words long and still incomplete. Though Bonham-Carter called it a memoir, the manuscript's length and lack of an ending also describe "Journey into America." Whichever manuscript it may have been, Bonham-Carter apparently returned it to Ducas, who claims he asked Fairlie if he should send it back. "He told me he had his original and I could dispose of my copy," the agent later wrote. So Ducas did. But Fairlie's copy has never turned up.

"The manuscript of what could well be one of the finest British autobiographies of the last part of the century has gone missing, and might have been destroyed," ran an item in the *Daily Telegraph* a few weeks after Fairlie's death. Where could it have gone? It's possible that Fairlie failed to keep a copy, in spite of what Ducas said. Or maybe he did keep one, but some unidentified party took it. Perhaps the likeliest scenario is that Fairlie kept bits and pieces of his manuscript and, after sending some chapters to his agent, never wrote any more. In a 1985 letter to Fairlie, Ducas mentions that he's sorry Fairlie "didn't finish his memoir." With both men gone, and neither of their archives yielding anything concrete, the fate of this tantalizing manuscript seems likely to remain unknown.

A few fragments of Fairlie's memoir do survive, however: an outline, some letters that refer to its contents, fragments of some early chapters. Using these as a guide, this collection attempts to fulfill the earlier book's mission. Whenever possible, stories Fairlie planned to include have been reprinted here, if in slightly abridged form. (A few deletions have been made silently, and if the title of a piece has been changed to give a clearer or fuller sense of its subject, the original headline is included in the source note. Footnotes in Fairlie's originals are preserved here with an asterisk; new notes are numbered.) These aren't his greatest hits, per se. He wrote many wonderful pieces that are too rooted in their historical moment to bear republication here. Nor is this book entirely representative of his work. The collection favors the broader columns and essays Fairlie wrote for weeklies and monthlies over pieces in the daily papers where he spent most of his early career.

Above all, the book emphasizes the pieces that best display a balance he struck as fully and gracefully as any journalist of our time: an anthropologist's eye for observing the world around him; an immense wealth of knowledge that lent perspective to his analysis; and a knack for adding just enough of his own experiences to give his writing liveliness and charm. If this book is skewed toward his later work, it's largely because the longer he lived, and the more adventures he had, the richer his writing grew.

Fairlie's work and—for all its travails—the way he lived while writing it prove that it is possible for journalism to be at once a humble and a noble calling. Even as the profession changed in ways that made his lifestyle seem all the more perverse and the rewards for abandoning it all the more attractive, he never gave up the freedom he'd left the *Times* in 1954 to attain, nor did his hardships embitter him. His writing is only one of the ways he proved himself a master at revealing the rewards and perils of independence.

Fairlie planned to conclude "Bite the Hand That Feeds You"

with what he called "a fitting climax to my story of the hazards of being a freelance journalist": an account of the stretch in 1982 when he lost the two regular gigs that provided most of his regular income. He shared his sad news with John Midgley, expecting the *Economist* writer to commiserate. Instead, his friend just laughed. "Personally, Henry, I think it's rather funny," he said. Fairlie had to agree. "There I was straddling the Atlantic, as I put it, for a year, with one column in London in the *Times,* and one in Washington in the *Post*—and, wham! bam! I lost them both in two weeks!" he wrote. "Who would be a freelancer? I would."

A GENIUS FOR CONFLICT
The Life of British Politics

The English "genius for compromise" is one of the fictions of the middle-class politicians and middle-class political writers who have dominated the discussion of politics in England since Palmerston died. The plain fact is that the English political genius is a genius for conflict. Against the alchemy of the "genius for compromise," I put forward the chemistry of substances in solution, and I have no doubt which is the more appropriate in the middle of the 20th century.
—*"A Genius for Compromise? A Debate on the British Party System,"* Encounter, *1956*

Sketches of MPs

In a major address to Parliament on March 1, 1955, Winston Churchill announced that Great Britain would develop the hydrogen bomb to deter Soviet aggression. "Never flinch, never weary, never despair," the eighty-year-old prime minister concluded.

One can leave aside the *Daily Mirror,* which has now reached the point of billing each great speech by Sir Winston Churchill as "Positively his Last Appearance," but there are still others of more serious intent who think that the Prime Minister has ceased to be a useful servant of the State. If they heard, or have read in full, his speech on the hydrogen bomb, they must either revise their opinion or be very deaf to the accents of leadership. Sir Winston Churchill uses oratory for a specific purpose: not to press home an argument or push a policy through, but to create a mood or an attitude. All his great post-war speeches have been designed to this end. His "Iron Curtain" speech at Fulton created the attitude of mind in the West which for the next seven years was to shape all discussions of foreign policy. His famous speech in May, 1953, after Stalin's death, in which he advocated high-level talks with the Soviet Union, created a new attitude, favourable to ideas of co-existence, which in its turn remoulded all subsequent discussion of foreign policy. He rarely, in these speeches, says anything "new." Mr. Shinwell was quite right, from that narrow point of view, in saying that there was nothing

Spectator, March 4, 1955, originally titled "Political Commentary."

original in his speech on the hydrogen bomb.[1] But he is the great synthesiser. He takes the facts, hopes, fears, doubts, speculations of the day and transmutes them into a single, coherent and intelligible challenge to the minds and hearts of his listeners. This is what he did again on Tuesday. This is leadership on a scale of which no other man alive today is capable—read the reactions of the world's press, including the headline which *Le Figaro* gave his speech, "Meditations on the Theme of the Apocalypse"—and the country cannot afford to dispense with it a moment earlier than is necessary. Let all the rumours be true. Perhaps he does tire quicker than before. Perhaps he does nod now and then. There still remains the creative, imaginative genius of the man. It is of priceless value to the free world, even if his afternoon nap is half an hour longer than before.

From the sublime . . . well, it is a rum collection of Labour members who decided to abstain on the Defence debate. The pacifists one respects, and there is nothing more to be said about them. But let us have a closer look at Mr. Maurice Edelman, the blue-blazer-and-brass-button boy of the Labour Party.[2] Mr. Edelman has been perfectly tailored, by whatever divinity shapes our beginnings, to be the star of the Purley Tennis and Badminton Club. (If Purley does not have a Tennis and Badminton Club, it should have.) But he is an adventurous soul, and has sought other worlds to conquer. Drop in at an embassy reception, and there will be Mr. Edelman, fresh with a quip which he picked up a month ago from M. Massigli.[3] Look in at

1. Emanuel Shinwell (1884–1986) was a long-serving socialist MP and, from 1951 to 1955, shadow minister for defence.

2. Maurice Edelman (1911–1975) was elected Labour MP for Coventry North in 1950.

3. Rene Massigli (1888–1988) was French ambassador to London from 1944 to 1954.

a literary cocktail party, and there will be Mr. Edelman again, this time with a delightful story about Claudel to cap the morning's obituary notices.[4] But, why politics? And, why the Labour Party? Watch him as he rises from his perch behind the Front Bench to put a supplementary question: the slight tug at the back of his jacket to make sure that it is lying straight, the deft rearrangement of his shirt cuff, then (and only then) the ever-so-modulated voice. "Are you ready now, Miss Horsbrugh?[5] Will I serve?" What is behind it all? One asks the question because Mr. Edelman is a man of most elusive convictions. There is no one in the Labour Party who, intellectually and temperamentally, stands farther to the Right than Mr. Edelman, but no one has taken more trouble to avoid identifying himself with the Right. He sits for Coventry North, a hot-bed of Bevanism, with Mr. Crossman rolling them in the aisles next door.[6] But, no, that cannot be the explanation. The mystery remains. What is Mr. Edelman in politics for?

Usually just in front of Mr. Edelman sits Mr. Woodrow Wyatt.[7] They are of the same generation, and they provide an interesting contrast. Mr. Wyatt clearly enjoys politics hugely. One suspects that when he tramps through the division lobby he puffs out his

4. Paul Claudel (1868–1955) was a French symbolist poet.

5. Florence Horsbrugh (1889–1969) was Conservative MP for Manchester Moss Side and minister of education from 1951 to 1954.

6. Aneurin Bevan, a charismatic Welsh socialist, led a left-leaning faction within the Labour Party. R. H. S. Crossman (1907–1974), Labour MP for Coventry East from 1945 to 1974, was a prominent Bevanite and journalist.

7. Woodrow Wyatt (1918–1977) was a Labour MP for Birmingham Aston (1945–1955) and Bosworth, Leicestershire (1959–1970). Wyatt later became a Thatcherite conservative columnist for *News of the World* and chairman of the Tote, the state-run betting service.

chest and says to himself, "Wyatt, MP, you are making history, you are treading where Chatham trod, you are shaping the universe."[8] It is easy, especially for some of the young cynics in the Labour Party today, to laugh at Mr. Wyatt's attitude. But he has a quality which lifts him above them all. He has the courage of a terrier. He is one of the most outspoken opponents of Bevanism—and it is not easy to be this when you are a young Labour MP representing a Birmingham constituency. But Mr. Wyatt has never felt that it was his duty to truckle to the opinions of his constituency party. Whenever he thinks his constituency party is about to go round the Bevanite bend he just takes the train to Birmingham and calls a meeting. He then tells them a thing or two which had perhaps not reached Birmingham before. There is courage among Left-wing Labour MPs who defy their party Whip, and they receive the praise they deserve for it. But the courage of Mr. Wyatt deserves to be acknowledged too. I have given some space to Mr. Edelman and Mr. Wyatt, because they seem to me, in the contrast between them, to typify one of the main anxieties about the Right wing of the Labour Party today. Many of the new post-war recruits to the Right wing—Mr. Edelman is a protégé of Mr. Hugh Dalton[9]— seem to be characterised by a lack of conviction and even spinelessness which together can be the death of any party. Mr. Wyatt may sometimes chase his tail round in circles in his excitement, but at least he instinctively feels that politics is about something important and is therefore worth getting excited about. You may approve of Mr. Wyatt's views or not, but at least

8. William Pitt the Elder, 1st Earl of Chatham (1708–1778), became one of the most famous and influential parliamentary figures of the eighteenth century thanks to his leadership during the Seven Years' War. He was also known as the Great Commoner.

9. Hugh Dalton (1887–1962) was a Labour MP and chancellor of the exchequer from 1945 to 1947.

a party composed of people like him can never be in danger of dying of anæmia. One of the reasons for the success of the Bevanite campaign has been the rank-and-file feeling that the Right wing is bloodless. The fault does not lie with the likes of Mr. Wyatt.

The BBC Attitude to Politics

There are two ways by which a political commentator can struggle through a Parliamentary recess. One is by substituting an "Economic Diary" for a "Political Diary." The other is by writing what journalists know as a "think-piece." During the next three weeks I am going to write three "think-pieces" on the causes of our present discontents—assuming, of course, that Sir Anthony Eden does not once more change the composition of his Government and that Mr. Gaitskell does not ask to see the Prime Minister again.[1] From time to time I am urged to make this column more "serious," and from time to time I succumb to the flattery that "seriousness" is worth striving after. But what do these advisers mean by "seriousness"? What they really mean is that political commentators should analyse politics in a cool, non-committal, quasi-academic fashion. What they are really concerned about is that a political commentator should not say anything which will disturb the smooth running of the present political Establishment in Britain. What they really want is a family of McKenzies and Butlers,[2] each reducing politics to

Spectator, January 6, 1956, originally titled "Political Commentary."

1. Anthony Eden (1897–1977), a Conservative MP, succeeded Churchill as prime minister in 1955. Hugh Gaitskell (1906–1963) was a Labour MP who served as chancellor of the exchequer and, from 1955 to 1963, leader of the opposition.

2. David Butler (born 1924) and Robert McKenzie (1917–1981) analyzed election-night returns for the BBC for many years. The two academics employed the "swingometer," a device that illustrates what the election would mean for each party's fortunes in Parliament.

sociological laws; and as long as the laws survive, Britain, freedom, the West and 500,000,000 souls can go hang.

Some of these reflections are, of course, prompted by an article about the present political condition of Britain which appeared in the *New Statesman* last week by Mr. Paul Johnson.[3] What has struck him, since his return from Paris, has been a journalistic protest against what he calls the Hydra—and what in this periodical, as in the *New Statesman*, has previously been called the Establishment. It is not for me to dissent from him that a journalistic protest is taking place. I am quite certain that during the past three years or so a new attitude to politics has been developed in certain journals in this country, and that a large part of the credit is due to Mr. Malcolm Muggeridge, who has acted as what I believe is called a catalyst.[4] But where I think Mr. Johnson went very wrong—and it is an important point— was in his insistence that the journalistic rebels have popular support—that the "popular wind is in their sails." I wish this were true. But I can find no evidence at all that the people of this country really object to the present set-up.

Let us, then, get clear what the protest is against. If I were asked to put it colloquially, I would say that it is a protest against the Mrs. Dale attitude to politics.[5] Some time ago it was pointed out that Mrs. Dale and her henpecked husband never seemed to read a book, listen to music or have any views about politics.

3. Paul Johnson (born 1928), a prolific journalist, historian, and sometime friend of Fairlie's, was, at this time, a liberal contributor to the *New Statesman,* which he later edited (1965–70). He subsequently shifted to the political right, defending Richard Nixon and advising Margaret Thatcher.

4. Malcolm Muggeridge (1903–1990) was a journalist, novelist, and TV broadcaster. He was credited with breathing new life into *Punch* during his editorship (1953–58), where he published Fairlie frequently.

5. *Mrs. Dale's Diary* was the first long-running BBC radio serial drama. Beginning in 1948 and running more than two decades, it chronicled life in a conventional middle-class home in a fictional London suburb.

Some of those who pointed this out obviously thought that it was possible for a BBC charade character to have an attitude to politics. But the truth, surely, is that Mrs. Dale is not a necessary popular evil of the BBC's attitude; she is its quintessence. What the BBC has striven to do over the past two decades is suggest that politics is a matter of little importance or, at most, a matter on which sensible men need not disagree strongly. Even in religious discussions—such as they have—the BBC producers set out to find the atheist (or agnostic) and the Anglicans (of course), who start from the lowest common denominator and, after half an hour's discussion, present their listeners with the highest common multiple of their views. Have you ever heard Mr. Grisewood, at the end of an *Any Questions?* programme, say, in his cultivated fireside manner, "Well, the team seems to be agreed about that"?[6] If you have, you have heard the voice of the BBC on politics.

The BBC is the summary and the voice of this attitude to politics. But it spreads far and wide. It is, to use Mr. Johnson's phrase, considered "noisy, vulgar and disreputable" to hold strong views about political questions, and by political questions I do not mean whether the purchase tax should be increased or not. That is the politics of candle-ends. Much, as readers of the *Spectator* know, though I admire Mr. Gaitskell, one of his most serious weaknesses is his tendency to believe that Parliamentary issues are political issues. The Parliamentary legend of Butskellism has been killed—by Mr. Gaitskell—but I am not at all sure that Butskellism is not as alive today as ever.[7] A political com-

6. Freddie Grisewood was the original host of *Any Questions?*, a long-running BBC Radio 4 program in which a panel of journalists and MPs fielded questions from a live audience.

7. Butskellism, the centrist economic philosophy shared by Britain's major parties in the years after the war, was named for R. A. Butler, the

mentator has to make only one disguised attack on someone like Mr. Roy Jenkins, and, one by one, the BBC politicians (of both parties) move in.[8] "Of course," they say, "Mr. Jenkins is a real Socialist. You were just inaccurate when you attacked him." But was I? Mr. Jenkins (and many others fall into the same category) seems to me a good Labour Party boy; but today that need mean no more than that he wants to see the Labour Party return to power and carry out some welcome reforms which he happens to have near his heart. I would certainly entrust Mr. Jenkins with the leadership of a Parliamentary Labour Party. But at the end we would be a country producing noiseless cuckoo-clocks.

I have tried, in the shorthand which is necessary in journalism, to give an impression of the attitude which seems objectionable to me and to some others. I will close by trying to make it clear why I think it is objectionable. One of the heartening things about the last fifteen years has been the revival of the British intellectuals' belief in Britain. The intellectuals have come to recognise that Britain, with all its faults, is the depository of certain standards and a certain experience which can be entrusted to no other country in the world. (Unless there are those who, M. Mendès-France having failed them, now pin their hopes to M. Poujade.)[9] But the attitude of most of these

left-leaning Conservative, and Hugh Gaitskell, the right-leaning Labour leader, both of whom served as chancellor of the exchequer.

8. Roy Jenkins (1920–2003) was a longtime Labour MP for Birmingham and later home secretary, chancellor of the exchequer, biographer of Gladstone and Churchill, chancellor of Oxford, and co-founder of the short-lived Social Democratic Party, which sought to energize the "radical centre."

9. Pierre Mendès-France (1907–1982) was the leftist French prime minister who ended involvement in Indochina during his seven months in office. Pierre Poujade (1920–2003) staged a shopkeepers' rebellion against

intellectuals is that Britain is a weak, second-class Power which is fighting an important but last-ditch battle. In this weak condition they think that both Britain and the values which it personifies must be protected in the cotton-wool of bipartisanship. My thesis is that Britain within the Commonwealth is potentially the strongest Power in the world, but that this potential will only be realised when political questions again become a matter of conflict.

---

the Fourth Republic in 1953 that broadened into a powerful, if short-lived, populist movement with nativist and anti-Semitic overtones.

In Defence of Ordinariness

Every reviewer should declare his interest; and I frankly confess that I sleep more soundly in my bed at night if I know that Parliament is sitting. It is becoming fashionable again to decry Parliament and its members. I wish, therefore, to use this occasion, not only to celebrate the second edition of one of the great constitutional textbooks of this century, but to celebrate also Parliament itself and its honourable members. It is one thing to criticise the activities of individual members of Parliament; it is quite another to criticise the activity of being a member of Parliament. It is one thing to look at Parliament with a cool, cynical and comprehending eye; it is quite another to belittle Parliament. At the risk of sounding like a nineteenth-century Liberal, I must assert that Parliament seems to me to be one of the glorious achievements of the human race. It is still, today, one of the surest bulwarks of freedom, continuing, as for centuries past, to teach the world by its example.

I opened this new edition of Sir Ivor Jennings's masterpiece* as a duty, in order laboriously to discover where and how he had revised it.[1] Before I had reached the end of his familiar opening paragraph (unchanged) I was reading with wide-eyed pleasure. There is lucidity, of course, but that conveys nothing of the gracefulness of the structure of the book and of the writing, a

Spectator, January 3, 1958.

*PARLIAMENT. By Sir Ivor Jennings. (C.U.P., 60s.)

1. Sir Ivor Jennings (1903–1965) was a constitutional lawyer and faculty member at London School of Economics from 1930 to 1940 and the author of several volumes explaining the English constitution.

gracefulness which is the property of the best of Cambridge scholarship; there is learning, but that gives no more than a hint of the unerring precision with which he illustrates his points; there is keen observation, but that gives only the smallest idea of his penetrating comprehension of what Parliament is about; above all, the whole is informed by his belief in the institution of Parliament, but that is a bald way to describe the disciplined passion which lifts the works so far above the level of most textbooks.

Sir Ivor Jennings has worked hard in revising his book, which was first published in 1939. But the overriding impression is of how little the changes matter. Since 1939 there has been a war, during which the Prime Minister enjoyed almost dictatorial powers; the first Labour Government to enjoy power has carried out a crowded and far-reaching programme of economic and social legislation; the changes in British society have made the problems of recruitment to the House of Commons (and the House of Lords) more difficult than ever before. Yet the differences between the Parliament of 1939 and the Parliament of 1957 are only slight. I defy any of those who nibble and niggle at Parliament to deny that this capacity for survival is of incalculable value in a shifting world. Parliament still unites freedom and order in a way which is the envy of the world, and probably its hope. Apart from Redlich's great work on Parliamentary procedure, there is no book I would rather see presented to the members of every new-born legislative assembly than this second edition of *Parliament,* accompanied by a cross-indexed copy of the first.

There is, for example, one instructive example of the way in which conventions grow and are accepted in the British constitution. In his first edition, Sir Ivor Jennings wrote of the choice of Labour Prime Ministers:

It was made clear when Mr. Lansbury was elected [Leader of the Parliamentary Labour Party] in 1931 and still more clear when Mr. Attlee was elected in 1935, that the Parliamentary Labour Party reserved its full liberty of action to elect whom it pleased if the party secured a majority, and thus to indicate to the King who was desired as Prime Minister.

In his second edition, Sir Ivor is able to point out that, in spite of this, George VI automatically sent for Mr. Attlee[2] in 1945, and that "when Mr. Gaitskell was elected chairman and leader of the Parliamentary Labour Party at the end of 1955 it seems to have been assumed that he would be the next Labour Prime Minister." For close students there is much of this kind to be found. There is also much else. What a wealth of social history is summarised in the changed hours during which the House sits on each day, not least in the fact that in 1939 the House could not be counted out between 8.15 and 9.15 in the evening, whereas it cannot now be counted out between 7.30 and 8.30.

There is also much to intrigue the close student of Sir Ivor Jennings. In his first edition, he only once let his passion off the leash. In his closing sentence, he returned to his persistent theme that the whole meaning of Parliament lies in the existence of an official Opposition. "The leaders of other Oppositions," he added in 1939, "are rotting in concentration camps or have joined the noble army of political martyrs—and the peoples are slaves." Why he should omit this sentence in the year after the Hungarian revolution it is difficult to understand. But the last chapter still remains a brilliant brief defence of Parliamen-

2. Clement Attlee (1883–1967) led Labour to a decisive victory in the 1945 general election, replacing Winston Churchill as prime minister.

tary democracy. He accepts Bagehot's definition of the real function of the House of Commons as being to "express the mind of the people," to "teach the nation what it does not know," and to make us "hear what otherwise we should not."[3] He argues that it does it "by defending and criticising the Government," and his book is an elaborate examination of how this process of give-and-take works.

It works because, as he says, the members of Parliament are "ordinary people with a fair slice of ambition. . . . What the democratic system does is to harness a man's ambition. . . ." Sir Ivor Jennings says that this is the worst that can be said about the members. It is also the best. The enduring virtue of the House of Commons, through centuries, is that it has been composed largely of ordinary people: drab, honest, foolish, bumptious, confused, worried, happy, unhappy, ordinary people. That they are ordinary people, that they will react, by and large, as ordinary people, especially at moments of crisis, which is what ultimately matters, is their virtue, their value and their glory. Take away their ordinariness and they will no longer be our defence against the extraordinary people who are always wanting to do extraordinary things to us. The man who will comment on politics must first acknowledge the virtue of ordinariness. This acknowledgment Sir Ivor Jennings makes in every judgment. Others, please copy.

3. Walter Bagehot (1826–1877) was the longtime editor of the *Economist* and the author of *The English Constitution,* a seminal study of the British political system.

On the Comforts of Anger

In 1963, Encounter *devoted its July issue to the theme "Suicide of a Nation?" Guest editor Arthur Koestler invited a range of prominent journalists and social critics to contribute a piece on the state of England. Fairlie was the lone contributor to strike an optimistic tone and to attack "State of England" writing itself.*

Anyone who writes a fair amount (and we all, these days, write far too much) about political and social issues is always in danger of writing what may briefly be called "State of England" pieces: editors, for one thing, like them; and they are, for a second thing, easy to write. You only have to make a certain kind of noise. Elsewhere, I have called them "Wurra-wurra-wurra-wur-aw-aw-aw" articles, for that is the noise which the lions make in *The Rose and the Ring* when they gobble up Count Hogginarmo; to this I have little to add, except that I have since discovered that Tigger makes almost exactly the same noise, "Worraworraworraworraworra," when he suddenly pulls the tablecloth off in *The House at Pooh Corner.*

All "State of England" writers remind me irresistibly of him:

> ... he jumped at the end of the tablecloth, pulled it
> to the ground, wrapped himself up in it three times,
> rolled to the other end of the room, and, after a
> terrible struggle, got his head into the daylight
> again, and said cheerfully: "Have I won?"

Encounter, July 1963. Reprinted by permission from the Estate of Henry Fairlie.

This is exactly how most articles on the "State of England" are written.

I am aware, of course, that this is a "State of England" number of *Encounter;* but it is just this grotesque fact which has prompted the moderate thoughts which follow. I was asked to discuss the current vogue of "almost nihilist criticism"—the phrase, I may be allowed to say, was not mine—and the more I have thought about it, the more I am convinced that the fault (if fault at all there is) lies here: right here, in the ceaseless articles, books and special numbers about the "State of England," which we keep writing and others keep publishing. I can hope only that this issue of *Encounter* will kill the subject.

"State of England" pieces (of whatever length) are preoccupied with England, with decline, and with crisis. Since we live in England, it is in decline, and it is buffeted by crises, this may not seem surprising. But what ought to be matters of interest change their character when they become obsessions. Problems which are real and manageable become part of a Problem which can never be tackled but only constantly written about. Changes which need to be quietly made are presented to us in terms of Decision, demanding the exercise of some kind of national will.

Moreover, we allow these obsessions to grow only because we ignore so much of what is real around us. The most important facts about England are that it is as free and orderly and kindly a country as any in the world. I can see no reason why it should not remain so: and I am not sure that I wish it to be anything more. Before I can share the concern of the "State of England" writers, therefore, I need to be shown what it is they wish to alter in our society or, to use their own language, what it is they wish to inject into it. If they reply, as they usually do, "vigour," or "dynamism," or "efficiency," or "greatness," I then need to be shown that these words do not conceal attitudes hostile to the kind of liberty I am accustomed to enjoying and the kind of order I am prepared to tolerate.

The first question to ask, when confronted by any "State of England" writing, is what we are being asked to exchange for what. I agree that the price to be paid for the kind of liberty and order we know may, to some, seem high. It probably means that our society will have less efficiency than economists would like, less sense of purpose than moralists would like, less simple priorities than sociologists would like, less doctrine than theologians would like. To these, unable to shape us as they please, it is no doubt all a little alarming; to the rest of us, less so. At least, it means that we still have some chance left of doing what we ourselves want to do, and not what they want us to do. To me, this seems a civilised state of affairs, if not the only civilised state of affairs.

A free society is necessarily an untidy, uncomfortable and apparently inefficient affair; and I suspect that one of the troubles with "State of England" writers is that they cannot bear the whole anxious process.* As the American conservative, Fisher Ames, said: "Monarchy is like a splendid ship, with all sails set; it moves majestically on; then it hits a rock and sinks for ever. Democracy is like a raft; it never sinks but, damn it, your feet are always in the water." "State of England" writers seem to me not to like getting their feet wet: it makes them jumpy company on a raft.

It is my belief that England's feet are no more than ordinarily wet; but, since this is not a "State of England" article, that is beside the point. What I am concerned with here are the language and attitudes which have helped to create the stereotyped

---

*A "stop-and-go" economy is both unavoidable and even proper in a free society. Certainly, it is no reason for creating an "atmosphere" of emergency: which is then used to justify restrictions of freedom.

impression (which may end up by acquiring substance) that, sitting on our raft, we are about to sink, unless we take drastic and unusual action: that we face some unique Crisis of Decision. Unless this language and these attitudes are challenged, we are in danger of acquiring other attitudes which should have no place in the thinking and aspirations of a fortunately free and orderly people.

There are such attitudes about. Here, for example, is a passage from a leading article in *The Times* of April 10th, 1963, entitled "The Kindly Dinosaur":

> The British, a naturally kindly people, are coming increasingly to believe that kindness is all that matters. Hardly any major modernisation or rationalisation can be proposed without protests that it will inflict hardship, particularly on the infirm or the elderly. That is considered reason enough for its abandonment. It is not enough. The dinosaur, for all we know, was good to its aged and did not eat its young. It may well have been the most benevolent giant that ever was. That did not prevent its lack of adaptability enforcing its extinction.

The argument seems innocent enough. In fact, it could be used to justify, in the alleged interests of society, the deliberate and callous neglect of the interests of any minority: especially, so it seems, the weak and the aged.

It needs to be extended only a fraction to justify, again in the alleged interests of society, any inhumanity: lack of adaptability to the supposed characteristics of the species sent a fair number of people to the gas ovens. It is this primitive Darwinism in the argument used by *The Times*, the lurking assumptions about the "survival of the fittest," which make me suspicious. The Pathetic Fallacy crops up in political as well as in other kinds of writing and, as our generation should know better than any other, it usually leads to nasty results. Before asking us to consider the dinosaur as a warning, *The Times* might have stopped to recall that nature is careless of the single life: *homo sapiens* usually claims not to be.

Arguments which, like this one, derive from false parallels with biological species or races are far too dangerous not to be recognised for the nonsense they are. It may therefore be worth quoting from *Fossil Amphibians and Reptiles* by Dr. W. E. Swinton, of the Natural History Museum:

> Thus the factors that led to extinction are many and complex. No one theory, no single event, can explain the disappearance during the closing stages of the Cretaceous and the dawn of the Eocene of groups that had hitherto had a long record of dominance. It may be, perhaps, that dominance itself is impermanent, for the organisms that have survived for the longest periods of geological time have usually been, like the brachiopod *Lingula*, obscure and unobtrusive.

The case, then, would seem to be for becoming ourselves obscure and unobtrusive, a small nation, brachiopod *Insula:* then we would survive. Heavy weather, all this may seem: but it is to such balderdash that almost all "State of England" writing, with its canting about "survival," can fairly be reduced.

A second quotation needs to be put beside the one from *The Times.* It comes from a letter which Mr. Correlli Barnett[1] wrote

1. Correlli Barnett (born 1927) was a British military historian who would later argue, in *The Collapse of British Power,* that the obligations of empire led Britain to overextend itself and that subsequent decline followed in part from unrealistic, unwordly values instilled in the nation's elites.

to the *Spectator* after I had expressed my doubts about the current cry for "leadership" and "sense of purpose." He took me to task for what he called my "talk of open and free societies." I was, he said

> faithful to 19th-century humanism, liberalism, and parliamentarianism. All these are luxuries possible only to a world empire with a huge navy, a vast bank account, and few rivals. What faces Britain to-day is the more basic matter of survival, and survival in terms of developments in technology (with all their colossal sociological consequences) that our political traditions simply do not encompass. What Britain must think about is Power. . . . Without it, you simply do not count.

Mr. Correlli Barnett is not uncharacteristic of today's tough young realists. He throws humanism, liberalism and parliamentarianism into the dustbin. We can hardly complain that we have not been warned. By the time we grow infirm and elderly, clinging to our out-of-date humanism and liberalism, what place can there be for us in the society which he and *The Times* appear to envisage?

These quotations could be matched by many more over the past twelve months, especially from leading articles which have called for "leadership" and a "sense of purpose," and have sought to re-introduce the awful distinction between the "useful" and "useless" members of society. (This distinction is most easily resisted by assuming that one is among the "useless" members.) I have given these quotations attention because they help to underline the carelessness about liberty—about the actual liberty which we enjoy in this country—lying behind almost all "State of England" writing.

Its motives can be seen most clearly in the writings of the economists and of those who have set themselves up as spokesmen of the technocrats. Their trick is an old and familiar one, which has been most recently described, in another context, by Sir Isaiah Berlin:

> It is one of the stratagems of totalitarian régimes to present all situations as critical emergencies, demanding ruthless elimination of all goals, interpretations, forms of behaviour save for one absolutely specific, concrete, immediate end, binding on everyone, which calls for ends and means so narrowly and clearly definable that it is easy to impose sanctions for failing to pursue them.

We are, of course, nowhere near a totalitarian régime in this country, but we are daily getting nearer to using totalitarian arguments to justify another large encroachment on our liberty: or, rather, on some of our particular liberties.

If this seems to be pitching it too strongly, it is worth noticing that the currently fashionable criticisms* which are made of the amateur and the politician are merely the old and insidious managerial criticism of politics presented in a new jargon. Like Lord Reith,[2] their dark prophet, they ponder the deadly question, whether it is

> undesirable to have elected representatives associated with the management of public services? Logrolling; ears to the ground; fear of the electors;

---

*These criticisms have become, in Orwell's phrase, one of the "smelly little orthodoxies" of our time.

2. John Reith, 1st Baron Reith (1889–1971), was the founder and first director-general of the BBC.

everything submitted to the criterion of the vote. Timidity, compromise, mediocrity—are these the inevitable concomitants of democracy. . . ?

The voice of the manager then, now the voice of the technocrat, proclaiming, as does every opponent of free institutions, that freed from the necessity to consult ordinary people, he could run their lives for them far more efficiently and beneficently than they can themselves. It is time that, against their evil doctrine, we re-asserted our right to be inefficient.

Do I exaggerate the dislike which our "new men" have for our liberties? I do not think so. The clearest proof is in their most familiar comparisons. We are invited by them to contrast our own economic performance since the war with the "economic miracles" of Germany and France. This point deserves, one day, to be refuted in detail. Here, I must be satisfied with bald assertions.

1. I am extremely doubtful whether we have anything to learn from either the Fifth Republic in France or the Federal Republic in West Germany about the manner of ordering and sustaining a free society; I am not even sure whether we have much to learn in the matter from the French and Germans as peoples.

2. I am extremely doubtful whether either the Fifth Republic or the Federal Republic will survive. I hope that they will develop—and so survive. But, for the moment, I am prepared to wager fairly heavily that our own social and political arrangements will outlast theirs. Any takers?

3. I am convinced that the strength of our society lies in the spontaneity of its social decisions. They are decisions taken by responsible and independent societies within our society. The process is slow, but the experience goes deep.

4. I do not expect Continentals to understand this. But I do

expect Englishmen and even Americans to understand it. We have ways of conducting our affairs which provide our society with huge reserves of energy when it is needed: in a crisis.

The result is in history, and I think again will be. I am not one who is apt to confuse *vox populi* with *vox dei*, but the one thing which the people of this country have shown they can do, over a number of years, is sort out their long-term aspirations. This is their wisdom; and they are wise also in knowing that so ticklish a task cannot be left to the professionals, by whom I mean all those extraordinary people who are always wanting to do extraordinary things to us. Mr. Simon Raven may seem an unlikely character to find voicing the instincts of the common people, but, when faced by the fashionable cant of Mr. Anthony Sampson's *Anatomy of Britain,* he burst out that he had no wish to be efficient, especially at the price which seemed to be being asked.[3] In this, I believe he represented a deep and proper instinct in the English people.

On the whole, I am prepared to rest again on an assertion: that the English people are working their way, far more clearly and calmly than those who preach at them, to a quite realistic estimate of their changed position in the world and also, which is much more important, to the kind of body of common sentiments which makes a people conscious of itself as a people. It includes all kinds of rum things: but, above all, there runs through it an insistence that consideration for the weak should

3. Simon Raven (1927–2001) was a bon vivant who wrote two dozen novels, including *Alms for Oblivion,* and contributed social commentary to the *Spectator.* Anthony Sampson (1926–2004) wrote the influential study *Anatomy of Britain* in 1963, using careful research to demonstrate how completely Britain was governed by a network of elites, linked through school ties or family connections. He called for widespread modernization to equip the government to thrive in the postwar world.

never too little inform public policy. (This was the dreadful mistake which the Conservatives made in 1959.) To the charge that they think that only kindness matters, they would probably assent. It would be appalling hypocrisy, but there are many worse images for a people to hold of themselves.

"State of England" writing, however, would never have obtained its hold if there did not lie behind it something even more serious than an ignorance of the quality of English society: an ignorance of the quality of the whole of our civilisation. It is essential to take one quick look, and one lusty swipe, at those who set themselves up as the popular scourges of our civilisation (and therefore of this country as part of it). Like Gregory of Tours (but with considerably less reason) they cry "Woe to our times." They stand in a long and distinguished line, but I think it is necessary to see where their gloomy spirits take them. Here is the familiar rasp of Mr. Malcolm Muggeridge:

> Such is liberalism; the disease, not the cure, of our
> sick civilisation, a major destructive force in an age
> of destruction. The winds of change on which it
> rides blow over a charnel house, and carry a stench
> of death; its liberating armies, marching as to peace,
> rape, kill, and enslave on their way.

I am the last to dispute that the promises of liberalism have been among the great delusions of modern man. But the dæmonic force of liberalism has always been released by men using exactly the kind of language which Mr. Muggeridge himself uses. If the world and its institutions and its doings are so evil, then scorch its earch.

Whether it is Luther, or Mr. John Osborne[4] speaking through

4. John Osborne (1929–1994) won fame as an Angry Young Man for *Look Back in Anger*, his 1956 drama about disaffected postwar youth. In

the mouth of his make-believe Luther, the fury is equally destructive: even if, as in the case of Mr. Osborne, only self-
destructive. The violence, in turn, provokes counter-violence;
the reformation, counter-reformation; and the moderate man is
left, querulously calling with Erasmus: "If the dove of Christ—
not the owl of Minerva—would only fly to us, some measure
might be put to the madness of mankind."

I was thinking of Mr. Muggeridge's words as I walked along a
platform at Paddington on the Monday morning after they appeared. At the end of the platform stood a large white van. I
had to step to the side to get round it, and I stopped to watch.
One by one, railwaymen were going into it, and coming out of
it. On the sides of the van were the words: NATIONAL HEALTH
SERVICE: MASS RADIOGRAPHY UNIT. How many railwaymen
(and miners and factory-workers) would waste with T.B. without this service? It is at this point that one stops finding the
age peculiarly vile, and our society peculiarly evil. Savonarola,
I suspect, would not have thought much about that van. He
would have been fretting about the follies and wickednesses of
Ascot.

I am not saying that services like these are enough, only that
they take us a long way along *one* of the roads that we ought to be
travelling, and glad that we are travelling. In so far, then, as "State
of England" criticism is part of a chastising (self-chastising)
criticism of our times, I think we should be very careful that we
are not led into a blindness to the humanity and compassion
around us, lest we should thereby be led into a rejection of the
opportunities to extend those areas of humanity and compassion.
This is the worst form of obscurantism. Indulging the kind of
despair to which Mr. Muggeridge gives popular expression can

1961, he wrote *Luther,* another play about the individual protesting against
powerful authority: Martin Luther rejecting the Catholic Church.

lead much too easily to indifference and lethargy about sending just one more medical unit to the Congo.

Until we again think of ourselves individually as members of an enlightened Western civilisation, whose values, methods, and sense of direction we trust, we will never learn how to look at our own society as a member of it. We will become insularly preoccupied with things which scarcely matter a whit: with stops and goes in the economy; with evidences of a class structure which are more imagined than real, and which are anyhow breaking down; with tea-break strikes; with demarcation disputes; with an unimportant Communist Party and an equally unimportant monarchy; with public opinion polls on this, and mass observations of that; with traffic jams; with Mr. Marples; with Mr. Anthony Wedgwood Benn's title.[5]

For it is the lack of sense of proportion in "State of England" writing that most depresses me. Perhaps it is because the Critic has for the first time become a well-paid member of society, expecting services from it which were previously given only to the most privileged. I sometimes have the impression that all their criticism comes from a bad digestion. The thing most likely to set them off is a tasteless *bisque d'homard* in a luxury hotel, or the inability to obtain a meal when they reach Ballachulish after 10 p.m. It is all very affecting. But I do not really think that you can begin a reformation by nailing the *Good Food Guide* to the door of a provincial hotel. And there, I suspect, is

5. Ernest Marples (1907–1978) was Conservative MP for Wallasley and, in the late years of Macmillan's premiership, minister of transport. Anthony Wedgwood Benn (born 1925), popularly called Tony, had been the Labour MP for Bristol South East for a decade in 1960 when his father died, making him 2nd Viscount Stansgate. Forced to forfeit his seat in the House of Commons because of his title, he pressed for the passage of the Peerage Act, which in 1963 gave peers the right to relinquish their titles and remain in Commons.

the cause of it all. Our oligopoly of "State of England" writers (beside them, satire is only a home-loom industry) are consumed with guilt at what they consume from society.

So let it be, but I wish they would chastise themselves in private and, if they wish to record it all, put it into novels, or poems, or autobiographies, and not pretend that they are engaged in an objective concern for the "State of England."

Evolution of a Term

THE ESTABLISHMENT

The term "the Establishment," as it is now popularly used, was introduced into the common language and speech of England on September 23, 1955. Since then, it has made an antic journey into the language and speech of many other countries, and it is now reaching the dictionaries and reference books. It seems time to examine both its origins and its uses.

When Guy Burgess and Donald Maclean, two officials of the British Foreign Office, disappeared, in 1951, I was a leader writer on the *Times* of London, which still occupied its old building, at Printing House Square, E.C. 4. It was a modest building, standing comfortably round a small quadrangle, where there were hitching posts to which members of the editorial staff had once tied their horses, and it contained within it—the walls actually existing within the walls of the later additions—the old Printer's House. This original part of the building was known as Private House; to have called it *the* Private House would have been as much a solecism as to refer to *the* Marylebone Cricket Club. Leader writers worked in large and carpeted rooms, with coal fires. We were not expected to touch these, but to call a messenger boy if they needed tending. In the afternoon, as we composed ourselves to write, we might have tea in our rooms, brought to us by waitresses, in always clean and always starched uniforms, who were hired from what was then (and presumably

The New Yorker, October 19, 1968, originally titled "Evolution of a Term." Reprinted by permission from the Estate of Henry Fairlie.

still is) known as the Buckingham Palace division of J. Lyons & Co., Ltd., a firm that runs a chain of inexpensive cafés and cafeterias but also handled (and presumably still handles) the catering for large Palace functions. If a leader writer was not writing that day, he might take his tea in Private House, and in the evenings it was available for dining. Having been kept late at the office, I was dining in Private House on the evening after the announcement that Burgess and Maclean had vanished. At the table were two or three colleagues of mine who knew one or both of them well—the same schools, the same clubs—and the idea, which was being openly canvassed in the rest of Fleet Street, that the two diplomats might have defected to the Soviet Union was lightly dismissed. Guy? Donald? They had been on binges before. They would turn up again. "After all," said Mr. Alan Pryce-Jones, "Donald stood me up for dinner the night he disappeared. He owes me that."[1]

For the next few months, the "popular" press (certain, but unable to prove, where Burgess and Maclean were) kept a close watch on Maclean's wife. The "quality" press—the *Times* and the *Observer,* especially—refused to take part, and the friends of Maclean and his family protested vehemently against the way in which the "popular" newspapers were badgering Maclean's wife and children. Sir Donald Maclean, the missing diplomat's father, had been a gifted and charming Asquithian Liberal, and it was no surprise when Asquith's daughter, Lady Violet Bonham Carter, as fiercely and tenaciously loyal as ever, wrote a letter to the *Times* expressing savage contempt for the newspapers that were molesting the innocent—what else was to be assumed?—Melinda Maclean. During the next two years, while I remained

1. British author, journalist, and critic Alan Pryce-Jones (1908–2000) edited the *Times Literary Supplement* from 1948 to 1959 before relocating to America.

on its staff, the *Times* would not meddle with the story. Mrs. Maclean used these two years to make the necessary arrangements for her and her children to join her husband in Moscow.

By the autumn of 1955, I was the political columnist of the *Spectator*. In the week of September 23rd, there was only one possible subject for a political columnist to discuss: the acknowledgment by the Foreign Office of Burgess's and Maclean's defection. I had to write before both the publication of the White Paper on the subject and the debate on it in the House of Commons. As I sat in my room at 99 Gower Street, staring moodily at the blank piece of paper in my typewriter, the whole atmosphere of the *Times* during the days and months after the disappearance, the memory of hints and pressures to which I had paid only casual attention at the time, returned to me. I went and played a game of bar billiards at the Marlborough, the pub the *Spectator* used, and returned and wrote. I left in the evening, having turned in a column that appeared to me to be rather mediocre, but understandably so in the circumstances.

The relevant excerpts from the "Political Commentary" that appeared in the *Spectator* of September 23, 1955, are as follows:

> I have several times suggested that what I call the "Establishment" in this country is today more powerful than ever before. By the "Establishment," I do not mean only the centres of official power—though they are certainly part of it—but rather the whole matrix of official and social relations within which power is exercised. The exercise of power in Britain (more specifically, in England) cannot be understood unless it is recognised that it is exercised socially. Anyone who has at any point been close to the exercise of power will know what I mean when I say that the "Establishment" can be seen at work in

the activities of not only the Prime Minister, the Archbishop of Canterbury, and the Earl Marshal but of such lesser mortals as the chairman of the Arts Council, the Director-General of the B.B.C., and even the editor of *The Times Literary Supplement*, not to mention divinities like Lady Violet Bonham Carter.

Somewhere near the heart of the pattern of social relationships which so powerfully controls the exercise of power in this country is the Foreign Office. By its traditions and its methods of recruitment the Foreign Office makes it inevitable that the members of the Foreign Service will be men (and the Foreign Service is one of the bastions of masculine English society) who, to use a phrase which has been used a lot in the past few days, "know all the right people." At the time of the disappearance of Maclean and Burgess, "the right people" moved into action. Lady Violet Bonham Carter was the most active . . . and how effectively they worked may be traced in the columns of the more respectable newspapers at the time, especially of *The Times* and of the *Observer*.

I am certain that "the Establishment" would not then have entered the language if it had not been for the correspondence that followed my original column. In its next issue, the *Spectator* published two vigorous letters. The first was from Lady Violet Bonham Carter, claiming that "such action as I took was solely relevant to the persecution of their families by certain members of the press." The second was from Mr. John Sparrow, the Warden of All Souls at Oxford, who defended the Foreign Office's methods of recruitment, and added "a word of general appreciation of Mr. Fairlie's Commentary," which he found "full of low

innuendo and false in almost all its assumptions and sugges-
tions." Neither of them used, or commented on, the term "the
Establishment." In the issue of October 7th, however, the fat was
put in the fire by Sir Robert Boothby, M.P. (now Lord Boothby).
In a correspondence that was to be marked by strenuous abuse
and invective, his was almost the briefest, and certainly the
sharpest, letter of all. Unelaborate and unadorned, it ran:

> I am not surprised that Warden Sparrow has weighed
> in with an offensive letter about Mr. Fairlie's article.
> . . . All Souls was the headquarters of the Establish-
> ment during the decade immediately preceding the
> Second World War; and it would be difficult to
> overestimate the damage then done to this country
> at that disastrous dinner table.

That did it.

If it had not been enough in itself, the other letters the *Spectator* published that week poured more fat onto the flame. Mr.
David Astor, the editor of the *Observer*, made the same defense
of his activities that Lady Violet Bonham Carter had done,
accused me of a libellous smear, and went on:

> . . . his picture of an "Establishment" of influential
> people wielding power in this country and secretly
> defending or helping one another . . . amounts to
> saying that the higher echelons of our public life are
> a racket. Here again, is he doing anything more
> than some rather wild and libellous "smearing"?

There followed a characteristic letter from Mr. Randolph
Churchill,[2] which, while awarding me a prize or two, added that

2. Randolph Churchill (1911–1968) was the journalist son of Winston
Churchill and one of the foremost figures in Fleet Street of the early post-

he had always thought that my bonnet "concealed a whole bee-hive of nonsense about what he terms 'the Establishment.'" This was followed by a pseudonymous letter, signed "Stephen Dumpling," that said there was no doubt about the existence of "the Establishment":

> It is a power in the land, possibly *the* power in the land. Mr. Fairlie sums it up with almost Orwell clarity. It can be seen at work, now and then, by standing on tiptoe from just beyond the pale. As it is sometimes necessary for me to rely on its good will,
> I sign myself
>   Stephen Dumpling

Finally, that week Lady Violet Bonham Carter herself referred to "the Establishment"—of course dismissing it as "a fictitious body."

I was now being asked to the more irreverent luncheon tables within "the Establishment," and for a time I found it interesting enough to sit, rather silent and rather distrustful, at them. But I was disconcerted by what already seemed to me a wrong interpretation that was being put on the phrase. I found "nothing sinister" in the existence of an "Establishment," I said in the *Spectator* of October 7th. Indeed, "I believe that it is desirable that something like the 'Establishment' should exist, because it prevents even worse influences from operating." My main point, I continued, was simply that the tentacles of "the Establishment" now spread wide:

> The spread of the "Establishment's" influence is due partly to the increase in the number of official and

---

war era. Defeated in several attempts to reach Parliament, he started the official, multivolume biography of his father.

semi-official bodies [I mentioned the Arts Council, the B.B.C., and the British Council], and partly to the *apparent* diminution in the *formal* powers of the "Establishment" which has made people less suspicious of the *actual* power and influence which its members exercise.

But the word already had its own existence.

In the *Spectator* of October 14th, Mr. Malcolm Muggeridge joined the battle, ending, with his familiar rasp, " . . . even the children [of the Macleans] should be able to acquire prestige by recounting, during the Marx-Leninism lessons, how their clever mother made complete mugs of Lady Violet, Mr. Astor, and others who constitute, in Mr. Fairlie's felicitous phrase, the 'Establishment.'" In the same issue, Mr. Colm Brogan, a far more eager controversialist than his brother Sir Denis,[3] addressed himself to Lady Violet Bonham Carter, finally leaving the issue of Burgess and Maclean behind:

> She believes that the "Establishment" is a malicious invention, like the "Cliveden Set." She believes it does not exist. The reason is simple. She does not believe in its existence because she is in the heart of it. The "Establishment" is the air she breathes. . . . A small group which quite readily admits valuable outsiders and maintains a fringe of hangers-on is all that really matters. They are England versus the Rest.

In the same issue, Mr. Churchill returned to the debate, and I replied to him in much the same terms as Mr. Brogan's: the

3. Colm Brogan (1902–1977) was a conservative journalist and author. Sir Denis William Brogan (1900–1974) was a British-born historian of American politics.

phrase would make sense to him only if he would "stand outside the Establishment for a moment and look in."

The term would not now lie down, and the *Spectator*, of course, was running one of the most enthralling correspondences to be carried by any newspaper or journal in Britain since the war. In the issue of October 21st, Sir Robert Boothby, describing himself as "one who has bumped into it, on and off, for thirty years—and seldom emerged unscathed," wrote that "the Establishment" as it had existed before 1939 "always included the reigning Archbishop of Canterbury, Editor of the *Times,* Governor of the Bank of England, and Secretary to the Cabinet." These members of "the Establishment," he said, "had no need to dine together in order to achieve their ends," for "they were in telepathic as well as telephonic communication with one another." In that issue, too, the dismissive voice of Mr. Hugh Trevor-Roper (not yet the Regius Professor of Modern History at Oxford; he had to wait for that until his own contact in "the Establishment," Mr. Harold Macmillan, had attained power) inquired what all the fuss was about: "No doubt you are right in supposing that there is an 'Establishment,' though it is hardly a novel discovery to observe that there is here and now, as everywhere and at all times, a governing class." The effect of this disdainful observation was a little undone by a letter from Mr. P. H. Sutton, describing the attitude of "the Establishment" toward those who had mentioned its existence: "These chaps aren't exactly breaking the rules, but it just isn't cricket."

With that, the *Spectator* closed the correspondence.

As I have said, I do not think that without this correspondence the term would have entered the English language. On the other hand, that the term did not die with the correspondence and the particular occasion suggests that it was needed—that it supplied a want. Before I turn to that question, however, it is necessary to see if the term can be traced back further than my use of it in the *Spectator*.

In my original article, it will have been observed, I wrote, "I have several times suggested that what I call the 'Establishment'..." Moreover, Mr. Randolph Churchill, in his reference to the "whole beehive of nonsense" about "the Establishment" which my bonnet concealed, seemed to suggest that he had known me use the expression before. Had I done so in writing? If I had, I am not aware of it, and no one has pointed it out to me. Professor Ronald Hindmarsh, of Smith College, has said, with a solemnity that does not appear to be mocking, "It is common knowledge that Mr. Henry Fairlie used and defined the term in his column in the *Spectator* of September 23, 1955. But, if I read him aright, he was using it in private before that date." He is quite correct. I and a number of friends were using the word familiarly, if not frequently, before I finally committed it to paper.

We were young then—grandly poor and irreverent. A group of hungry young journalists, intent largely on enjoying ourselves at the expense of our elders and betters—and of our readers. They were the years before Suez. I think we knew that something like that was going to happen. Our recurring topic of conversation was "the state of England," long before anyone else (except Mr. Muggeridge, who was then editing *Punch*) had got hold of the subject. Our dislike of the secularization of English life since the Reformation underlay all our attitudes, and Mr. John Raymond[4] was intellectually the most daring among us in his insistence, night after night, that the common law had replaced religion in England and that in the secular idols erected

4. John Raymond (1923–1977) was a critic and literary editor of the *New Statesman* whose books include *Simenon in Court*. He was a close friend of Fairlie's.

or sustained under the common law could be found the cause of most of our evils. His vehemence against Edward Coke, for so long held up by Whig historians as the greatest common lawyer of all time and one of the founders of English liberties, was almost personal, as if Coke were still alive. To us, he was. It is true that several of us were Catholics—but very English Catholics, much in the spirit of Ronald Knox's reply when he was asked why, although he was a monsignor, he had never visited the Vatican: "I see no reason why a first-class passenger should go down to the engine room." Most of us were not Catholics, however. The point was not religion but the substitute that had been found for it: the total secularization of English life and thought—and feeling, also—which had left England with nothing it could fall back on now that physical power and material wealth were departing. We felt the loss of power before Suez confirmed it. Once the Suez adventure had begun, the more right-wing of us romantically, if a little desperately, supported it. But our common reaction was one of anger at England's futility, which was vividly summarized by Mr. Raymond when he upbraided the Third Programme for meeting England's hour of crisis "with a tinkle of Scarlatti."

When, some time later, Mr. Richard Crossman, now Lord President of the Council, said, "If anyone deserves to be called 'the first of the Angry Young Men,' it is Mr. Henry Fairlie"—a remark that he did not intend, and I did not take, as a compliment—he was pinpointing us as the precursors of a mood. But our own mood, in which we gaily found the word "Establishment," will be misunderstood if it is represented only as one of anger, and, in particular, of Look *Back* in Anger. We loved— and we hated—England. But we loved it—as we hated it—with a particular flourish that is now hard to find. Socialists and Conservatives—we were one or the other; there was not a Liberal among us—we were, in a sense, restorers. Conservative or

Socialist, we wished to restore England's truth—or, rather, wished that those who ruled England would stir themselves to restore it. And, Conservative or Socialist, we saw the barrier as the Whig lie that had governed England since 1688. Mr. Harold Macmillan once said that no governing class in all history had ruled for so long and with such ease as the Whigs in England between 1688 and 1886. The whole "Establishment" that the Whigs had erected and maintained for two hundred years, and that was still perpetuated in the prevailing ideas and institutions of the country, was our enemy. The rights of property, the common law, the Established Church, the vulgar little monarchy brought from Hanover, a landed class that was irrelevant but still influential, a moneyed class that feared enterprise because that would disturb its hold on the City, a governing class that wished merely to play Box and Cox in office, and the characteristic Whig invention of semiofficial bodies, such as the B.B.C., where valuable hangers-on could serve the Whig lie—all these seemed to us to be the cause of the irreligion of England, which had been tolerable while wealth and power were guarantees of spaciousness but was not now that we felt our country on the Gadarene slope. With this hodgepodge of attitudes and instincts, not unlike those of "Young England" in the nineteenth century, it was quite natural that we should use the term "the Establishment," which for so long in England had in effect represented both the Established Church and the vast network of interests of which it had been both the spiritual and the temporal front.

No sooner had the term caught on than Mr. A. J. P. Taylor, who often joined our company, could be heard murmuring that he had used it some years earlier.[5] Although the actual reference

5. A. J. P. Taylor (1906–1990) was one of the best-known and most controversial British historians of the twentieth century; his works include *The Origins of the Second World War.*

has never been publicly identified, I believe it can be found in a book review that he contributed to the *New Statesman* in the early fifties. By October, 1957, in a special number of the *Twentieth Century*, Mr. Taylor regarded the phrase with as much enthusiasm as if it were a bunch of sour grapes. Mr. Fairlie was believed to have started it, he said, but he had seen its origin ascribed to himself. Anyhow, he regretted the idea, whoever had had it, and he felt that we would have done better to revive William Cobbett's[6] much older term, "THE THING":

> That sugggests much better the complacency, the incompetence, and the selfishness which lie behind the façade. THE THING exists for the sake of its members, not for ours.

There, by and large, the matter was left until Mr. Hesketh Pearson put in a bid. In the final essay in his book "Extraordinary People," published in January, 1965, one found an opening sentence of just the aplomb that one associates with the circle of which he and Frank Harris and Bernard Shaw were the most talkative members:

> As I appear to have given general currency to the word "Establishment" used in a secular sense, I will here explain how it eventually appeared in my biography of Henry Labouchère, published in 1936.

In 1913, he explained, he had been struck by the virulent antagonism of "the dons" to Frank Harris's biography of Shakespeare, and had concluded that it was due to "the fear of originality

6. William Cobbett (1763–1835) was a prolific journalist, a member of Parliament, and a fearless critic of corruption in the British government. He agitated for the Reform Act of 1832, and he is perhaps best remembered for *Rural Rides*, an account of his travels in the English countryside.

always displayed by people with conventional minds, who in self-defence form a mutual-protection society which in effect becomes an establishment." At that date, Mr. Pearson concedes, he did not actually use the word, but, jumping twenty-two years, he went on:

> When I was writing his [Labouchère's] life in 1935, I happened one day to be discussing the whole question of institutionalism with Hugh Kingsmill and Malcolm Muggeridge. I remember we laughed heartily over the fact that Charles Darwin, whose evolutionary theories had horrified the Church of England in 1859, was yet buried in Westminster Abbey twenty-three years later. . . . In the course of our talk, we certainly bandied the word "establishment," and I developed the theme under that name in my biography *Labby*.

Turning to "Labby," one finds that Mr. Pearson had indeed used the phrase in one of the senses it has currently acquired. Samuel Butler, he said, had discovered that

> the Church was not the only organisation that had an Establishment. Science had one too, with its priests and high-priests, its excommunications and anathemas. The world of painting also has its Royal Academy, medicine its Association, while economics, politics, letters, law, the army and the navy have their sacred inner rings which it is the ambition of everyone in the outer circles to placate or penetrate, though the genius knows instinctively that he must stand alone, unbuttressed by his professional Establishment.
>
> Labby . . . saw through the Establishment of pol-

itics. . . . Although the Establishment draws the line at genius, which is uncontrollable, it does not object to talent, because the occasional indiscretions of talent do no harm and in a way reflect glory on the Establishment, which must surely be a very sound and wonderful institution to find room for such gifted and outspoken members.

Mr. Pearson was using the phrase as many use it now, to suggest merely those who control any institution or profession; this is a very different matter, of course, from the single "Establishment"—the whole pattern of official and social relationships in Britain—that those of us who were using the word in the nineteen-fifties were attempting to describe and knock.

Mr. Pearson's, anyhow, was not the earliest bid that could be made. Some eager investigator discovered that Ford Madox Ford had used the phrase in private, as Douglas Goldring recorded in "The Nineteen Twenties" (1945):

It was a head-on collision between two acknowledged leaders of the literary avant-garde and the powerful forces of what Ford Madox Ford used to call the Establishment.

The collision to which Mr. Goldring was referring was between Wyndham Lewis and Roy Campbell, on the one hand, and R. Ellis Roberts, who was then responsible for the literary side of the *New Statesman*, on the other. (Ellis Roberts had refused to publish Roy Campbell's review of one of Wyndham Lewis's books.) Mr. Goldring does not explain precisely what Ford Madox Ford meant by the phrase. The silence from the grave is tantalizing.

Attempts to trace the word even further back have been made from time to time, but they have always rested on an elementary confusion over the traditional English use of "Establishment" to signify the Established Church. Many of the political struggles in the nineteenth century, and even in the early years of the twentieth, were precisely struggles of Nonconformists or Dissenters, who felt themselves both social and political outsiders, against "the Establishment" and all whom it supported and all who supported it. In England, at any rate, the ecclesiastical meaning of "the Establishment" cannot help informing the current use of the term in its secular sense. It is especially interesting, therefore, that the earliest use I have come across of the term as we now popularly employ it was in a country whose constitution expressly forbids "an establishment of religion." One weekend, I was casually reading a lecture on "The Conservative" that Emerson gave on December 9, 1841, at the Masonic Temple in Boston. The lecture takes the form of an imaginary dialogue between a reformer and a conservative, and Emerson identified the conservative as "an upholder of the establishment, a man of many virtues." Emerson then has the conservative describe how Friar Bernard set out from his cell on Mount Cenis to "reform the corruption of mankind" but was overwhelmed by the generosity and kindness of the rich families he met in Rome, and returned home crying, "... these Romans, whom I prayed God to destroy, are lovers, they are lovers; what can I do?" It is a classic description of the influence that the bland and insinuating manners of an "Establishment" are supposed to have. "The reformer concedes that these mitigations exist," Emerson continued dryly, and that "if he proposed comfort, he should take sides with the establishment." The palm, I think, has to be given to Emerson, since his use could only be secular. And there the search for origins may be brought to an end.

Although the term has begun to reach the reference books, it has not yet reached any dictionary that is built on historical principles, giving as precise references as possible to a world's earliest use. To expect to see the new edition of the Oxford English Dictionary is to ask for a life running much longer than the allotted Biblical span, and even the latest edition of the Shorter Oxford English Dictionary (one of the masterpieces of dictionary-making) has no addenda recent enough to include the word's current usage.

For this we have to turn to "modern and mechanical man," as Hazlitt described the American. In the addenda to Webster's Third New International Dictionary, there appears the following entry:

> **establishment,** *n. often cap.* 1: a group of social, economic, and political leaders who form a ruling class (as of a nation) ⟨the prince of Wales . . . frightened the *Establishment* because he sympathized with the starving miners of Wales—W. J. Igoe⟩ 2: a controlling group ⟨the Welsh literary *Establishment* . . . kept him out of everything—Keidrych Rhys⟩ ⟨the movie [*Establishment*] . . . has existed for perhaps a dozen years—Hollis Alpert⟩

The most arresting feature of this entry is that the first two illustrations both refer to Wales; it makes one wonder about the reading of lexicographers.

In Webster's New World Dictionary of the American Language, College Edition (1966) is this:

> **the Establishment,** 1. the Church of England. 2. the Presbyterian Church of Scotland. 3. In England, a complex consisting of the church, the royal family, and the plutocracy, regarded as holding the chief measure of power and influence. 4. the ruling inner circle of any nation, institution, etc.

Although these definitions contain one howler—a proper Establishment is the enemy of a plutocracy—their general direction is sound, and more satisfactory than those of the parent dictionary.

In the Random House Dictionary one finds:

> **4. the Establishment,** the existing power structure in society, a field of endeavor, etc.; institutional authority: *The Establishment believes exploring outer space is worth any tax money spent. Young writers feel that the literary Establishment is unjust.*

One of the difficulties with this definition is that it is lumped together with ten other meanings, or alleged meanings, of the term, ranging from "the act or an instance of establishing" to "a fixed or settled income." The Random House Dictionary distinguishes finely between the state's recognition of an established church and a church so recognized, but those definitions are the ninth and the tenth entries, whereas the popular and secular use is the fourth. There is not the slightest hint, therefore, of historical origins and connections. A second difficulty is that the definition does what no dictionary has a right to do: it borrows another equally recent, equally vague and shapeless term to do the work of definition. The phrase "power structure" has grown into the language almost simultaneously with "the Establishment." To define one by reference to the other abdicates the responsibility of lexicography. One turns, of course, to see if the Random House Dictionary enters the phrase "power structure." It does:

> **pow′er struc′ture, 1.** the system of authority or influence in government, politics, education, etc.: *The state elections threatened to upset the existing power structure.*
> **2.** The people who participate in such a system: *He hoped to become a part of the power structure.*

At first, there seems to be another fine distinction made, between a system of authority and influence and those who—who what? There's the rub. The definition says "the people who participate in" the system. But even the poorest and humblest worker who, wanting to keep body and soul together, acquiesces in and serves a "system of authority or influence" participates in it, whether he is the saddler who made harness for the Earl of Westmorland or the factory worker who today makes a small piece of upholstery for Henry Ford II. But although they participate in a system, they do not compose it in any significant sense. The Random House Dictionary, in fact, defines "the Establishment" in terms of "the existing power structure," which it then defines poorly, and this confusion, although partly the fault of the editors of the dictionary, serves as a warning of how imprecise are many of the terms we now use in discussing politics.

In the most recent, "completely revised and modernized" edition of Roget's Thesaurus (1965), "the Establishment" appears in the index thus:

Establishment, the
influence, 178n.
master, 741n.
upper class, 868n.

If the term is an alternative to all of these, it has not only travelled far and wide but become meaningless in doing so.

Brewer's Dictionary of Phrase & Fable is an admirably handy reference book. At the turn of a page, it tells one what city was known as the Carthage of the North, where Castle Terabil was supposed to stand in Arthurian legend, and the meaning of "Touch not a cat but a glove," which is the motto of the Mackintosh clan. I have to confess to some disappointment that the

1963 revised edition consented—so early—to give its recognition to "the Establishment":

> A term which has recently acquired a special meaning denoting the hierarchy in any particular sphere of the community, or the hierarchy taken collectively. It has the slightly derogatory implication that the hierarchy is stolid, unimaginative, and reactionary.

That is, all the same, the austere manner of the old Brewer's. But the reference book that has handled the phrase with most disdain is Fowler's Dictionary of Modern English Usage as revised by Sir Ernest Gowers (1965):

> **establishment.** *Their enthusiasm is tempered by the coolness of the E. "Space travel," said the Astronomer Royal recently, "is utter bilge."/ Some of the blame must go to the Theatrical E. Their influence on the theatre is disastrous in every way./ Sir Oliver musters the women's colleges, 23 heads of houses, 4 heads of halls, and 9 professors. If anything, a vote for Mr. Macmillan is a vote against what many dons regard as the University E./ In his career he has shown enviable ability to drop bricks without disaster, to keep the respect of the E. but retain the liberty to hold advanced opinions./ The fusty E. with its Victorian views and standards of judgement must be destroyed./ Today the membership list of the Yacht Club is studded with E. names./ Mr. Crossman has suggested that it is the duty of the Labour Party to provide an "ideology for non-conformist critics of the E."* The use of *establishment* illustrated by these quotations leapt into popularity in the nineteen-fifties. It was started by the use of *Establishment* by certain writers as a pejorative term for an influence that they

held to be socially mischievous. In their choice of a word for the object of their attack they have been too successful. *Establishment* has become a VOGUE WORD, and whatever meaning they intended to give it, never easy to gather with precision from their various definitions, has been lost beneath the luxuriance of its overgrowth. As one of them has sadly recorded: "Intended to assist inquiry and thought, this virtuous, almost demure, phrase has been debauched by the whole tribe of professional publicists and vulgarizers who today imagine that a little ill-will entitles them to comment on public affairs. Corrupted by them, the *Establishment* is now a harlot of a phrase. It is used indiscriminately by dons, novelists, playwrights, poets, composers, artists, actors, dramatic critics, literary critics, script writers, even band leaders and antique dealers, merely to denote those in positions of power whom they happen to dislike most" (Henry Fairlie in *The Establishment,* Anthony Blond, 1959).

It is perhaps not surprising that I regard this as the most valuable of the definitions of and comments on the phrase which have so far appeared in the reference works. Certainly the attempts that the dictionaries have made to give the phrase a clear meaning suggest that we are indeed using a corrupt term, which, besides not assisting inquiry and thought, may actually be obstructing them.

As has been seen, I tried to wriggle away from the success of the word almost as soon as I first used it in print. But when I made my contribution to Mr. Hugh Thomas's anthology of essays,[7]

7. *The Establishment* (1959), edited by Hugh Thomas, featured long essays on the phenomenon Fairlie had identified four years earlier. Fairlie contributed an essay on the BBC, which he called "the voice of the Establishment."

from which Sir Ernest Gowers took his quotation, a reviewer commented that the spectacle of me trying to rid myself of the word was like that of "Mr. Rockefeller trying to throw away his millions." Even more aptly, when I was bewailing one evening what had happened to the word since I first used it, Mr. Joseph Kraft[8] (who, among American political columnists, most deserves to be called a precise user of words) remarked, "To introduce an idea like that is like giving drink to the working classes." It has certainly been like giving drink to working writers.

Before the great French historian Marc Bloch was tortured and finally executed by the Germans, he wrote a personal testament, which has been published under the title "Strange Defeat." It was written in an appalling moment, in terrible circumstances, yet Bloch never forgot the manners of his civilization ("the sacred soil of France from which, in the past, so many rich harvests have been taken") or the discipline of his craft. In his description of the French collapse, Bloch referred to "the utter incompetence of the High Command," but then, a few paragraphs further on, he wrote, in the middle of his passion:

> I referred a while back to the "High Command." But scarcely had my pen written the words when the historian in me was shocked by their use. For the ABC of my trade consists in avoiding the big-sounding abstract terms. Those who teach history should be continually concerned with the task of seeking the solid and the concrete behind the empty and the abstract. In other words, it is on men rather than functions that they should concentrate their atten-

8. Joseph Kraft (1924–1986) was a highly respected American journalist who covered politics for the *Washington Post*, the *New York Times*, and *Harper's* and who authored a widely syndicated column.

tion. The errors of the High Command were, fundamentally, the errors of a specific group of human
beings.

Political reporting and comment today—written by men who
face not a firing line but, at most, a mere deadline—are full of "the
empty and the abstract" as a substitute for "the solid and the
concrete." We are always reading, or always writing, about "the
Pentagon" or "the Senate Club" or "the White House" or
"Whitehall" or "the Quai d'Orsay," and "the Establishment" is
simply the last and most general of these "empty and abstract"
terms, which, precisely because of its vagueness and its shapeless-
ness, can be used in almost any country about almost anything.

It is not, I think, a coincidence that the term will be found
frequently in the Sunday edition of the New York *Times* but only
rarely in its daily editions. During the week, when reporters are
about their proper business of describing "the solid and the
concrete," there is no place, as there is no need, for a concept
such as "the Establishment." On Sunday, however, the journalists (and outside writers performing like journalists) feel im-
pelled or compelled to abandon "the solid and the concrete" and
take us into what I still like to spell as "aëry" regions. Similarly, I
think it is no coincidence that the term appears with regularity
in magazines whose writers feel driven to offer the idea behind
the event and the forces behind the idea. This is teleological
journalism, infirmly based on the doctrine that final causes exist,
and that, whereas they cannot be discovered or discussed in
ordinary daily journalism, they can be explored in more leisurely
columns. Intrepidly, these writers invite us to come with them
up a river so that they may show us its source, but again and
again the only source they find is an uncharted lake called "the
Establishment." They fall in, and we with them.

The idea of inner circles and hidden forces and final causes can very easily be translated into a theory of conspiracy, and this, I think, goes far to explain why the term has become so popular. A significant proportion of the random examples given above use "the Establishment" to hint at conspiracy—to hint at it so vaguely that the writer can never be pinned down to actual names, but also so suggestively that the reader is persuaded he need not ask for names. The success of the term is, in part, a response to a desire to explain our politics in terms of conspiracy, and we are left with the question of why this desire should be so strong today. The most apparent reason I can think of is that many of the Western democracies have experienced various forms of radical or left-wing government and have found, at the end of the day, that the ways in which a society is governed or managed remain much the same as before. The popularity of conspiracy theories, or near-conspiracy theories, today is an in-fantile replacement for the political utopianism that no one any longer has the heart to nourish.

One of the most noteworthy characteristics of today's youthful dissenters is their pessimism, contrasted with the traditional optimism of the young. The term "the Establishment" is tailor-made for them, since it carries the implication that they will always be defeated. Indeed, the implication in the term itself prepares the way for the inevitable consequence. As one watched the hapless demonstrators—not their leaders—on the streets of Chicago in August, one could not help contemplating that their energies had been misdirected: that, having been persuaded to oppose a nonexistent Establishment, they were now being beaten about the head by a very existent Mayor Richard Daley, the source of whose power they could not identify.

I am a Conservative—a term of some respectability in England —and I do not think it is unimportant that it was a Conservative, in a Conservative journal, who launched the term "the Establish-ment" in England. It was immediately adopted, of course, by the vociferous left wing. But not the least important incident in the history of the term was an early attack made on its use by Mr. Anthony Crosland, who is now a prominent member of the Labour Government. Although Mr. Crosland has often been accused (as his friend Hugh Gaitskell was) of being on the right wing of the Labour Party, he showed in his books while he was in opposition, and has shown in his actions since he has been in office, more genuine and accurate Socialist determination in attacking the causes of inequality than most of his colleagues and critics. The idea of "the Establishment," he said at the time, was a distraction, which diverted attention from what really needed to be changed to a nonexistent conspiracy. In a way, he was right, and, having launched the term as a Conservative, it is as what Miss Helen Waddell, in that great achievement "The Wandering Scholars," called "a conservative of letters" that I wish the language could be rid of it.

Chips of Memory

My career as a movie actor was not long. But it had a certain dramatic unity to it. One line in one scene in one film. No critic gave my performance a bad review, and even today, when the movie is shown on the late-night shows, my appearance is passed over by the viewers in silence, the tribute of their unspeakable satisfaction and surrender.

To explain why I gave up so promising a career, I need to tell the story from the beginning. I was the son of Scottish parents who moved to London, my father having thrown up his patrimony of some of the richest farmland in Scotland to become a journalist, a sin that has been visited upon his son as a punishment. They chose to live in Highgate, once a handsome village just north of London, but by then a suburb. Halfway up Highgate Hill is the spot where Francis Bacon carried out his scientific experiment in refrigeration, stuffing the carcass of a chicken with snow, and catching a cold from which he died, which has always made me question the prudence for which his Essays are renowned.

Not far away is Highgate Cemetery, where both Karl Marx and Radclyffe Hall are buried, although not side by side. The disciples of *Das Kapital* place ornate wreaths on Marx's grave—they obviously get enough out of the book to do well out of the system—while the devotees of *The Well of Loneliness* put knots of violets on its author's tomb. At the top of the Hill, every house

The New Republic, July 1, 1978, originally titled "Reconsideration: Chips of Memory." Reprinted by permission from the Estate of Henry Fairlie.

seems to have a literary or historical association, especially with the romantics. Coleridge died there, still excitably talking, we must believe, through the last dose. Among such ghosts I was raised.

But my most vivid association is with the schools where I was sent. At the age of five I went to a kindergarten kept by the Misses Legge. The romantics had left their names all over the place, and the kindergarten was called Byron House School. This unfortunate name did not help the Misses Legge to inculcate much seemliness in their little charges. Some years later a girl who was to become a film actress—Elizabeth Tailor, was it, or Elizabeth Tyler?—was also a pupil at the school which by then took anyone. But clearly the Byronic influence was still working strongly.

Under the instruction of the Misses Legge, my Scottish accent was diluted, but it was still noticeable when, at the age of eight, I crossed the road to Highgate School. It was founded in 1565, when English poetry was flowering, as may be seen from the school song:

> In fifteen hundred and sixty-five,
> When Glorious Bess was still alive,
> Up Highgate Hill, sedate and slow,
> As a Lord Chief Justice ought to go,
> Rode Sir Roger Cholmley—O!
> > Cholmley—O!
> > Cholmley—O!
> As a Lord Chief Justice ought to go,
> Rode Sir Roger Cholmley—O!

He had founded the school, and I am an Old Cholmleian for ever.

Highgate was what the major public schools—rather uninventively—call a minor public school. It had the best traditions of both. The headmaster was a cleric in the Church of England and, true to his orders, appeared before the whole school in various states of intoxication. The birch was frequently laid across our behinds, once across my bare behind, because I had put a football bladder in my shorts to soften the blow. One master had played soccer for the Arsenal, one of the most famous professional teams in London, and was assigned to teach us French. I learned how to say "Le soccer." He also had a habit of breaking open the skin on my knuckles by rapping them with the metal edge of a ruler. The German master used to pull the short hairs at the back of our necks, as he hammered in some metre from Schiller, which prepared us to confront the Nazis. T. S. Eliot once taught English there, which literary critics should take into account.

Year by year my Scottish accent was diluted still more, a fact which appalled my Scottish grandmother. "I dinna ken why your mother abides it." I also did not like losing my accent, but I accepted that this was my lot, and the school did its best with rod and insult.

Then one day our school OTC was taken in buses to MGM's studios at Denham, where they were filming the original version of *Goodbye, Mr. Chips*.[1] When the OTC marches off to war in the film it is from Highgate. In the Christmas holidays, the studio called again. The crowd scenes were being done by boys from Dr. Barnado's Home, one of the largest orphanages in London, but unfortunately they did not have the right accents for the small speaking parts. Could the school gather a reserve of about 24 boys, between the heights of 5′4″ and 5′8″, from which the studio could draw the number it needed each day?

---

1. The Officer Training Corps (OTC) is a program of the British army offering leadership instruction to students. During the Second World War, it functioned at both the public school and university levels.

The responsibility fell on me as the boy in charge of the dramatic society. (I was only 13 at the time but the remains of my Scottish accent had enabled me to give a convincing performance as the Second Witch in *Macbeth*.) I chose the schoolfriends whom I liked. Boys who did not usually speak to me began to come round to my home. I told them not to call me, I would call them. Each day we were collected by a studio bus at about 5:30 a.m., and before we were taken home in the evening the casting director told me how many boys were needed the next day. This meant that I stood up in the bus—gazing indifferently at the cherubic faces—and singled out the six who would be collected in the morning.

They were paid £1 a day, which was riches to a schoolboy then, while I earned £2 as the organizer. I of course also went every day, and that Christmas earned about £50. If I had stuck to being a casting director, I would now have a house on Malibu Beach.

They were filming two other movies at Denham at the time. One of them was *The Four Feathers,* that magnificent story of heroism and cowardice in the Sudan after Gordon's death, on which Alexander Korda of course spared neither money nor his fertile imagination. But it created a hazard for us. Dressed in our Eton suits and collars, we would be ordered from our dressing rooms to the set. We would thread our way through the labyrinthine studios, suddenly to find ourselves surrounded by a thousand dancing dervishes of the Mahdi, while Ralph Richardson stood alone and at bay on some promontory. It was all that I could do to keep my small band together, and get it to the right set where Robert Donat was preparing a Latin lesson.

Robert Donat was infinitely kind to us—Greer Garson was more standoffish, but then the leers of schoolboys must be tiresome—and he often ate with us in the cafeteria. When he was made up in the morning as an old man, he acted as an old man throughout the day, even when he was off the set. He explained that he had been brought up on the stage, and that he could not get used to slipping in and out of a part for the short takes in making a movie, so often at lunch he would cup his ear and say, "Eh? Can't hear you, Fairlie. Speak up, eh!"

I was showing the organizing genius of a Carnot, keeping the egos of 24 budding stars in rein, but I suddenly realized that, because of my duties, I was not being given a line, whereas the boy Webber, whom I had almost not chosen anyhow, had already had three lines. I went to the casting director with whom I had some leverage, since he relied on me to keep the other boys under my thumb, and said that I could not promise to go on if I did not get a line. "All right, Fairlie, you'll have one."

He was true to his word. One line, no more. It was handed to me the night before the shooting. I was to run into Robert Donat as the old Mr. Chips in a doorway, lift my cap and look up at him and say "I thought you were away for the hols, sir!" You may think that such a line is easy to memorize, especially when you have had to learn the whole of *The Ancient Mariner* in one night. But memorizing is not the whole of acting. When many years later I told my story to Peter Finch, he agreed that the two "s's" running together between "hols" and "sir" would have tested the enunciation of Laurence Olivier. I practiced the line all night, before a mirror, and was silent on the bus in the morning.

At last the moment had arrived. I had drawn a clean suit and collar and cap from the costume room. I went to the set. This was not a crowd scene. I was alone with Robert Donat. I was starring. The American director, Sam Wood, was in his canvas chair. He took no notice of me. Behind him sat a rather prim man, on the back of whose chair were the words, "Adviser on English Public Schools." I was placed on one side of the doorway, my co-star on the other. The clapper board clapped: "Scene 76. Take One." I sprang to the doorway, met the billowing gown of Mr. Chips, lifted my cap and said, "I thought you were away for the hols, sir!"

Sam Wood's voice rang out. "Cut!" The cameras stopped whirring. The lights were cut. Everyone in the studio looked at Sam Wood. I felt they were looking at me. What had I done wrong? Sam Wood turned over his shoulder to the Adviser on English Public Schools: "Do they have Scotch boys in English public schools?" (He would say Scotch, which is a drink.) My accent had betrayed me, even though it was now barely noticeable. My line would be taken from me. But the Adviser on English Public Schools nodded that they did indeed have Scots boys.

Lights! Roll cameras! "Scene 76. Take 2." I repeated my performance, and looked again at Mr. Chips: "I thought you were away for the hols, sir!" Again the voice rang out: "Cut!" I waited for the judgment. It came: "But do they have little Highlanders like this?" The Adviser on English Public Schools, who was in fact the classics master at Rugby, stirred in his chair, but not so much as to disturb his languor: "Yes, we have them. In fact it is one of the functions of the English public school, Mr. Wood, to take the barbarous accent out of little savages like him." My pride was wounded. My heart black with fierce hate. But my line was saved.

"Scene 76. Take 3," and in a flash it was all over. Robert Donat said later that it had been a pleasure playing opposite me. I replied that I had felt the same. Keep your wits about you and you will see me and hear the line when next you see the film. I am also in the choir in another scene, but that was not a speaking part. One of the other scenes in which the camera was fixed on me and the detestable Webber for some time was cut from the final version. But there I am in celluloid in what *The Filmgoer's Companion* calls an "immensely successful" movie. Who made it so, I ask you.

If I had answered my Scottish blood as it rose in my veins, I would of course have drawn my dirk from my sock and plunged it into the breast of the classics master from Rugby, but I had to think of my career as a film star. In the event, as my father gave up his rich farms, to become a journalist, so did I give up my career in the movies, to follow him to Grub Street. The sacrifice may seem to have been foolish. But I can always console myself with what might have been.

Playing opposite Elizabeth Tiler: two stars from Byron House.

Fairlie's memory seems to have played a trick on him here, one harder to correct in the pre-home-video era in which he wrote the story. He does indeed have a line in the film, but it differs slightly from the transcription he offers. And his big moment may not be a "crowd scene," per se, but it's not quite the intimate two-hander with Donat he recalls, either.

A Volcanic Flash

WINSTON CHURCHILL

Never Despair: Winston S. Churchill, 1945–1965 by Martin
Gilbert

The opening sentence of this eighth and final volume of the
official biography of Winston Churchill finds him sleeping late
on the morning after the surrender of Germany. He was 70.
Within two months the British people would throw him out of
office; but any fear that the rest of his life will be an anti-climax
is at once dispelled. He awoke that day to news of the capture of
Rangoon, "the splendid close of the Burma campaign," he telegraphed to Mountbatten; the struggle against Japan must continue. He lunched in bed, his most favored desk. To Truman he
telegraphed that it was his intention "to adhere to our interpretation of the Yalta Agreements." Tito's forces had already
marched into the Italian province of Venezia Giulia, one of the
territories at issue at Yalta, and entered the Austrian province of
Carpathia. Communism, established by force of arms in Eastern
Europe, was trying to push to the West. On that first day of
"peace" in Europe, Churchill telegraphed Tito, warning him
that if he attacked the allied forces in Venezia Giulia, the British
commander "has already the fullest authority to reply." (Eleven
days later, under Churchill's pressure, Tito's forces withdrew.)

The New Republic, December 26, 1988, originally titled "A Volcanic
Flash." Reprinted by permission from the Estate of Henry Fairlie.

But the most ominous news was that 15 Polish leaders, all approved by Britain as possible members of a provisional Polish government, had been seized by the Soviet authorities and taken to Moscow as prisoners. In the hour of victory, the cold war was begun . . . by the Soviet Union.

There, at its very beginning, is the frame of this volume, and the justification of its length. Some have criticized the method of Martin Gilbert's work. It is true that Gilbert has not provided an interpretative biography, nor drawn on the multitude of other sources that are available; he has left that more congenial task to later historians. But I think that Gilbert has been, in his way, correct. He has stuck to the thankless task of furnishing a documentary record, overwhelmingly from Churchill's own papers and those of his immediate circle, of the life, decisions, actions, concerns, and style of a statesman who was at the center of affairs from his election to Parliament in 1900 almost until his death. The modesty of Gilbert's method is appropriate to the magnitude of his subject.

Churchill's activity was so unceasing, his interests so far-ranging, his knowledge of men and affairs so comprehensive, his understanding so profound, his political sense so realistic *and* so visionary, his influence so large and beneficent and needed, his humanity so various, that it was first necessary that a conscientious historian should labor in the vineyard to give some structure to this life as it was lived. This Gilbert has splendidly done. Perhaps the attention span of some reviewers has been shriveled by television. Personally I would reduce the new volume by only a dozen pages or so (there are sometimes too copious extracts from the less important speeches). Otherwise there is good advice to the reader in the title: never despair.

In these pages we contemplate the last 20 years of the life of an old man. In 1953, when Churchill was 77, and again prime minister, he suffered the most recent of three arterial spasms or minor strokes, and there were warnings of the major stroke to come. His doctor, Lord Moran, and his private secretary, Jack Colville, a man of superior intelligence and character, went to Lord Salisbury, the elder statesman of the Conservative Party, who suggested that Churchill should be persuaded (that is, forced) to repair to the House of Lords, while nominally remaining prime minister. Even Salisbury knew the idea was foolish: "I am afraid he regards us in the Lords as a rather disreputable collection of old gentlemen." (Offered a dukedom by two sovereigns, Churchill never accepted a peerage.) And who would be the unfortunate wretch who would tell Churchill that he was to be put out to lordly pasture?

But they had misjudged him. Churchill had immediately to meet a dangerous motion of censure in the Commons; and to the amazement of all the moaners and the nail-biters, he whipped the opposition in his speech, ran it yelping from the field. Nigel Nicolson, a backbencher at the time, wrote to his father of the occasion, "He is looking white and fatty, a most unhealthy look, you would say, if he were anyone else, but somehow out of this sickly mountain comes a volcanic flash." That nicely captures the moving and elevating story that this volume tells.

Gilbert devotes his first 650 pages to the years in opposition, from 1945 to 1951. This may seem excessive. Yet he enables us to see for the first time Churchill's sustained and often electrifying energy and inspiration out of office. We are jolted, almost at once after the defeat of Germany, even though we know it will happen, by his defeat in the 1945 general election. The votes were not counted for three weeks, so that the ballots of the men and women on active service around the world could be flown home. I remember many foreign journalists, including Americans, saying that in their own countries no one would have believed that the ballot boxes could be kept for three weeks without tampering by the government. In the interval Churchill flew to the opening of the Potsdam Conference. There, on the night before he returned home for the counting of the votes, he had an "unpleasant dream. . . . I dreamed that life was over. I saw—it was very vivid—my dead body under a white sheet on a table in an empty room. I recognized my bare feet projecting from under the sheet. It was very lifelike. . . . Perhaps this is the end." Two days later, even before they had finished counting the votes, he submitted his resignation to the king.

Was life over? In the Commons and in public life he was gracious and magnanimous beyond even what we expected from him. But only from Gilbert's record do we now see how deeply, and for how long, Churchill felt the wound. It was only painfully that he overcame his "vain repinings." Above all, perhaps, he was dejected because he had not been entrusted with the conduct of affairs when, as he told a reunion of veterans of Alamein in 1950, "destiny compels us after all our victories, to face new, strange, gathering dangers." But it was precisely this sense of the danger that drew him out of his despondency and galvanized him into action.

Wishing to warn and to advise, Churchill was greedy for information, especially about Soviet military strength (as the British and Americans were rapidly demobilizing), and about Russia's political intentions. He reached to an extraordinary range of contacts abroad, as he had done before the war to estimate Germany's strength and Hitler's intentions. In the Commons he pummeled the Labour government with the facts that this "private citizen" had collected. He also passed on some confidentially to Clement Attlee, who had succeeded him as prime minister, and regularly communicated his all-too-accurate forebodings to Truman.

Churchill first met Truman at Potsdam. He liked him "immensely," he told his daughter Mary, and found him "a man of exceptional character and ability, with . . . simple and direct methods of speech, and a great deal of self-confidence and reso-lution." Out of office, Churchill built on this relationship, and in March 1946 the president of the United States escorted him to Fulton, Missouri, where Churchill delivered the speech that defined the nature of the Soviet threat and introduced the Iron Curtain.

Gilbert's method draws our attention to the pertinacity of such personal relationships. On the day after the German sur-render, Churchill found the time to telegraph to three former French prime ministers, to Léon Blum, Edouard Daladier, and Paul Reynaud, his congratulations on their liberation. No one would have blamed him if he had held at least the last two partly responsible for France's collapse in 1940. And later that year he sprang to the defense of a fourth, Pierre-Etienne Flandin, who was being tried for treason for collaborating with the Vichy government in its early days. The court was stirred when Chur-chill's letter was read; the serious charges were dropped, and Flandin was released from custody.

These four French names provide only one example of the network of contacts he maintained around the world. One of the weaknesses of the Western alliance today is that American pol-iticians, notably those aspiring to the presidency, have few, if any, sustained relationships with politicians, soldiers, and intel-lectuals in other countries. They would do well to recall the extent to which Churchill was his own source of intelligence even out of office. This "greatest citizen of the world of our time," as Attlee called him after his death, was the least of Little Englanders, the least of chauvinists. He found his own way into the details of the politics of other nations.

Churchill did not despise intellectuals, as many of our con-temporary conservatives affect to do. Of course intellectuals on politics can be fatuous. But Churchill knew that they also en-gage in an activity for which there is no alternative, that crosses all frontiers, that limns our first intimations of the future, not least in its interest to explain the past. Churchill always wanted to know where we have come from. One of his most severe critics after the war was that almost "pure" intellectual in politics, R. H. S. Crossman, the extreme left-wing product of Winchester and New College, Oxford, darting and mischievous, devious, conspiratorial, capable of standing common sense on its head, and playing pingpong (as I can vouch) with a deadly venom; yet with a value, even seriousness, to which one was stupid not to attend. It is characteristic of Churchill to find him on vacation in Marrakech in 1950 reading *The God That Failed,* the essays by six former communist intellectuals that Crossman edited. If Churchill was going to warn the world of the dangers of Soviet communism, he wished to know for himself what he called in a letter to his wife "an impressive study of Communist mentality by those who have recovered from the disease." Here was a politician who would not have worried about a question about what books he had read recently.

The Fulton speech was not popular at the time, especially in America, although Truman read it on the train to Fulton and was enthusiastic in his approval. Churchill merely told truths too bluntly. It is valuable to have Gilbert's full account of its preparation, delivery, and reception; Churchill could justly claim in a letter to Thomas Dewey in December 1946 that by then it "would be criticized as consisting of platitudes," and three days later to Frank Clarke in Florida, "Fulton holds its own."

I remember reading the speech the day after its delivery. Europe had just struggled through the first bitter postwar winter. Britain itself was tired, short of rations, dreary. The continent was shattered, exhausted, unfed, unclothed, unhoused. We dreaded each election in France or Italy, because Soviet communism, even with the tyranny, at least seemed to offer some kind of an answer. Then there came this familiar growl from a small Midwestern campus no one had ever heard of. It compelled us to look still more bleakly at the reality. And suddenly there was hope. It was always Churchill's genius to extract hope—even in 1940, when Hitler had the continent writhing under his heel— by staring at the harshness of reality. He would wring hope from the very brutality of the truth.

Out of office after the war, Churchill did what one would have thought only a government could do: he was the main founder, inspirer, guiding spirit, and ultimately the proclaimed formal leader of the United Europe movement. It was a consuming passion. Again Gilbert's copiousness displays its worth. We find it hard to believe that an aging man could so replenish himself, and us, and Europe, and America, in a cause that was so far-reaching in its vision and its urgency. Churchill loved Europe— America—the West—Christendom (a term he was not afraid to use)—as no one else in our century has known how to love it. Within him was the whole civilization.

So, thrown out of office, he put himself into harness. He was all muscle in the cause. "Without the resurrection and reconciliation of Europe," he wrote in 1946, "there is no hope for the world." He tried to pull in allies from almost every point on the political compass. Before the vital European conference at The Hague in 1948, he wrote a six-page letter to Léon Blum to try to prevent a European socialist boycott of it. He wanted the socialists in, too. Blum, recall, an intellectual, a literary man, a Jew, a socialist, the creator of the Popular Front in France, was the enemy, one would have thought, of everything that the high-born Tory represented. Yet to Churchill, Blum was Europe.

So Churchill drilled his passion to the laborious task of forming the United Europe Movement. From Churchill's inspiration, as George C. Marshall stated when he announced the Marshall Plan, came not only that Plan, but NATO itself. Churchill's eloquence in peace matched his eloquence in war.

> President Roosevelt spoke of the Four Freedoms, but the one that matters most today is Freedom from Fear. Why should all these hard-working families be harassed, first in bygone times, by dynastic and religious quarrels, next by nationalistic ambitions, and finally by ideological fanaticism? Why should they now have to be regimented and hurled against each other by variously labeled forms of totalitarian tyranny, all fomented by wicked men, building their own predominance upon the misery and the subjugation of their fellow human beings? Why should so many millions of humble homes in Europe, aye, and much of its enlightenment and culture, sit quaking in dread of the policeman's knock?
>
> That is the question we have to answer.

We can speak too glibly of Churchill's sense of history, as if it was unearned; as if he saw some technicolor panorama of the centuries, rather like the English codfish now served up as "Masterpiece Theatre." Gilbert allows us to appreciate more fully the energy of his sense of history. Behind it was a sense of geography. He seems always to be in the Map Room. Yet he didn't really need a map to know where Carpathia was. He knew the *limes* of the Roman Empire—its wooden, manned frontiers —and knew why geographically, strategically, economically, they were drawn where they were. He had served as a young officer on the North West Frontier of India; he had been with Kitchener in the Sudan. What remained of a sense of empire in his case was an embrace of the globe. He ruled no one out.

His magnanimity to foe as well as friend is celebrated. After the First World War, as Gilbert records, a French municipality asked him to devise the wording for its war memorial. Churchill proposed the words to be set out as written:

IN WAR: RESOLUTION

IN DEFEAT: DEFIANCE

IN VICTORY: MAGNANIMITY

IN PEACE: GOODWILL

These words, as Gilbert says, "stand in the opening pages of each volume of Churchill's war memoirs, under the heading: 'Moral of the Work.'" Having defeated Germany, he was the first and the clearest, after the war, in seeking re-entry of Germany into the European community. Even in Berlin in 1945 he said that "hate had died with their surrender." At the European Congress in The Hague, he proclaimed, in the spirit of Heine, that one object was to "revive the ancient fame of the German race."

I remember how he spoke, shortly after the end of the war, in Strasbourg. The ancient city of Strasbourg has always been a shuttlecock between Germany and France. When they go to bed at night, its citizens have rarely been sure if they will wake up the next morning German or French. In a newsreel cinema in 1945, we watched Churchill address the rapturous multitude in Strasbourg from the balcony of the Hôtel de Ville. He rose to his feet, silenced the crowd, peered over his small spectacles, and said, in a caricature of his most grave English accent, syllable by syllable, *Pre-nez-garde. Je-vais-par-ler-fran-çaise.* We chortled at the cunning old dog. With a joke, Churchill had made the men and women of that city feel not French or German, but European. He was a healer, like Lincoln. Churchill, the conqueror of Germany in a war that had to be fought, as Lincoln knew the Civil War had to be fought, set out at once to bring the Germans back to us.

Out of office, Churchill threw himself also into another passion. He was, remained, and proclaimed himself to be a Zionist. Few of his attacks on the Labour government that succeeded him were more brutal, more contemptuous, than his criticism of its Palestine policy. Ernest Bevin, the great trade union leader brought forward by Churchill during the war as secretary of labor, and then dramatically made foreign secretary by Attlee (one of Attlee's soundest judgments)—a man who had fought communism all his life in the unions was unlikely to back down before the Soviet menace—was unquestionably pro-Arab, even anti-Semitic. Churchill, with all his admiration for Bevin, made Bevin look like the scoundrel he was over Palestine, which was, in Churchill's mind, the historical entity of Israel. Why? Churchill loved the rowdiness of the Jews. He welcomed members of Parliament banging the lids of their desks in the chamber; and the best desk-lid bangers in history are the Jews.

No years in opposition, of any statesman, were as creative as Churchill's. Then came his years as prime minister from 1951 to 1955. I was a young journalist at the time, an editorial writer on domestic politics for the *Times*. I watched him, I listened to him, I wrote impudently about him. Gilbert's account corrects some of my judgments, but reassures me that I was not entirely wrong. Yes, there were the declining powers, of which one was well aware; but also there were the volcanic thrusts.

Consider Russia. A big country. Every country in Europe has lived for centuries under the threat of Russia's push forward. It is an unceasing source of amazement to Europeans, therefore, that America has no sense of a historic Russia. Americans appear to believe that Russia was born in 1917 at the Finland Station. Churchill was aware, as Gilbert shows us, of the huge presence of Russia. He understood that Russia is permanent; and that it is almost dangerously religious. He understood also the attraction of communism, a little like the attraction of Cavafy's barbarians, who were "a kind of solution," though he opposed it bitterly. On the death of Stalin, and on the rise of Khrushchev, Churchill saw a new possibility (as he would have seen, I imagine, in Gorbachev).

The real importance of this volume is the tale it tells of Churchill's turn from the defeat of one totalitarianism to the fight with another, with new forms of aggression, and a wholly other country. The differences between these two struggles, in Churchill's mind, are striking. The most consistent and forceful opponent of appeasement before the war resisted those after the war who used "appeasement" as a shibboleth to oppose any accommodation with Russia. In 1950, in opposition, he welcomed Attlee's assurance that there would be no appeasement, but then asked that the word "be more precisely defined. . . . Appeasement in itself may be good or bad according to the circumstances." This was a man whose mind was not locked into the past. As prime minister, in advocating in 1954 a policy of "peaceful coexistence" with Russia, he warned that there is "a vast ideological gulf between the idea of peaceful coexistence vigilantly safeguarded, and the mood of forcibly extirpating the Communist fallacy and heresy."

The last years make one ache. Churchill wished only to be released from his mortal coil. He was miserable. Even at the time, one thought of a more or less lifeless whale beached on his overlong, no longer fruitful, life. Gilbert refers a lot to Alan Hodge, the young man who helped Churchill with his remarkable *A History of the English-Speaking Peoples* (notice the plural). Hodge was one of my liveliest companions in London. The old man, Hodge related, liked to watch old movies in a private cinema. Like all old men, he nodded off in the middle of it. And like all old men, he would wake up with a start, and say to young

Hodge, "Tell me which are the baddies and which are the goodies, and then I can work out the rest for myself." Which, of course, was more or less what he did with Hitler and Stalin.

Hodge told me of a wonderfully haunting moment. Churchill did not like to be alone, though he felt alone. Once he summoned Hodge to be with him in one of the houses lent to him by rich friends in the south of France. In the chill evening, Churchill stared into the fireplace. The pine logs were spitting and hissing as they burned. Then the familiar voice growled: "I know why logs spit. I know what it is to be consumed."

What gave this man his embrace? Nothing is more important in Gilbert's last volume than the disclosure, even though we knew it vaguely before, of Churchill's unbelievable lack of nastiness. He could not be mean for more than a minute. This odd giant never stopped seeing others as mattering as himself. He may well, in the hurly-burly of great affairs, have driven his colleagues to distraction. He had things to do, and believed, rightly, that he was the only person who could do them. But never—never—did he fail to look to the people in his private life.

The extensive letters to his wife in this volume are a resource in themselves. (So are Clementine Churchill's spirited rebuttals.) And there was his moving relationship with his youngest daughter, Mary, and her moving love of him; his anxious, caring love of his only son, Randolph; the dear love of his fraught daughters, Diana and Sarah, and their abundant reach to him. In a very special circumstance, half public, half private, Randolph Churchill once told me that the mess of most of the lives of Churchill's children, including Randolph, was not the fault of his father, Winston, but of his mother. "Our mother loved Winston Churchill so much that she had no time for her and his children. It wasn't my father's fault. No one invited us more to be part of his busy life. He always found time for us. Always."

The volume, the work, the life, end, as they must, with the funeral. For once I wish Gilbert had abandoned his severity. It is totally plausible that Churchill planned his own funeral; it was, after all, the most gorgeous display of pageantry this side of a coronation. Surely nobody but Churchill could have thought that his body should be taken by barge, like a Tudor sovereign, from a pier near to St. Paul's Cathedral to a pier near to Waterloo Station, where it would be borne by train to the Marlborough burial plot at Blenheim. In the event, however, the most heraldic feature of this departure was none of Churchill's doing. As the barge progressed down the Thames, the dockside cranes all dipped as it passed. The sight of these bowing cranes moved a nation (and me) to tears. For dockers, stevedores, are a nation's most Bolshie workers. In Britain, certainly, none of them ever could have voted for Winston Churchill. Yet they, these proud proletarians, by their own bidding, on a day off, and not on the orders of their employers, lowered their cranes like guardsmen making an arch of their swords over the passing of a monarch.

THE LAST, BEST HOPE
FOR MANKIND
American Space and Time

There is a malaise now in the United States: a lack of conviction in the American idea, of confidence in American society, and of certainty in American purpose. If the outsider expresses his own conviction, confidence, and certainty in the American experiment, he is usually dismissed as naïve. It is therefore pleasant to believe that as the American winds his way through the survey that follows, he will be once more encouraged. It is the enjoyment of his own country which the outsider would like the American to rediscover: the enjoyment of its trials, which are its own, as well as of its achievements, which are unique.

—Spectacle, *unpublished manuscript, 1975*

A Cheer for American Imperialism

Is America an empire? It is a question which no American cares to ask himself and, if you ask it of him, he returns a hasty negative. "Imperialism is not in our blood. You are still thinking in terms of the British Empire." I have got used, by now, to the answers. But it seems to me a question which needs not only to be asked but to be answered with some frank regard for the facts. To an outsider, the fact that America is an empire is the most obvious fact of all.

The idea of empire, I realize, fits uncomfortably into the severe and sparse conception which the Americans have of their destiny. Their nation began its life in rebellion against a colonial power, and consequently the mere suggestion that they may themselves be an empire is taken immediately as an accusation. "It is that word. It is just that word," says one American with whom I have discussed the question over and over again. Call it, then, by another name—though none is so short and convenient —but the fact will remain.

"I am a Berliner," President Kennedy proclaimed, in perhaps the most far-reaching words he ever used, and, if they meant anything at all, they implied a shared citizenship. That is what he said. But a shared citizenship of what—if not an empire? "I am a Berliner" has no meaning if all he was talking about was a treaty obligation to defend West Berlin. But that, precisely, was what he was not saying. To say "I am a Berliner" is exactly the

The New York Times, July 11, 1965. Reprinted by permission from the Estate of Henry Fairlie.

same as to say *civis Romanus sum* and *civis Britannicus sum*.
Common to all three is the idea, not simply of protection, but of
protection arising from common citizenship of an empire.

But I should begin by enumerating what seem to me the facts
of empire, as distinct from the plainer facts of America's power.

(1) International police, or "peace-keeping," operations are
in themselves the most obvious obligation of empire;
and no serious person that I know (whatever his view of
the specific actions in Vietnam and the Dominican Republic) denies that America must, from time to time,
engage in such operations. To employ force abroad without the declaration of war is, in fact, the first attribute of
empire.

(2) More specifically, to endow American forces with a
combat role—a phrase which could have been rendered
so simply in Latin, and would have been understood by
any emperor or, for that matter, any legionary—is to
endow them with the same responsibility as once belonged to the Roman and the British soldiers on the
frontiers of empire. That American soldiers in far-flung
provinces of the world should have a combat role seems
peculiar only if one does not acknowledge the fact, and
so the duties, of empire.

(3) When military police actions lead directly to a local and
political engagement in these far-flung territories, empire
exists. As one American commentator wrote recently of
the Dominican situation, "Despite Washington's carefully
orchestrated campaign to cloak the political negotiations
in the trappings of the Organization of American States,
they remain very much a United-States-managed opera-
tion." Exactly, and that is empire.

(4) "Until the international community is ready to rescue

the victims of clandestine aggression," Adlai Stevenson said the other day, "national power will have to fill the vacuum. It is the most costly, the most dangerous and the least desirable kind of peace-keeping." May be. But, meanwhile, this stark admission that, in the absence of any other world order, national power must fill the role is as clear an acceptance of imperial responsibility as one could wish for.

(5) Empire means that the need for it is accepted in the provinces perhaps even more readily than at the center; and, freed from the necessity to mince his words, Mr. C. Rajagopalachari, ironically one of the leaders of India's struggle for independence, wrote recently to The New York *Times:* "There is not the slightest doubt that if America withdraws and leaves Southeast Asia to itself, Communist China will advance and seize the continent ' . . . and the empire of China under Mao and his successors will be firmly established." To resist this empire, he looks to the protection of another.

(6) Near Phoenix, Ariz., 500 *Luftwaffe* pilot officers are now being trained by the United States Air Force for tactical command duty, including the delivery of nuclear missiles. Some of them have already passed the course, with appropriate graduation ceremonies, and been awarded the freedom of Arizona. In much the same way, the Roman legions were recruited from native populations, the legionaries themselves becoming privileged citizens; and Sandhurst turned out superb native officers for service in the empire. Symbolically as well as actually, the *Luftwaffe* officers are, however ironically, the representatives of empire.

(7) Above all, there is the achievement of Secretary of Defense Robert McNamara. He has created, during his

years in office, an American force which can be disposed around the world with a minimum of difficulty and domestic disturbance. To an outsider, this force seems to have the inspiration as well as the practical attributes of empire; its mission, certainly, is the peace and security of an empire. But, perhaps even more significant, this is the achievement of Mr. McNamara which has been least questioned, which has been almost tacitly accepted by the American people—as if they understood their unending and inescapable imperial role.

So one could go on. Even the American critics of America's present policy use the language of empire. Whatever may be said for or against the idea that there are distinct spheres of influence properly "belonging" to one or other of the great powers, it is an imperial conception. Certainly, those who use the notion of spheres of influence as an argument for American withdrawal in any part of the world are relying on no more lofty intellectual or moral categories than the Administration in staying there.

All, some or much of which may be accepted by Americans, but still they shy from the idea of empire. It seems important, therefore, to try to explain why I think the idea of empire is useful. For one thing, certain time-worn propositions can immediately be stated frankly, even if they are not accepted.

No empire can contract and hope to survive. It must either be strenuously maintained or disintegrate. No empire, it follows, can selectively withdraw from its frontiers without inviting another empire to advance—by steps which have thus been generously preselected for it. The ingenious idea that America can abandon her responsibilities in one part of the world, without sacrificing them elsewhere, can be countered by the simple question: Who will do the selecting?

Perhaps if it were done by all-wise and all-seeing men, it would be feasible. But once the process is begun no one can foresee how, by whom, under what pressures, for what motives, in response to what seductive arguments, it will be continued. It is impossible to abandon any frontier of an empire without establishing precedents, both of argument and of action.

An empire has no justification except its own existence. It is, therefore, pointless to ask (as is so often asked today) why America is "here" or "there." There can be no answer that is militarily, politically, intellectually or morally satisfying. When Arthur Schlesinger Jr. said recently that America's initial involvement in Vietnam was a mistake, he may or may not have been right. But when he went on to say that, once that engagement had been made, America could not withdraw, he was (although he might be horrified to have it put in this way) simply drawing attention to the facts of life of empire.

An empire is always open to the strongest attack where the arguments for its remaining seem to be the weakest. An empire is normally defending, not its heart, but its frontiers. By their nature, frontiers are difficult to defend, both in logic and in practice. A frontier is always dangerous. It is where interests meet, and may collide. It is where the claims of others seem to be strongest, and one's own claims most open to question. It is distant. It is costly and hazardous to defend. It is usually uncommonly messy. It is not surprising, therefore, that an empire is continually engaged in small wars or actions precisely where the arguments for disengagement are the most appealing. But this is the trap. Frontier wars are the inescapable moments of truth for an empire. By the time one is left defending the heart alone, the game is already lost.

An empire wastes treasure and life. There is nothing more apparently wasteful than the defense of far-distant frontiers. For long years Britain's civil officers and soldiers kept guard on the northwest frontier of India—bartering with the tribes for their loyalty and, when this was not successful, subduing them. The "waste" (in both action and inaction) was undeniable. But, as a result of their watch and only as a result of their watch, two huge empires, Britain and Russia, remained locked in peace where their interests threatened to collide most dangerously. That America is now "dissipating" her resources in small wars and actions around the world seems to me, therefore, a meaningless criticism.

Implicit in all this there remains what seems to me the most useful perspective which the idea of empire can offer. Americans —and this is the firmest conclusion that I have drawn from watching and listening to the current debate on American foreign policy—have not yet learned that foreign policy does not produce "results" and, what is more, is not intended to produce "results."

The foreign policy of a country in the position which America now occupies can never be much more than a ceaseless attempt to stop six holes in a dike with only five fingers. This is what foreign policy is. There is no respite, for it is a fact of empires, as it is a fact of dikes, that the pressure on them is continuous and continual. No sooner has one stopped one hole than the water begins to trickle through elsewhere—as often as not, where one thought the dike was strongest. As Dean Rusk obliquely observed the other day, there are, in an average year, between 30 and 40 changes of government in the world—"and many of these, you can be sure, will run contrary to your expectations."

The only thing to do in this situation is to live with it, and sleep well at night.

But there is more to it than this. An empire with the world-wide responsibilities of America can never be certain where not only changes of government but changes in any of the existing circumstances may lucklessly involve her. She can never be certain that she has no involvement in a particular area until a threat has appeared there; and, when the threat appears, the calculations which must be rapidly made are full of imponderables. An empire can never make a tally of the extent of its commitments, or even establish any order of priority among its commitments.

All that is clear is that the empire is one, and that the effect of its actions in one of its parts is likely to produce incidental reactions in all of its other parts. An empire does not exist apart from the will at the center—in the metropolitan country—and that will cannot be shown to be weak in one area, without its being assumed to be weak elsewhere.

At the beginning of the fifth century the Britons, harassed by the invading barbarians, sent a desperate appeal to Rome for the help and protection of the empire. Honorius's reply—and it is one of the most melancholy documents in history—was that the empire no longer had the strength or the will to protect them, that they must fend for themselves.

Within a few years, Britain had slipped into the dark ages—but, of course, not Britain alone. Steadily and selectively, Rome continued to withdraw from her frontiers, as the barbarians realized that the empire had lost its will, until Roman civilization could survive only obscurely in Byzantium, and Rome herself, the nearest man has come to establishing a successful world order, fell forever. None of this, in the early days, was inevitable. But once the process had begun, it could not be arrested.

An empire must grow used to the fact that its commitments—the empire itself—are without rhyme or reason. One of the greatest of American commentators said to me the other day that what I called the American empire was, in very large part, a holdover from the Second World War, that America had simply found herself occupying positions which had formerly been under the protection of Britain and that there was no real reason why she should now stay in them. All of this is, no doubt, true; but it is how empires grow, and their illogicality is no criticism.

Even this commentator was not, then, consistent. He went on to admit that, for sentimental reasons, America recognized an obligation to defend Australia and New Zealand. Why? Because Australia and New Zealand are white, while India (which he is prepared to abandon) is coffee-colored? Because Australia and New Zealand are part of the family of English-speaking peoples? At this point I found not only a great deal more illogicality, but a great deal more immorality in the attitudes of my American critic than in my own conception of the American empire. An empire cannot decently distribute its favors in this fashion according to its prejudices.

But I cannot leave it there. One of the most thoughtful and experienced of British correspondents recently visited Vietnam, and returned home across the Pacific and across America. From Washington he filed his firmest conclusion: "THANK GOD FOR EMPEROR LBJ," read the headline over his article. It may be brash, but it is to the point. I, too, am prepared to celebrate the American empire and, in celebrating it, I believe I give voice to the inarticulate feelings of millions and millions of ordinary people of the world, where they have access to the truth.

Where the Strategic Air Command is, where the Tactical Air Command is, where U.S. Marines may quickly be brought into action, where United States paratroops stand on the alert, where the American fleets plow the seas or ride, ready to strike, in their great bases, where the ultimate deterrent spreads its benign protection: there is peace—not certain, for only the foolish man looks for certainty—but at least more likely. If I sleep soundly in my bed at night, if I expect my children to be able to live peaceful and fruitful lives, it is because I count myself and them as citizens of the American empire.

Not long ago I was arrested in Yugoslavia, along with a photographer who was accompanying me. It is not the easiest thing to find a consul in Sarajevo on a Saturday morning, and we discovered to our dismay that there was, in fact, no British consul in Sarajevo.

Was there, then, an American consul? Yes. We were immediately relieved. We knew at once that the arm of the empire to which we belonged would stretch to us even there. But there was more to it than that. As we sat moodily under the eyes of our guards, I remarked to my companion that the wonderful thing was that we had not the slightest doubt that the American consul would count us as one of his own. But we knew more even than that. We knew that the American consul represented an empire which understood our claims, which rested on opposition to arbitrary arrest, detention and inquisition.

We were, in fact, released after a prolonged and angry interview with the chief of police, while the search for the American consul was being made. But neither I nor my companion had the slightest doubt that we owed our release to the threat, which I constantly reiterated, to involve the American consul. What is more, neither the military who arrested us nor the police who detained us questioned our right as *British* citizens to summon the *American* consul to our protection. They, at least, assumed the existence of the American empire.

In both the large and the small considerations, this protection, this duty of empire, is sublime.

For this is the last thing that I wish to say about the conception of empire—and perhaps only an outsider can say it. Empire can be—and the American empire is—a lofty enterprise.

The superiority of the American to the Russian or the Chinese empires is partly a matter of interest, partly a matter of methods and partly a matter of purpose. There is nothing peculiar or difficult in my saying as an Englishman and Mr. Rajagopalachari's saying as an Indian that we would prefer to live within the American empire rather than the Russian or the Chinese empires, simply as a matter of calculated self-interest.

That we calculate our interest in this way is, in turn, the result of the methods of empire which we have seen used. The American empire has never depended on the arbitrary use of military power, whereas neither the Russian nor the Chinese empires would exist without it. Moreover, this difference in methods reflects a difference of purpose. Gibbon spoke of the emperors of the second century as "pleased with considering themselves the accountable ministers of the laws," and the phrase might be applied to the successive administrations which have discharged America's imperial responsibilities since 1945.

Even more than the Roman and the British Empires, the American empire unites power to law. It unites power to the search for a world order. It unites power to the desire of men in a rich and advanced society to bring succor to the poor and the backward who live in the province of their care. I have no doubt in saying—although it will horrify many—that the Peace Corps seems to me an exact and lofty imperial enterprise. The only tragedy is that, whereas the young district commissioners of the British Empire had no thought of returning home, at least until the end of their lives, the members of the Peace Corps abandon their mission after only a few years. Deny it though they may, and will, the volunteers in the Peace Corps are driven, first and foremost, by a deep sense of imperial mission.

But perhaps the most obvious type of an imperial officer is a man like James S. Killen of the Agency for International Development. Trying, in turn, to bring some economic order—to bring food—to the people of Pakistan, of Korea and now of Vietnam, he remarked the other day that the business ethics in Vietnam are "probably no better and no worse than anywhere else in the so-called developing countries." It was, recognizably, the saddened, the disillusioned, but the benevolent voice of empire.

Nothing seems to me more urgent than that America should find some way of building up a corps of civil officers—not volunteers, not *ad hoc* recruits—who can, as their life's work, undertake the decent mission of empire. Almost 200 years after her own Revolutionary War, America requires her own altered form of a Colonial Office.

It could not, of course, be called that—such is the touchiness of our world to words which represent reality—any more than the name of "empire" can be used by either America or the great number of its subjects. But it is not the word, the name, with which I am concerned. I am concerned that America should recognize that the responsibility she has undertaken is inescapable, is indivisible, is without logical defense but also without practical substitute; is wasteful and often repugnant but ultimately merciful and needing no apology. For 20 years now—so short a time—the United States of America has fulfilled her imperial obligations with a maturity, a generosity and an enlightenment which cannot be paralleled in all the history of the world. If ever a country had the grace for empire, it is this.

What is more, I believe that this is understood by the ordinary people of America. The "cloud of critics" at the center, as Gibbon contemptuously dismissed them, may react nervously to every exercise of their country's power. But I have traveled already in some of the states and have found, in the mass of her people, a sense of purpose, even a clearness of mission, which is truly imperial; which is lordly, benevolent and touchingly aware that the task they have undertaken is a task which will not fall from their shoulders for generations more.

If this steadiness and clearness are not empire—then find another word for it. For it is there.

In Defense of Big Government

There is something more than a little deceitful in a presidential candidate who tries to get to Washington by saying that he is running "against Washington," and hopes to be elected to the most powerful office in the world by proclaiming that he is against "big government." A saloon-keeper might as well justify his application for a license by saying that he is a member of the Temperance Reform League. It is as if Julius Caesar had exhorted his troops to cross the Rubicon by saying that the purpose of their march on Rome was to restore the city to the size of a village.

One could dismiss it in this way if it were not that the parrot-talk about "Washington" and "big government" is so unthinking, and so fashionable; and it is fashionable because it is merely one expression of the current drift in the United States to a reactionary and selfish conservatism. Moreover, it is not only in America that this drift is evident. Western Europe is now profoundly right-wing. The attack the Labour government in Britain has just made on public expenditure must be seen in the context of a reactionary mood growing in the country: part of what the *New Statesman*, in a phrase that I personally would not use, but that may be allowed as shorthand, has called a "middle-class backlash."

The reaction is intellectual as well as political. The conservative counterattack on democracy has been building for most of

The New Republic, March 13, 1976. Reprinted by permission from the Estate of Henry Fairlie.

the 20th century, on both sides of the Atlantic; and the essential leadership the West needs from America this year—and that means from the Democratic party—is a supreme affirmation of the possible efficiency of democratic government. It needs to be confidently and explicitly stated that strong and efficient central government is the foundation of a 20th-century democracy: its resource and its emblem, the very ground of its legitimacy.

We need to remember this year that, when democracy was similarly in retreat and disarray in 1933, it was Franklin Roosevelt who—in the face of Mussolini, in the face of Hitler, in the face of Stalin—demonstrated the ability of democracies *to govern* in a crisis; and by governing efficiently to succor their peoples, without keeping them in order with storm-troopers. If democracy is to survive at all, this is the demonstration that is needed; and it can come only from America. Anyone who thinks that I am exaggerating should take a close look at Britain and Western Europe, before he lets his eyes travel east to contemplate the awful spectacle as the night falls on India.

Since one of my purposes is to criticize the "new conservatives," it will be helpful to emphasize the ground from which I argue. In the terms of my own country, I have generally been regarded as a Tory, rather than a conservative. Indeed, the *Sunday Times* in England once called me "the only romantic Tory we have," and *Newsweek* in England has called me an "eccentric Tory"; and these are not labels that even now I refuse. There is in England such a breed as the Tory Democrat, and I might in England still be one.

The characteristics of the Tory, which separate him from the conservative, may briefly be summarized: 1) his almost passionate belief in strong central government, which has of course always been the symbolic importance to him of the monarchy; 2) his detestation of "capitalism," of what Cardinal Newman and T. S. Eliot called "usury," of what he himself calls "trade";

and 3) his trust in the ultimate good sense of the People, whom he capitalizes in this way, because the People are a real entity to him, beyond social and economic divisions, and whom he believes can be appealed to, and relied on, as the final repository of decency in a free nation. The King and the People, against the barons and the capitalists, is the motto of the Tory.

This tradition is absent in America; and as a result, whenever conservatism holds power in the United States, unless it has chosen a political neuter like Eisenhower as its leader, one has only to wait for it to be nasty: to show its colors, and be narrow-minded and selfish and mean-spirited. This is one reason, although it is by no means the only one, why the English Tory feels at home with the Democratic party, while the Republican party fills him with a puzzlement that gives way to desperation and at last to contempt. No attempt to civilize and broaden conservatism in America in this century has yet succeeded.

But I wish to push my point further, even at the risk of seeming to trail my coat. I have been told that the one young conservative American political columnist for whom I have the highest regard—George F. Will—has been heard to sigh of an evening that he wished that there were such a thing as a Tory Socialist. He should stop sighing, and realize that there is such a beast, as emblematic as a griffin; and if he wants to find at least the makings of one, he should look between his legs, like Eeyore trying to find the tail he thought he had lost. We do not need to subject the word "socialism" in this context to too rigorous an analysis; there have been Tory Socialists in the past, such as Richard Oastler; and there are many who sigh with George Will today that they wished that the creature existed again. For the truth is that, if one takes the three characteristics of the Tory as I have described them, they make it not unnatural that he often feels inclined, and in the past 150 years has often shown his inclination, to seek his allies among the Socialists.

But it is on the question of the role of government that one can see how so intelligent and serious an American conservative as Will gets into trouble. He knows that what is called "capitalism"—"private enterprise"—in America, as in the rest of the West, is now protected and subsidized and indeed served by the government. He can disturb one's Sunday breakfast with the sheer intellectual impatience with which he exposes the buffoonery of the International Trade Commission in seeking to keep out foreign shoes that are good and cheap, in order to favor the inferior and more expensive shoes of American cobblers.

But he knows that the same criticism—and many that are worse—can be made of almost all that is still called "private enterprise" in America. General Motors and General Foods, Lockheed and Boeing, are socialist principalities. I am not the most unblinking admirer of John Kenneth Galbraith, but once he had put his finger on the intimate and necessary connection that now exists between the decisions of the great corporations and the decisions of government, he at least had the courage to follow his insight to its only conclusion: that there is very little that an honest man can now be except *some kind* of Socialist. The prophetic remark of the Gladstonian Liberal Sir William Harcourt 80 years ago has been realized: "We are all Socialists now."

It may again be put simply. We have all been taught that the Magna Carta was—and is—one of the foundations of "Anglo-Saxon" liberty, and, yes it was and is; and I have no objection to my own country sending it across the Atlantic as a part of its own one million dollar celebration of its defeat by a few rebellious colonists 200 years ago. But there was something to be said for King John; and "Anglo-Saxon" liberties were in fact wrought as much by a strong monarchy as by the selfish privileges that the barons managed to extract for themselves at Runnymede. Sellars and Yeatman in *1066 and All That* were being quite profound when they catalogued each of the "liberties" that the barons had secured, and added "but not for the common people."

Too many of the "liberties" now being claimed from "big government" seem to me to be essentially "privileges" only for today's barons. It may be too much—it might even be wrong—for the Democratic party to begin this year to speak the language of socialism. But it is time that it was acknowledged that there are now only two choices: one can be either for *strong government for the few and the rich,* or for *strong government for the unrich and the many.* There is no longer a third way. This is what the American election this year is about: not whether there should be "big government" or not—that is a false issue—but whom the "big government" should serve.

The Democratic party must not, if it wishes to be true to its own tradition, and cannot, if it wants to win, appear to say "me too" to the conservative attacks on strong central government. On the assumption, which seems to me safe, that President Ford will be the Republican nominee, there is no chance that he will, in the actual election, run "against Washington." An incumbent President who ran "against Washington" would put himself in the preposterous situation of running against his own incumbent administration.

Ford's campaign speeches make it increasingly clear that he has already realized this: he is the "man from Washington." But he seems also to have realized more, that the vast majority of the ordinary people of this country, not just "the poor," need the federal government and, beyond a limited extent, they do not trust their state and local governments to supply what they need. My impression is that Ford began to realize this during his first sallies into Florida, where it is clear that the un-poor old in Miami are as anxious about their Social Security as any poor Puerto Rican in New York.

We all respond to our own "vibrations" of what the people are supposed to be thinking; every journalist has his own taxi-driver whom he elevates into the *vox populi*. But to me it is obvious that, although the American people may today be against inefficient government, against abnormally corrupt government, against overweening government, perhaps even against the pretensions of government by which they were excited between 1961 and 1963, against just plain lousy government, they are not against "big government" as such. They need it, and they know that they need it. They are not fools, and the Democratic party will box itself into a corner if it takes too seriously the current and glib talk about "big government." If one asks to be allowed to govern, one had better believe in government.

One of the difficulties is that much of the glibness comes from articulate men and women who are at least on the margins of the Democratic party, infesting its raiments. In response to the Vietnam war and to Watergate, they are recklessly careless of democracy's need for strong central government. They will believe nothing that the government says. Out of any mistake of the executive, they will bend their spite to prove malfeasance. They will not even allow the government to have its secrets. The work of government that is done by loyal and conscientious men, according to their own lights, earns from them hardly a sniff of regard. Having downgraded the work of Congress for 30 years, they suddenly find that virtue is encapsulated in the report of any congressional committee or subcommittee that chooses to seize some publicity by criticizing the government, no matter how flimsy the testimony on which the report is based, or how shallow its conclusions. Congressmen and senators who must have thought that they would end their careers in obscurity are now amazed and cheered to find that they can walk with their heads high, trailing clouds of glory, in the gutters of a press that believes them as credulously now as so recently it believed the President.

Of course there are corrections to be made in the working of the system; but one does not correct one's balance by turning a somersault, or repair an institution by tearing at its fabric. If the current mood continues much longer, thoughtless and unprincipled, America will soon have as heavy a price to pay for tearing at the fabric of government, as it had recently to pay for refusing to recognize that the fabric had been worn out of shape. I can hardly be accused, as an outsider, of having been slow to realize that the presidency had got out of hand. My first criticisms of the "Imperial presidency" were made 11 years ago, when it was not all that popular to make them. But to resist the pretensions of the presidency is not the same as repudiating the legitimate claims of government; and the Democratic party in particular should make the distinction.

But the kind of malignant suspicion of government to which I am referring would not have become so reckless if it was only a reaction to the Vietnam war, to Watergate, and to the "dirty tricks" to which the agents of government will reach when they are inflamed with a sense of an imperial mission. Behind many of the apparently "liberal" and "radical" attacks on government today lie years of "conservative" preparation. In the resentment of "big government" as such—not of its pretensions or its errors —one hears the voice of privilege as it has been insinuated for so long. Radical chic has made its unholy alliance with a naked conservatism; and its accent may be heard most nights in the sneer of David Brinkley at whatever a government may strive to do. But what matters about it is that it is the sneer of patronizing and vaulting privilege at the needs of ordinary people that can be served only by government. It is selfishness given the appearance of moral concern.

Not for a hundred years has personal selfishness been so viciously presented as political prudence. What I have called "The Spoiled Child of the Western World" is not only American: he is all over the Western world, the child of "affluence," cunningly saying that all he wants is to be left alone to do "his own thing," and he will leave others alone to do "their own things," which of course means that he will leave them alone to be poor, to be uneducated, perhaps even to starve. If there is one thing that India does not need today it is a shabby version of its own forms of spiritual passivity, yet the hippies journey to India with their degrading little visions, telling the Indians just to do "their own thing," while all the time, as an Indian said recently with contempt, for them there is always the check at American Express.

This seems to be not much worse than the boast of Karl Hess, the former assistant to Barry Goldwater, that he is a "full-time welder"—even a blacksmith—in the Appalachians! He is no more a "full-time" welder—or blacksmith—in any real sense than the hippie in India is in any real sense a follower of Krishna. For both there is the check at American Express, the passport out, whenever they wish to take it; and I find it objectionable for Hess to puff up his little haven of privilege in the Appalachians (while keeping his ties to the Institute for Policy Studies, of all places!), as if it is an answer for any but the privileged to the problems of modern technology and the "big" governments and corporations and unions which it demands.

But what do we expect of an assistant to Goldwater, except precisely this kind of selfish "libertarianism," as he loftily describes it; and what do we expect of Garry Wills, for that matter, who has also travelled from the conservatism of the *National Review* to a position that borders on anarchy, if not indeed of nihilism? Neither has changed his spots; they are conservatives still, but in the current mood, they are able to give their conservatism a cunning flavor of "libertarianism," of the assertion of individual freedom against the supposed oppressions of "bigness." Each indeed is the "spoiled child"; and as spokesmen of the social indifference of their generation, they are important.

There are other influences that can be traced, but my purpose here has solely been to show how the reaction against "big government," virtuous as it can be made to seem, is deeply related to the conservative reaction that has been building in the Western world for so long. For the sake of brevity, in what is no more than a shot across the bows in this election year, I will catalogue my main convictions:

- Far from democracy's being the enemy of individual freedom in the modern age, as the "new conservatives" would have us believe, the extension of the democratic power is the only reliable defense of our liberties.
- Put in another way, this means that the extension of equality is now the only justification of our liberty.
- When the private power—of the barons, of the corporations—is necessarily as great as it is in modern society, it can be checked only by a dynamic assertion of the public power. When a George Wallace attacks big government *and* big corporations *and* big unions with equal vehemence, one knows that the winner will be, whatever he says, the corporations.
- The scope of all power in the modern world is such that the scope of government is the most reliable of our resources. The central government needs to be not only strong and efficient but wide-ranging in its activities.
- By democracy in our age, we can mean only what used (so short a time ago) to be called *social democracy*. The most valuable definition of social democracy was given by Aneurin Bevan in *In Place of Fear:* "the sustaining of passion in the

pursuit of qualified objectives," and we need a return of that passion in our defense of democracy, confident that in a free society its objectives always are qualified.

Finally, if we may look out from that private welder's shop in Appalachia, democracy has to acknowledge that, one day soon, it is going to have to confront the ever-widening gulf between the poor nations and the rich nations. Oh! what a yawn comes from the "spoiled child." Yet it is ultimately by its ability to bridge that gulf that the future of democracy will be decided. It cannot be done by weak government, by small institutions, by village communes. Nothing goes to India from that welder's shop in Appalachia. If the actions of Indira Ghandi are shameful, she has at least this justification: that the great and prosperous democracies of the West have given no demonstration of the ability of their own governments to do it in any other way. When 400,000 new men, women and children arrive in New Delhi every year, it is a little ridiculous and it is certainly deceitful to suggest that anything but "big government" can help.

And this points exactly to the kind of awkwardness with which the Democratic party is faced: that when there is a resistance to foreign adventures—as in Vietnam, as in Angola—that resistance all too easily topples over into a resistance to any foreign concerns at all. But with all the mistakes that it has made—and they have only been mistakes, they have not been wickednesses—the Democratic party in this century has searched to find the ways of avoiding so intolerable a contraction of the moral concerns of a great and free nation. It has been the most thoughtful, the most unprejudiced, the most tolerant, the most effective instrument of the democratic vision in the world. It has sought, intellectually and politically and morally, for the balance between liberty and equality, between authority and freedom, between action and unjustified interference. As I have said, there are now, as always, corrections in the balance to be made, but it will be a tragedy for untold millions in all parts of the world if the Democratic party surrenders even temporarily its conviction that strong government is necessary. And that a strong government not only can be free, but is the source of much of our new freedoms. The selfish "full-time" welder in Appalachia owes his privileges, not to the Republican party, but to the Democratic party, not to a narrow "libertarianism," but to a succoring democracy.

Let the Convention Be "a Brawl"

Nothing could be more exhilarating or more healthy for the American political system than a Democratic National Convention this year at which the nomination of the presidential candidate runs to 36 ballots.

Perhaps it is too fanciful to expect it at the Republican Convention, but why not at Madison Square Garden? Why should the nation not be kept on tenterhooks as three and a half votes from Indiana at last switch from Birch Bayh on the eighteenth ballot, while on the twenty-fourth ballot the favorite son from West Virginia still holds his delegation—until at last a vote in the Illinois caucus puts one candidate over the top?

The belief that a candidate must go from the primaries to the convention able to win on the first or at the most the second ballot is a distortion of the political process in America. It leaves the conventions with no real function, so that they are in danger of becoming mere registers of a will that is not their own. In turn, this means that the role of the parties is diminished. If "the party is over," it is partly because we will not let the conventions hold a party. Conventions should in part be national binges.

The primaries were always a questionable "reform," and any purpose that they were intended to serve has now been perverted. They have become a form of "sudden death," as in tennis and football.

In tennis in the past, a match might go to a hundred games, a

The Washington Post, January 21, 1976. Reprinted by permission from the Estate of Henry Fairlie.

single set to half a hundred, a worthy victor at last triumphing 6-3, 9-11, 14-16, 6-2, 29-27. But now the game is strangled as it becomes interesting. There is no ultimate test of will and endurance. In the primaries it is even worse: The "sudden death" takes place before the game has really begun. Who would not cry when on the stump in New Hampshire?

In the primaries, the wrong qualities are tested in the wrong way at the wrong time by the wrong people for the wrong reasons. The nomination of candidates ought to be done by a different voice from that which will ultimately elect them. Even if the voice which is heard in the primaries were truly the popular voice, it is still being allowed to make itself felt too early in the electoral process. But of course it is not truly the popular voice of the country at large. "We, the People" vote in the primaries in different numbers and in different combinations from the election that follows, from different motives and even from different whims.

The nomination of candidates ought to be done by the regular and active members of their parties, assembled in their conventions, forced by the intensity of the occasion to take into account the multitude of factors that press on them.

It may be excessive to let the nomination of a candidate run to 103 ballots, as it did at the Democratic Convention in 1924, but even that worked in its way. The victor may now be forgotten, but it has been said rightly of John W. Davis that "Few men were better qualified to be President."

But more to the point, how invigorating was the struggle of Franklin Roosevelt at Chicago in 1932! On the first ballot, he was 100 votes short; on the second, he went up 16 and a half votes, Smith down 7 and a half, Garner holding his own; on the third, Roosevelt gained 5 more votes, Smith lost another 4, and Garner gained 11; on the fourth, William Gibbs McAdoo of

California broke the deadlock, and opened the gates through which the others poured.

But all through the process, the real power of real politicians from real states was at play: Mayor Cermak of Chicago refusing to deliver Illinois; Sam Rayburn rounding up the Texas delegates from hotel bedrooms and speakeasies to force them to a narrow vote; Huey Long on the telephone to Roosevelt, bargaining on a point of policy.

When the names of the states were called in those days, it was like the summoning of the earls in a play of Shakespeare: "Come, Mississippi, to arms.... And you, our faithful Arkansas, to horse. ... Oh, honest Texas, blazon the lone star on your shield. ... Comeliest of our lieges, sweet California, from Angeles let angels come to bless our cause." Real men of real power from real states.

We talk of the alliance of interests that Roosevelt formed to sustain himself for 12 and the Democratic party for 20 years. But that alliance was drawn tight in the bargaining of a convention.

It is proper that a man who is to be President should be forced to discover where power lies, and to demonstrate his skill in engaging that power in his own cause. The primaries are not tests of power or of the ability to manage it. After all, almost the only significant victories that George McGovern could at last count were given to him by the Democratic (i.e. Kennedy) machine in Massachusetts and by Richard Daley in Cook County. Where had fled the states he had won in the primaries?

So, damn the primaries, and let there be 36 ballots. Let the Convention grow hot and steamy, exhausted and intoxicated, even if simply with its own life. Let the bands play, the demonstrations muster, the balloons soar, the bunting fly. Let it be vulgar and alive, almost a brawl. Let there be a waste of spirit, and a waste of energy, as a great party meets in a jamboree to perform its one sublime and heady task.

The democracy of America has few occasions on which to celebrate its own genius: the way in which powerful interests have for 200 years been held in a creative tension with the popular voice. It is at the conventions that this tension should be pulled most tightly into a knot, able to take the strain, not only of the election, but of the responsibilities of power that may follow.

Politics is too important to be left to the prissy. "Ah, the governess," said Disraeli when the political philosopher, John Stuart Mill, rose in the House of Commons; and the governesses of the conventions today are the television reporters and commentators.

They tut-tut at any show of boisterousness: they have no stomach for a bloodletting. There cannot be a genuine disagreement or an honest duel but they say that the party is tearing itself apart. The reporters on the floor with their walkie-talkies are like men from Star Trek, accustomed to the cleaned-up world and morality of their spaceship, disdaining the untidy affairs of mortals.

If the people have grown weary of the parties and the politicians, is it not in part because the real life of politics is concealed? In the primaries, the politicians have only to tell more lies. In the conventions, the truth of politics ought to be played out to the full—and move us.

The Importance of Bathtubs

FAIRLIE AT LARGE

In order to reconcile their pupils to the spartan regime which they were forced to endure, the headmasters of English public schools used to warn them that the decline and fall of the Roman Empire was caused by the decadent habits of the Romans, and especially by their habit of lolling about in warm baths.

In the depth of winter, therefore, when icicles hung by the wall, and Dick the shepherd blew his nail, and Tom bore logs into the hall, and milk came frozen home in a pail, little English schoolboys were forced to immerse themselves, perhaps once a week, in bathtubs filled with ice-cold water. Building up character, it was called, and we did not question it. Ours not to reason why. Ours but to do and shiver. But even so, the British Empire was not saved.

This childhood experience may seem to justify Joseph Alsop's firmly held belief that Englishmen never take a bath from one end of the year to the other. He has even been heard to express the opinion that, so encrusted is it with dirt, an Englishman's suit will stand up by itself even when he is not in it.

Such calumnies hardly need answering. But the rituals that are attached to bathing are interesting in all cultures—the Japanese wash before they get into their baths, which seems to me to be carrying things a little too far—and it is perhaps interesting that I did not encounter the shower until I first visited America.

The Washington Post, January 22, 1978. Reprinted by permission from the Estate of Henry Fairlie.

Like others throughout the world, I have since adopted many American habits—such as beginning the day by pouring a glass of orange acid into my stomach—but the pleasures of taking a shower still elude me, and in a caustic mood I would even say that the practice has elements of perversion.

I have no doubt that it makes Americans clean. But as the Romans knew, cleanliness is not the purpose, at least the only or even primary one, of performing the rituals of bathing. There is no ritual to showering that is worth talking about, except perhaps trying to get the nozzle to eject water at the speed and in the direction one wants. The Americans can fly to the moon, and make cans that do not need can openers, but they cannot make a nozzle that works for a shower.

A bath—by which I mean a warm and sometimes even a hot bath—is to lie in. To lie back in. To loll in. To be silent and alone in. To muse in. To think in. To ponder in. It can also be to read in, although this requires some practice if one is not to get the pages so wet that one cannot turn them, and the novice should be warned that, if one lets the entire Sunday edition of *The Post* fall into the bath, the sight is not pleasant.

None of this can one do in a shower. One really would not get very far with Proust if one tried to read *A la Recherche du Temps Perdu* in one's morning shower. (There are some of us who would admit that we cannot get very far with him anyhow.) But where better to read him, if read him one must, than in a bath? For a bath is above all a place for the "Remembrance of Times Past," and lapped by the water and his prose, the two all but indistinguishable, one would not have to stir for months, except to run some more hot water now and then, and even then to do it by no more exertion than turning the tap with one's toes.

Turning the tap with one's toes is the mark of the true bather, and few sensations are more pleasurable than, when one's bath has become a little tepid, feeling the new hot water slowly lap up one's body, until once again one is wrapped in it.

When someone has run a bath, and closed the door, one hears nothing from within, except occasionally the sound of a slight movement, like the dip of an oar in a lake at night. All is silence. All is peace. But from a shower there comes only noise, splashing and slapping and jumping about, and occasionally a voice breaking into, not the gentle lilt of the true bather who sings softly, but raucous and jolly snatches of songs from the locker room.

It is no wonder that Americans have a reputation for being always on the go, never able to take things quietly for very long, if they start the day by standing upright for five minutes under a jet of water, which they deliberately aim at themselves.

These thoughts had their origin in a serious conversation which I was having the other day with an American woman. We were trying to explain people's obsession with their "feelings," why they are so turned in on themselves, so concerned with what they "feel," rather than being turned out with interest and exuberance to what is other than them. I said that this concern with one's own feelings is what one used to take away by oneself and "think about in one's bath." But having thought about them there, one then got out of the bath and turned to meet the world again. If you are a true bather, you already have your own transcendental meditation, but with not much fuss about it. Insulated in one's bath, one muses and puts things in perspective, but once one gets out, one puts aside one's self-absorption.

My companion immediately seized the point. She has a friend who says that lying in a warm bath is like being back in the womb, and there for a time she lies, but then to get out and start all over again, which is a way of being born again with not much pretension to it.

I remember a woman in whose house I was once staying, who at the time was down in her spirits and altogether out of sorts. She once returned from work, obviously in no mood for conversation, poured a bourbon, picked up one letter from the pile waiting for her and went upstairs, ran a hot bath for herself and closed the door. For more than an hour, all was silent, except for an occasional lap of water or the gush of more hot water being run.

When she at last reappeared, she was glowing, and said to the assembled company, "Well, let's go!" She added, as an aside: "There's nothing like a letter, a bourbon and a hot bath," and the emphasis in her voice was on the bath. If she had a shower, after all, she could not have had either the letter, or the bourbon or spent an hour under it.

Servants in England, when they used to wake their master or mistress in the morning, inquired gently: "Will I draw your bath now?" There is something about the phrase, "to draw a bath," which tells it all. The preparation of a bath is a ritual, as much as the bath itself. If America took the time for the ritual, there would be far less need for all the artificial and expensive rituals of the "human potential" and "self-actualization" therapies that now abound. Only a nation that showers instead of taking baths would have to pay money in order to be taught how to meditate and relax.

In 1969, an American firm of plumbing manufacturers sent five of its experts to Europe for a tour of "great historic baths." This is a hopeful sign. I hope they went to the Savoy Hotel in London, where people have been known to stay in one of the suites overnight in order to use the long, deep baths with their great brass taps. But it still says something about America that they had to be sent.

In most American houses, the bathtubs are so small that one cannot lie immersed in them in comfort and, if one is more than 4 feet 10 inches long, not immerse oneself in them at all. Yet

Americans pay vast sums, not only to be taught how to meditate and relax, but in order to enjoy devices like saunas, which are only an extended form of baths or rather, I would say, a limited form. America keeps inventing ingenious ways of compensating for what it rejects. So be it.

Mencken's Booboisie in Control of GOP

FAIRLIE AT LARGE

To say so is of course a kind of apostasy from the true faith of a journalist in this country, but I am not a great admirer of H. L. Mencken, and will lay no wreath on his grave when his centenary is observed in September.

Here and there his wit is coruscating, but usually it is labored, and too often he writes like a brewer. His denunciations of his victims can be pure savagery, and one cackles at them, like the old women sitting and knitting at the foot of the guillotine, but what else does one gain? The sad truth is he had little to say. For the most part, he is an unholy bore.

His prejudices are as lumpish as those he arraigns. As the young Randolph Bourne, a journalist of 10 times his quality, said of him very early, he went "heavily forth to battle with the Philistines, glorying in pachydermatous vulgarisms," and quickly became a moralist himself, "with the same bigotry and tastelessness" as the enemy. He could in his writing be as much a boor as them.

Yet there I was crying as I watched the Republican convention, "Mencken! Thou shouldst be living at this hour!" Wishing that someone would spatter buckshot into the Joe Louis Arena. Wishing that he would come among us, still the guttersnipe, and scrawl his graffiti on the walls. For there was his *Homo boobus*, indeed, elevated to be a sovereign. We needed someone

The Washington Post, July 27, 1980. Reprinted by permission from the Estate of Henry Fairlie.

to break from the yoke of mere happenings, and say that here was the common man and, yes, the common woman, too, come to take possession of their century at last.

Those who warned the prophets of the common man that they would not like his visage when they saw it had only to point to the floor in Detroit. There it was, polished now for television, the face of Caliban, come smirking to rule. With their noses wiped, taught some manners for the screen, clean handkerchiefs in their pockets, there were the *booboisie.* Narrow minded, book banning, truth censoring, mean spirited; ungenerous, envious, intolerant, afraid; chicken, bullying; trivially moral, falsely patriotic; family cheapening, flag cheapening, God cheapening; the common man, shallow, small, sanctimonious.

The common man, exactly as Reagan said of himself in his prime time. We have been warned of his coming. Not only Mencken inveighed against him. Sinclair Lewis gave us the half-baked stereotypes. It was Walter Lippmann, commenting on the characters in Lewis' novels, who pinned them down: "They are the creatures of the passing moment who are vaguely unhappy in a boring and senseless existence that is without dignity, without grace, without purpose. They are driven by they know not what compulsions, they are ungoverned and yet unfree, the sap of life does not reach them, their taproots having been cut." They were there, in their own soap, on the convention floor. They may deserve our concern, for they are deprived; they do not deserve our approbation.

But how understanding of them we are now asked to be. They are the middle Americans. We must explain them as neutrally as do the sociologists. We must not criticize them. Not so long ago, the drawings of Norman Rockwell were mocked, as they should be, as a false representation of stunted lives. They are a celebration, not of what is good in those lives, but of what is banal and deformed, but today we must cherish them.

The Norman Rockwell of today is Norman Lear. How cleverly he seems to caricature the prime-time, soap-opera lives of the characters whom he portrays. But in fact he celebrates them, is gentle with them, and of course he exploits them. There is no line drawn between his characters and his viewers. He makes them both acceptable. Their lives are empty; they are trivial, the lives of helots. He justifies them.

The powers-that-be should pay him a fortune, for he takes the lives which they have deformed, and he makes them seem shapely. He makes a joke out of bigotry, he turns prejudice into a whimsical pleasantry.

Look at almost any of his characters: they might have sprung to the screen from the cover of the Saturday Evening Post of 30 years ago; not least Mary Hartwell with her brainless and meaningless efforts at self-expression; her life bounded in the narrowest possible compass; her mind in braids.

Much of what we today call "nostalgia" is a tolerance, justification and celebration of small-town America. The abandon with which the high culture in American today flirts with the popular culture has the same effect. What is common and low is legitimized. The "metropolitan" in America, to use the words of Lippmann in this context, is surrendering to the "provincial."

The metropolitan in America has always been much weaker than in Europe. New York may seem to extend its sweep over the whole culture. But it has nothing like the hold of Paris; its influence has never cut as deep as that of London. Today it is capitulating. What is called "neo-conservativism" is largely a New York phenomenon; its most prominent figures have in common their access to the New York media; and one by one the neo-conservatives are announcing for Reagan. Taking sides with the Reaganites. It is no less than a *trahison des clercs.*

What has always disturbed the European (and English) conservative is that the American conservative has barely even a whispering of aristocratic sentiment. He will support a Nixon. He will support a Reagan. These men are not evil. They are not even reactionary. They simply are vulgar. They are in person the common man. This does not seem to worry the American conservative. If he thinks he needs the masses, as Ortega y Gasset used the term, he will take them on their terms, in the persons of their nominees. He is then surprised when later he has the devil to pay.

Just as Americans in general do not have the habits of deference, so the conservative in America does not have them either. Ultimately he does not defer even to the country's institutions. If one of these institutions, such as the Supreme Court, makes decisions he detests, he will defame that institution. He is as ready as is the common man to bypass the institutions he ought to defend.

The American conservatives may resist the Equal Rights Amendment. But the overwhelming majority of proposals for amending the constitution in recent years have been put forward by conservatives. They even wish to control the budgetary process, which traditionally is in the keeping of the representative institutions, by constitutional amendments to reserve it to the popular voice.

They may have opposed the initiative and the referendum when these were introduced; but it is they who now use them most indiscriminately as vehicles of popular discontent. Just as it was Goldwater who first captured his party from the grassroots, so it is the conservatives who now reap the benefits of the primaries and caucuses, as the common man is stirred to subvert the traditional methods of politics. Those who have carried Reagan to the very threshold of power are exactly the ungoverned but unfree whom Lippmann described half a century ago.

Ungoverned and unfree and so in the end ungovernable; this is exactly what Ortega foretold in the coming of the common man;

and it is what the conservative in America seems to have no resource to resist. No traditions to which to appeal; no habit of deference to authority; no patience with the bridle of institutions.

Europe shudders today, not so much at the three men who have emerged this year as candidates, as at the political illiteracy of the popular voice which has chosen them, the America they most fear. The politicians will come and go, and do less good and harm than is supposed, but what of the people who chose them?

The America which Europe fears is the America of the Reaganites. The America once of the Scopes trial; the America of prohibition; the America of ignorant isolationism. The America then of "better dead than red"; the America of McCarthyism; the America of the last fundamentalists of the 1950s. The America now of the new evangelicals; the America of the Moral Majority; the America of a now ignorant interventionism; the America which can see homosexuals as a conspiracy; feminists as a conspiracy; perhaps even women as a conspiracy. The America of fear. For it is in fear that the ungoverned and the unfree are doomed to live. And there was this America in control at Detroit.

It is time that we reminded ourselves, and said aloud and more often, that it is from these people that nastiness comes. It is time that we pointed out to the neo-conservatives that democracy has never been subverted from the left but always from the right. No democracy has fallen to communism, without an army; many democracies have fallen to fascism, from within.

The Reaganites on the floor were exactly those who in Germany gave the Nazis their main strength and who in France collaborated with them and sustained Vichy. If the neo-conservatives cannot sniff danger, surely the rest of us can be alert.

The Voice of Hope

FRANKLIN D. ROOSEVELT

"Fairlies don't cry," my mother told me. Even when I was a small
boy growing up in London and my father arrived home dead in a
taxi, my tears had to be contained until I was among my friends
at school. I was therefore all the more surprised when, a few
years later, on the morning of April 13, 1945, she came into my
bedroom with tears of her own. She had to wake me, a lazy
undergraduate on vacation. "Mr. Roosevelt is dead!" she announced, and added, choking, "It's on the wireless!" I can remember no other occasion when I saw my mother weep. I did
not again see a Briton cry at the death of an American until
November 22, 1963.

FDR's voice was known not only in America but across the
world. When my mother said that the news of his death was
on the wireless, she was talking of the instrument which had
brought him into our home. Franklin D. Roosevelt came, from
3,000 miles away, with Jack Benny. The main image I recall from
those years is of the radio set in people's homes. It was not only in
occupied Europe that people had to huddle round their sets, lest
the gestapo discover them listening to the BBC's broadcasts. My
memory is of huddling round the set even in Britain and in
peacetime. Radio sets then were not very powerful, and there was

The New Republic, January 27, 1982, originally titled "The Voice of
Hope." Reprinted by permission from the Estate of Henry Fairlie. Editor's
note: *The New Republic* devoted this issue to the centennial of Franklin D.
Roosevelt's birth.

always static. Families had to sit near the set, often at a table, with someone always fiddling with the knobs. It was like sitting round a hearth, with someone poking the fire; and to that hearth came the crackling voices of Winston Churchill, of George Burns and Gracie Allen, and of FDR. The fireside chats, we need to remember, were radio talks. It was not FDR who was at his fireside—the mistake Jimmy Carter made on television—it was we who were at our firesides.

From across the Atlantic, Roosevelt came to our firesides, a friend. It is as a friend across the seas that I remember him. Not only during the war, but even, when I was only a boy, before it. The voice itself was friendly, and it seemed always to say friendly things. If he was giving money to the unemployed in America, he would give pocket-money to me in England. Generous-hearted—one could tell that from his voice—and trustworthy. He would not let one down. It is perhaps hard to convey what his voice meant to us in London, second only to Churchill's, as Britain stood alone and the bombs rained down. If Churchill's was the voice of resistance, Roosevelt's was the voice of hope. It was during the darkest days in Britain that Churchill pointed across the Atlantic: "But westward, look, the land is bright."

It would not have seemed so bright if there had not been Roosevelt. We knew his voice, and it was cheerful. Even as a boy, and later as an undergraduate, I thought he seemed different from Woodrow Wilson, the first President really to matter to Europe. Wilson was a little governessy; he was always lecturing. He would say "Tut, tut!" if one skipped one's homework; but Roosevelt—just this once—would understand.

But behind it all was something that really counted. There across the Channel were those lunatic dictators: Hitler, Mussolini, Franco, Stalin. My boyhood was marked by the disappearance, one by one, of every democracy on the continent. "What is the difference between Chamberlain and Hitler?" went one schoolboy joke. "Chamberlain takes his weekends in the country. Hitler takes his countries at the weekends." And against the fearful spectacle of all Europe lying under a great terror, with not a free people left, stood the reassuring spectacle of a free and confident and working democracy—Roosevelt's America. When Churchill spoke of the Anglo-American friendship in that summer of 1940—"Like the Mississippi, it just keeps rolling along. Let it roll. Let it roll on in full flood, inexorable, irresistible, benignant, to broader lands and better days"—we believed him partly because FDR was to us one man who had made it work.

The radio in FDR's day carried farther and more immediately than any means of communication had done before. The Atlantic Charter, which Churchill and Roosevelt signed in 1941, even before America was in the war, was a radio document. With its proclamation of the Four Freedoms to all the peoples of the world, it was endlessly chattered to them over the waves of the BBC's Overseas Service, and it was then written into the original charter of the United Nations.

We are tempted to scrutinize FDR's fireside chats as if they were no more than exercises in public relations. They certainly were that. He was not averse to publicity, not uninterested (he would have appreciated the word) in his "image." But he had an extraordinarily quick and deep sense of the opportunities and significance of the new instrument. Even as Governor of New York, if he wished to force the hands of the legislators at Albany, he appealed to the people by radio. He gave his first fireside chat only eight days after assuming the presidency. As early as 1929, he said: "It seems to me that radio is gradually bringing to the ears of the people matters of interest concerning their country which they refused to consider in the daily press with their eyes." We miss the point if we see his use of the radio only as a device for the "selling" of the candidate or the President. He realized that it had changed our notion of "the people," as the popular press had done; that it had expanded the "democracy," made politics more democratic by making the people as a body more accessible; even that it had altered the size of the world—"one world" is a phrase from the radio age.

His immediate understanding and skillful use of the radio were only part of the innovating spirit which was his most striking characteristic as a politician. The man who took to the radio like a duck to water was the same man who, in his first campaign for the New York Senate in 1910, hired an automobile, a two-cylinder red Maxwell, with no windshield or top, to dash through (of all places) Dutchess County; and it was the same man who broke all precedents twenty-two years later when he hired a little plane to take him to Chicago to make his acceptance speech. (It would, after all, be broadcast.) Ignore his willingness to try everything, however new, and one ignores the spark which lit first a nation and then the world, each time bringing hope where there had been none.

The willingness to try everything was how Roosevelt governed. The memoirs of those who served him are as bountiful as the reminiscences about any politician. None are more jolly to read. How he stirred up those around him—pitting them against each other—to stir up any ideas that they might have. How he put off what he was not yet ready to decide—appearing to be maddeningly indifferent—then to make his decision when they were least ready for it. Only FDR could have avoided listening to the chairman of the Federal Reserve, Marriner Eccles, who was seeking what he believed to be an important decision, by addressing himself, throughout most of the meeting, to the mess Fala had made on the carpet. "Do you see what Fala has done?" The presidential eyes deliberately wandered, refusing to focus on Eccles.

It is easy to tell such stories merely for their jollity. But in the method was the genius; in the genius was the policy. Rexford

Tugwell[1] could say of the early Brain Trust days: "We could throw out pieces of theory and perhaps they would find a place in his scheme . . . ; and perhaps the inventiveness of the suggestion would attract notice. But the tapestry of policy he was weaving was guided by an artist's conception which was not made known to us." In the end, a Harold Ickes or, more sourly, a Henry Wallace, said the same.[2] In that method lies the answer to those who say that the New Deal did not really change much, that it had no concept, that it was only a series of improvisations which added up to more wind than water. That was not how it seemed to Americans at the time, or how the news of it reached even a schoolboy in Britain. Were we all, then, just taken in?

Whenever one reads the revisionist historians of the recent past, they seem to have forgotten so much of what it was like at the time; or perhaps, many of them being so young, never knew. They are able to write of the Marshall Plan and the Truman Doctrine, for example, as if it is of little account that Europe in that terrible winter of 1947 was a hell frozen over. They forget that Europe had collapsed as an organized industrial and political community, and that this was the reality that faced the Americans who had to decide and act. The trouble with the revisionists is that they seem to have only the documents. They appear to have no memory; not only no memory of their own, but no sense of historical memory. They work busily on the documents, but with no historical imagination. They fail to take into account the voices of the ordinary people who lived through

1. Rexford Tugwell (1891–1979) was an original member of FDR's "brains trust" and an important adviser on his New Deal programs.

2. Harold Ickes (1874–1952) served as secretary of the interior for all four terms of FDR's presidency. Henry A. Wallace (1888–1965) served as secretary of agriculture from 1933 to 1940 and vice president from 1941 to 1945. A progressive inclined to pro-Soviet views, Wallace ran a losing third-party candidacy for president in 1948.

that time. I believe it when I read that, after FDR gave his First Inaugural, half a million Americans wrote to the White House.

Of course the New Deal was not revolutionary. Did Roosevelt ever claim that it was? Someone has pointed out that the left-wing revisionists of the New Deal during the 1960s were really only complaining that it was not a socialist program. But then who ever thought it was socialist, except the conservatives who detested it at the time? Or even radical, for that matter? The radicals were persistently critical of what they thought was the inadequate liberalism of the New Deal. It is true that unemployment was *not* significantly reduced until the war; that fundamental power relationships were *not* basically changed; that the New Deal did *not* address itself to the blacks or even really to the very poor. (Basic poverty was not brought onto the unfinished agenda of the nation until the Kennedy and Johnson Administrations. It was the concern of the Great Society, not the concern of the New Deal.) All of that, and more, is irrefutable. But what is most significant is that America was made—for the majority of Americans—a far better place in which to live than it had been.

It makes not a scrap of sense to say that some sort of New Deal would have had to be introduced by Hoover if he had been reelected. (It is even said that he was already moving in that direction. If one believes that, one will believe anything!) Roosevelt was the New Deal, and Hoover was not Roosevelt. Even if one were to say only that Roosevelt liked politics and enjoyed being President, while Hoover did not much like politics and hated being in the White House, one is saying more than those who pick over only the legislation and executive orders realize. For what was the New Deal but a President jollying and chivvying lots of people to get things done? What was it but a rabbit warren of a hundred agencies and ten thousand people, with a Scottish terrier (a rather large terrier) scuffling at the entrance, barking happily and wagging his tail as he made the rabbits scurry everywhere?

To say that the New Deal wrought no institutional changes is poppycock. For what was the New Deal but the agencies, with their bewildering array of acronyms, which popped up all over the place—not only in Washington—and then grew into a coral reef which no one since has succeeded in breaking down? Everything in the New Deal was introduced as temporary, "for the emergency," but what appeared to be improvisations quickly grew into institutions. The most striking fact about the New Deal is its rapid institutionalization, and no one can read the memoirs without realizing that FDR knew exactly what he was doing. It has often been said that the genius of English politics in its heyday was that the substance of its institutions was changed without having to change their appearance. Similarly, Roosevelt avoided taking on, say, the great departments and their clients by creating new agencies. It took a politician of supreme confidence as well as skill to let loose so many oddballs at so many desks to do so many things, and still manage to weave them into that tapestry.

The institutions of a country are not only those that occupy the great edifices of government in its capital. To bring millions of people into a party who were not in it before, to include those who were excluded, to make the trade unions strong, is to work not merely a political but an institutional change. It is sometimes said that the rapid advances in technology, especially when spurred by the war effort, would have given the Americans prosperity in any case. But who brought so many Americans into the mainstream to enjoy so large a share of that prosperity? It was not the technology, it was a man; it was not the economy, it was government. It was a politician feeling his way with his fingertips to the millions upon millions of immigrants and descendants of immigrants who were at last ready to claim that the promise of America should be translated into performance for them.

Of course he felt his way to them partly to win their votes, and formed the famous New Deal coalition partly to give himself a political base. But as Isaiah Berlin once said of Chaim Weizmann: " . . . in his case, as in that of virtually every statesman, personal motives are inextricably mixed with, at the lowest, conceptions of political expediency and, at the highest, a pure and disinterested public ideal."[3] It is always absurd to ask that our politicians "do something," and then complain when they get it done by acting as politicians. If we think that the personal ambition or the political expediency in some way lessens the idealism, we had better go back to the beginning, and sift through the murky personal motives and political maneuvers of the noble Pericles. You do not get the right architect to build the Parthenon without first finding the political base to supply the funds. Roosevelt built a political base—and then post offices and park benches.

But the method would not have worked if it had not been held together by character and by vision. The two, in him, are inseparable. He was a large man. Even listening to him on the radio, one felt that he was physically large. (Churchill was quite tiny; yet one thinks of him as large.) There is not an apprentice cartoonist today who could not draw FDR blindfold; and there is no possible cartoon of him in which the jaw, the cigarette holder, the hat, the smile, the sheer zest of him would not spring from the page. "Everything I saw and heard," said Tugwell after his first meeting, "was merged in an impression of vitality." We may be grateful that Doris Kearns did not have the opportunity to go to work on Roosevelt, and scrape around his edges to discover the insecurities in so large a frame. It is in fact remarkable after all these years how little has ever been said of him that

3. Chaim Weizmann (1874–1952) was one of the early leaders of the Zionist movement and the first president of the State of Israel.

is small or distasteful; and those who were small about him in his life, not least those who served and then left him, only made themselves seem small.

There was a popular song at the time, "Franklin D. Roosevelt Jones," which we sang even in England. It was about a boy who was a winner in every way. Roosevelt was a winner; one never doubted it, in peace or war. His zest in the game was partly what carried him through, and in turn enabled him to carry through so much. But in the zest, in the fun, was also the vision. The largeness one felt in him, the generosity of spirit, was also a spaciousness of vision. What remains forever daunting to explain is how an aristocrat from the Hudson Valley—a man who had every reason for thinking that America was the property of the Roosevelts—had so generous a conception of America. There was no one he wished to keep out, not even out of his office, for if he disliked them, he would simply taunt them; and not out of the whole wide-open space and unfinished story of America. He was the first and last politician who translated the spaciousness of America—simply the Idea of it—from the wilderness and the frontier to the cities and their sidewalks.

The openness, the generosity, the inventiveness, the innovation, the experimenting, the embrace: they were the unfailing welcome of one man to a land that had been created to make welcome. He did not wish to close down America. He did not think that small is beautiful. He thought that big was beautiful, the bigger the better, for then more people could be accommodated. Dedicated (like a Roosevelt before him) to conservation, he then used conservation to create jobs. How simple the idea: who else dared it? When he was told that artists and writers felt that they also were workers, and should be helped by the WPA, did he hem and haw about the folly of spending money on painting and literature? He just said: "Why not?" He did not bankrupt the budget; he just expanded the country. The

Democrats today need to learn most from the spaciousness, and remember that America is big, was made to be big, and waits to be made big again. Big countries are big governments.

People will not understand FDR's war leadership if they fail to realize that to Europeans as well as to Americans he had given this picture of America as still large and spacious and open, vital and confident and young. No other country has ever come forward at a moment of crisis, and largely by his decisions, with such superb supreme commanders and such brilliant field commanders. The command of the American forces during the war —and he was unmistakably the commander-in-chief—saved countless lives in enemy as well as allied countries. The commanders were responsible for their rigorous training, but it was FDR's expansiveness that gave America the heart and muscle to do it. The factories went to work—as early as December 1940 he pledged that the U.S. would be "the great arsenal of democracy" —and then the troops came. Some of their officers were billeted on my college at Oxford, Corpus Christi, while they waited for D-Day. It was the first time that I had actually seen Americans. What strange habits they had! But how young they seemed (even to an undergraduate), how confident and *democratic!* (They called *anyone* by his first name!) Some of them had names that ended in "baum," or "berg," or "owski," or "tino"; and all were Americans, and confidently Americans—Americans who had finally been made Americans by Roosevelt.

I will not here discuss his diplomacy in the war. It was often at fault, but the fault, I believe, more of an American view of the world than simply his own. To the English and to Europeans, as much as to Americans, what he had done earlier in peace was the foundation of his leadership in war. I can never forget the feeling that the navy-blue mantle he wore during the war had been thrown round me as I slept under the kitchen table during the Blitz; round my mother as she slept under the basement stairs; round all the huddled peoples of Europe. He brought into the war an America which, by policies that earned him the accusation that he was a traitor to his class, he had made strong and well and united. He brought into the war a working democracy—which made the dictatorships seem unfrightening—and one doubts if anyone else could have done it. We really did believe that westward the land was bright; and when the GIs arrived, going to war with cameras and Camels, they confirmed it. Across the Atlantic there really were broader lands and better days—for one man had made them so for millions of Americans. When an American lieutenant who was billeted on my college called me Hank one day, I knew that democracy had come to my country.

Sometime at the end of May 1945, that American lieutenant, who had become a friend, left my college. The convoy of American army trucks roared through the narrow streets of the old city, the American commanders then to lead their men over the whitened bones of their fathers in Europe. A few days later, he was killed. The symbol of my college is a pelican. A few months after the end of the war, two live pelicans arrived for my college. They were sent by some of the American officers we had come to know, in the names of their dead buddies and themselves. It was the most characteristic act of American generosity I had yet encountered, and I could not help feeling that Franklin D. Roosevelt, if he had known, would have sent such a gift, as he had sent Lend-Lease. And there had been the "Bundles for Britain." Why be surprised then, when the Marshall Plan's aid came, a few years later? Who had made America, not only so generous, but so able to be generous? Two live pelicans from Louisiana to a "dead" college in Oxford—that was the inspiration of Roosevelt's America to exhausted Europe.

My America!

I had reported from some twenty-four countries before I set foot in America. I will never forget the first shock—even after having been in every country from the Sudan to South Africa—at realizing that I was in another place entirely, a New World. In the casbah of Algiers during the first referendum called by de Gaulle in 1959,[1] when the women hurrying down the steep streets to vote for the first time pulled their yashmaks around their faces as they passed a man (which seemed to me only to make their dark eyes more fascinating), I was still in the Old World, however strange it was. But here in America it was all new.

I had been in the country about eight years, and was living in Houston, when a Texan friend asked me one evening: "Why do you like living in America? I don't mean why you find it interesting—why you want to write about it—but why you *like* living here so much." After only a moment's reflection, I replied, "It's the first time I've felt free." In the nine years that have passed since then, I have often reflected on that answer, and have found no reason to change it. What I mean by it is part of the story to be told here.

Other memories come to mind. One spring day, shortly after my arrival, I was walking down the long, broad street of a suburb, with its sweeping front lawns (all that space), its tall trees

The New Republic, July 4, 1983, originally titled "Why I Love America." Reprinted by permission from the Estate of Henry Fairlie.

1. On September 28, 1958, Charles De Gaulle organized a referendum on a new constitution, returning to the presidency and creating the Fifth Republic. (Fairlie erred in placing it in 1959.)

(all that sky), and its clumps of azaleas (all that color). The only other person on the street was a small boy on a tricycle. As I passed him, he said "Hi!"—just like that. No four-year-old boy had ever addressed me without an introduction before. Yet here was this one, with his cheerful "Hi!" Recovering from the culture shock, I tried to look down stonily at his flaxen head, but instead, involuntarily, I found myself saying in return: "Well—hi!" He pedaled off, apparently satisfied. He had begun my Americanization.

"Hi!" As I often say—for Americans do not realize it—the word is a democracy. (I come from a country where one can tell someone's class by how they say "Hallo!" or "Hello!" or "Hullo," or whether they say it at all.) But anyone can say "Hi!" Anyone does. Shortly after my encounter with the boy, I called on the then Suffragan Bishop of Washington. Did he greet me as the Archbishop of Canterbury would have done? No. He said, "Hi, Henry!" I put it down to an aberration, an excess of Episcopalian latitudinarianism. But what about my first meeting with Lyndon B. Johnson, the President of the United States, the Emperor of the Free World, before whom, like a Burgher of Calais, a halter round my neck, I would have sunk to my knees, pleading for a loan for my country? He held out the largest hand in Christendom, and said, "Hi, Henry!"

Small anecdotes? But I wish to suggest that it is there, in the small anecdotes, that the secret lies. America has—if one opens oneself to it—a bewitching power. From the very beginning the stranger feels its influence as a loosening. At first this can be disquieting. After all, one is not in an exotic land, where the differences are immediately striking, easy to see, so that one may be fascinated without really being touched by them. Yet from the beginning in America one feels this power, unsettling all that one had thought was familiar, fixed by the ages. To some—I have known them—it is alarming. For there do come moments when one realizes, more than in any other country not one's own, that here one may be being remade. If here history still invents itself, then here also, still, one may invent the future. But suppose that means that one may also invent oneself? Max Ascoli, the Italian Jew who fled from Fascism and founded and edited in America a remarkable magazine, *The Reporter*, once wrote: "It did not cause me any trouble to become an Italian, but my becoming an American is my own work." Every immigrant will know what he means; millions are still working on it in their own lives.

I remember also the time when I still resisted the very power of America to attract. After I had been here in Washington, D.C., a little while, I noticed one day that all the Americans who had befriended me were preparing to participate in some ritual, and that I was not invited. It was the Fourth of July. I presumed that they were being tactful: How could they ask me to celebrate a British defeat? So I accepted an invitation from Patrick O'Donovan, then the Washington correspondent of *The Observer*. What could we do on the Fourth? We looked at the television listings, and were delighted to find that there was a midday rerun of the original *Scarlet Pimpernel*, with Leslie Howard as Sir Percy Blakeney. We may have been defeated by the Americans, but one Englishman, single-handedly, had outwitted Robespierre's police. So we sat with our elbows on the lunch table, watching Leslie Howard be English, brave, and debonair, and even when the table leaf gave way with a crash, it did not interrupt Sir Percy or our absorption.

Later in the afternoon, Patrick—who had been a strapping young Irish Guards officer during the Second World War, as handsome (as they say) as the devil—opened the screen door into his Georgetown garden, and peed. "It does one good," he proclaimed, "on the Fourth of July, to piss on American soil." But he let in an enormous bug—one of those gigantic bugs that

make it all the more inexplicable why Americans like barbecu-
ing on their patios in the fetid summer—which then banged
from wall to wall, sometimes wheeling to dive-bomb us. "You
shouldn't have pissed on America," I said to Patrick. "George III
tried to piss on it, and look what happened to him." But Patrick was by now cowering behind the couch—all six-foot-four
Irish Guards of him—shouting to his wife, " 'Mione, 'Mione,
HELP!" She came downstairs, took one pitying look at her
brave Britishers, got a can of Raid, and destroyed the American
intruder. Patrick got up from behind the couch, drew himself up
again to his full height, and said as if he were addressing his
troops in the desert, "Henry, I cannot *bear* the tropics." By the
time the fireworks began on the mall—"More shots to be heard
round the world, I suppose," grumbled Patrick—we had the
Dutch courage to ignore them. We had drunk our way—what
else for exiles to do?—through the Fourth of July.

But as I stayed and felt America drawing me to it, I inevitably
began to think of the others who have come. The curiosity about
the country which first brought and kept me here scarcely entitles me to claim that I have shared the experience of most immigrants. I have no right to make it seem as if I came here traveling
steerage, like the political refugees or those who simply had
neither food nor hope in their native lands. But I will say this
about the Statue of Liberty. It was an act of imagination, when
the French proposed raising the money for it to celebrate the
American Revolution, to choose such a site, and not Washington or Mount Vernon or Philadelphia, and to put on it
that inscription, recalling not the English colonists who made
the Revolution, but the millions upon millions of others who
have come here since. They were drawn by the promise of this
land; the land has performed for many more of them than it has
failed; and they in turn have helped remake the nation. And still
they come.

The story of the immigration cannot be told bloodlessly. It cannot be drained of what Osbert Sitwell caught so well, in this hauntingly lovely passage from his *The Four Continents*, published in 1954: "New York, with all its faults, is yet the greatest and the most moving of modern cities . . . built by refugees to shelter and protect their dreams on alien soil. . . . For that is what it is, a metropolis of dreams realized and unrealized . . . dreams of every age and intensity. . . . So when in the small hours you open the window, and the cool of the darkness flows into the heated room, it is on a beautiful and improbable city of dreams that you look, some tragic, some naive, but many of them practicable and to be achieved in the future, near or distant, by the labors of these same dreamers when awake during the working day. Thus in the main the dreams will be fulfilled, and the hopes that prevail over fears are justified." How can one lose the sense that something quite miraculous has happened in the making of one nation from so many different peoples?

No other immigration into any other country has had anything like the same meaning for the rest of the world, for those who did not migrate, lifting the imagination of the world to horizons beyond even the expanse of this continent. The name of America still lends to countless millions its own dreams for them to dream themselves.

An English economist once said that it was America that had taught the world that it need not starve. Consider that. It cannot be denied. The achievements of American agriculture are one of the wonders of the modern world. Americans consume each year only a third of the wheat which American farmers produce; there is no other valley in the world which has been made, by irrigation, as fertile as the Central Valley of California. But it is not only such facts and figures that tell the wonder. One must look down the vastness of the Middle West, as the English poet Louis MacNeice did in 1940, "astonished by its elegance from the air. Elegance is the word for it—enormous plains of beautifully inlaid rectangles, the grain running different ways, walnut, satinwood or oatcake, the whole of it tortoiseshelled with copses and shadows of clouds. . . ." It is common for the American when he is in Europe to gasp at the hedgerows of England or the terraced vineyards of Italy, kept for centuries. But the gasp of the Englishman is no less when he gazes on a continent, immense in scale, still fabulous in its diversity, which not only is cultivated but has by its cultivation been given its own coherence; which unlike Europe has been made one. Who but the Americans would, so early, have made the Great Plains yield so much—those semi-arid lands which even they, at first, called "the Great American Desert"?

But let us return to small things. If America was to produce, it had also to invent. The English critic T. R. Fyvel once told a story of a friend, also English, who had "found himself for a fantastic weekend in a society of Texas millionaires who whizzed around in their private aircraft, dropping in on parties hundreds of miles away." The friend found this unexpectedly refreshing. He was even more impressed when he saw the children of his host "buzzing around in special little pedal motor cars which were air conditioned." But one night his Texan millionaire host turned to him and said something like: "You know, Bob, I ask myself if our machine civilization isn't shot all to hell." The Englishman, horrified, burst out to his host: "Don't have those decadent thoughts! Don't have any thoughts! Leave them to us—while you stay just as you are!" I understand his response. There seems to be nothing, however fanciful, that the American, with his unflagging inventive genius, will not attempt.

Matthew Arnold was amazed at the warmth of American houses. "We are full of plans," he wrote to his daughter from Philadelphia in 1883, "for putting an American stove into the Cottage," when he got back to England. In 1912 Arnold Bennett was amazed that, whereas "the European telephone is a toy," in America it was regarded as an indispensable convenience for everyone. In 1942 Sir Philip Biggs was amazed by the supermarket, "where you grab what you want and wheel it to the cashier in steel perambulators made for the purpose," and leave "laden with a variety of food, beyond the range of English households even in peacetimes, from the A & P stores." (Twenty-three years later, on my very first morning in America, the wife of the English friend with whom I was staying took me, not to the Washington Monument, but to a supermarket—just to stare.) In 1963 T. H. White, who made a lecture tour in his old age, accompanied by the eighteen-year-old sister-in-law of Julie Andrews as "my secretary, but really as a protectress," was amazed at the change machine in the automat restaurant on a train: "In went a dollar bill which was inspected and out come [sic] four silver quarters. Why couldn't we put in bits of newspaper cut to the right size?" But he found more to wonder at: "In Long Island fishermen can buy *worms* from slot machines"; and again: "I also learned of *tab-opening cans.* You can open a beer can and, it is to be hoped, you will soon be able to open any can, without a tin opener." They were all responding to something I could not imagine America without.

How I have come to take it all for granted was brought home to me not long ago, when I was sitting in my house with a friend visiting from England. It was a quiet afternoon in early summer, the windows were open, I could hear the birds chirping in the garden. My friend suddenly exclaimed: "How can you bear to live in all this noise?" What noise? "All this noise in the house," he said. "Something is always switching itself off or on, humming or purring." He had destroyed my own peace, for I noticed it from then on. It is no wonder that America consumes so much energy. The electric gadgetry in an American home makes it its own Disney World. But to most Englishmen it is the physical evidence of a society that does not tire of innovation; which by its inventiveness still seems to keep the future open; and in whose inventiveness ordinary people find convenience.

The inventiveness and gadgetry of the American reflects the spirit of a society which echoes the song: "It ain't necessarily so." If houses are insufferably cold, you invent a stove, and then you invent central heating; and if anyone writes in to say that the Romans had central heating, the important point is that the common man in Rome did not have it. Ben Franklin invented a prefabricated stove which could be produced for the common man; such a stove in Europe at the time would have been produced by craftsmen for the few. But then it has always been the American way as well, when faced with any injustice or harshness in this society, to say that "it ain't necessarily so," and to do something about it. If ever this spirit is allowed to languish, whether in the invention of things or the improvement of its society, America will have ceased to be what it means to the rest of the world.

When the cafeteria was first invented, the English responded to it with delight, from Clare Sheridan first being taken to one by Upton Sinclair in 1921, when she followed him as "he first took a metal tray from a column of trays," to S. P. B. Mais's description in 1933:

> You put your tray on a slide, help yourself as you rush along to orange juice, puffed rice, eggs, rolls, coffee, marmalade, or whatever it is you eat for breakfast, and when you reach the end of the counter a girl checks your loaded tray with lightning calculation, says "Thirty cents"—or whatever it is— and you take your tray and eat your breakfast at a table. The whole time spent in getting your food is thirty seconds.

The cafeteria has, of course, spread all over the world. But what these first encounters tell, above all, is of their convenience, and the fact that this convenience is liberating, as electrical gadgets (or Clarence Birdseye's invention, frozen foods) are liberating in the home. What they tell secondly is that these conveniences are not for a privileged few. Like the Franklin stove or the Ford Model T, these amenities were meant for all.

What I am trying to show is that, to other Englishmen besides myself, there is a meaning to the material progress of America which has traveled, and is still traveling, to the rest of the world, beyond the physical benefits which it bestows. It was a critic of fastidious taste and judgment, Cyril Connolly, who said in 1952:

> All American influence on Europe, however vulgar, brings with it an improvement in the standard of living and the dissipation of certain age-old desires. Should Europe oppose this influence? Europe, which has destroyed so many exotic civilizations, without even providing them with the democratic optimism which America brings with its films, its gadgets, and its *lingua franca,* the demotic language which obliterates all class distinctions.

But Connolly left out the most significant American influence of all: the spread of the manners of a society which has always been more informal, less stiff, less bound by convention, than any other in the world; in which a person is accepted, as Thackeray said during one of his visits, for what he is. The impetus to informality in America is, at least in part, the source of one of the most striking changes in our century: the change in the relationship between one individual human being and another, and so in their relationship to their society.

The informality is one characteristic which at first both jarred and drew me. By far the most infectious account of this characteristic of America was given by Dom Hubert van Zeller, an English monk who often preached retreats in both countries, and enjoyed America, but was still astonished at this scene:

> In a hall at Denver I had the privilege of being listened to by upwards of six hundred nuns, assembled from different communities, all of whom were eating ices off the ends of sticks. The distribution of the ices, effectively conducted by a member of the home team, took place during the earlier phase of my address, so from the elevated position which I occupied on the platform, I was able to lay bets with myself as to which religious order would finish first.

This is the public informality—often noticed in Congress, in the courts—but the training begins early, with the freedom given the American child.

The children, like the informality, can at first jar. But the true mark of American society is that its informality forms its own patterns and codes. Although the outsider cannot at first detect it, there is a rhythm of American life. This rhythm is a constant improvisation, a flexibility that will accommodate the wishes and whims of every member of the group. No one voice in the typical American family takes precedence over the rest. Someone is always leaving or coming back; someone is always asking if he or she can have the car; someone is always going to the refrigerator for a snack instead of a meal; someone is always arriving late at a meal or leaving it early. The rhythm of the American family is to be found in a system of communications by which the improvised activities of each of its members is made known to all so that they can be taken into account. What holds the home together is a pattern of wires and castings, as hidden from view as the inside of a transistor radio, along which a ceaseless flow of messages is carried, and accommodations made to them. Messages left on the refrigerator door can for days be the only visible form of communication between members of a family who otherwise succeed in never running into each other as they come and go.

This is one reason why Mom and Dad, Lois and Junior, are so noticeable as tourists, and look so uncomfortable. They are not used to doing things as a unit. One can notice this even in an ordinary restaurant in America, when a whole family has for once come out to have dinner together: one by one, each grows restless to get away, and the meal degenerates into a pitiless nagging of the one person (usually, the mother) who is actually having a good time, and so is holding up the rest. What has happened is that they are not using their transistors; since they are all together, the flow of messages has been interrupted; having to do the same thing, at the same time, their common life has lost its rhythm.

I noticed at once the general American aversion to sitting down to a meal, and the time spent, if you are a guest, sitting in an armchair, or a canvas chair on the porch, always with a low table within handy reach. What then happens was perfectly caught in 1952 by the English journalist Mervyn Jones:

> Darting in and out of the kitchen, your hostess keeps the table constantly loaded with sandwiches, plates of cheese, nice little things on crackers, bowls of fruit, nuts, olives, pretzels, rolls, cakes, cookies, and other refreshments. Gin, whiskey, beer, and coffee are on tap without a moment's break. You are urged, in case there should be anything you lack, to help yourself from the two or three vast refrigerators. . . . People arrive in cars, sit down, stretch out

their hands with the same air of unthinking habit as a horse reaching for a clump of grass, nibble for a while, get into their cars, and go—to be replaced, no matter what the hour, by other nibblers. All sense of time is lost. . . . You have, however, eaten twice as much as though you had sat round the table for three square meals.

The fact is that a wholly different manner of life was invented in America, contrasted with that of Europe (before it began to spread there from America): with more flexibility, more activity, more fragmentation, but still with its own patterns. American society is a kaleidoscope, in which the original pattern is always being rearranged. This is itself freeing, simply in day-to-day behavior, in the opportunities to meet other people, but also in deeper ways.

Though there are classes in America, there is no *class system.* When I answered, "The first time I've felt free," one thing I meant was that I was free of class. How could a class system be fastened onto a shifting kaleidoscope? If you imagine that you have discovered some symmetrical pattern in American society, you have only to change the angle at which you stand to it and the pattern changes. As Martin Green wrote in 1961, "America is not dominated by any single type, much less [a] class-limited one"; and he added, referring to Britain, "In these two ways, America stands for health, and we for sickness." This is strong, but it is just. Class—accent, vocabulary, dress, manners—not only confines the lower class in England, it also confines the upper class. It is much easier to mix here with people who are unlike oneself. To whom can this be more important than the immigrant making his way into the mainstream? Why the barriers remain so difficult for blacks to cross is too large a question to go into here, and the disappointing results so far of the Puerto

Rican immigration (of which Nathan Glazer and Daniel Patrick Moynihan expected so much in *Beyond the Melting Pot*) also raise disconcerting questions which are beyond the scope of personal response. I will merely say that the sheer rise of the present colored—Asian, Latin American, Caribbean—immigration seems bound to present challenges which will make Americans again consider the virtues of assimilation.

Other lines than those of class are also more easily crossed: those of sex, for example, and of age. When the English have come to America they have always written at length about American women. "And what luncheons," exclaimed Clare Sheridan, ". . . and apparently all for themselves. There is never a man. They even pay one another compliments. I wonder if they can be contented." (There has often been this ambivalence in the consistent praise of American women.) I too would comment when I first came here on the numbers of women lunching together in restaurants. But I soon came to believe that it is partly from her associations with other women that the American woman draws, not only a strength and subtlety of feeling for her own existence (a part of her superiority which almost every English visitor has acknowledged), but also her capacity for friendship with men. It is the American man's capacity for friendship with women which is in doubt, and I attribute it to the shallowness of his associations and lack of intimacy with his own sex. In a moment I will show why that last observation is not thrown in just to provoke a riot.

But first I must emphasize what it is in American women which, especially when they began to arrive in England in large numbers a century ago, took the English by storm. In 1907, Lady Dorothy Nevill, calling her "bright and vivacious," said, "it is by the American girl we have been conquered." As early as 1864 Lord Bryce, who later married one, thought that American women had "so much more freedom in their manners; . . . the absence of primness was a very agreeable relief." To Rudyard Kipling in 1891, "the girls of America are above and beyond them all. . . . They have societies, and clubs . . . where all the guests are girls . . . ; they understand; they can take care of themselves; they are superbly independent." But the essential point was made by Jerome K. Jerome in 1904: "The American girl has succeeded in freeing European social intercourse from many of its hidebound conventions. There is still work for her to do. But I have a faith in her."

The barrier of age is also crossed. My first editor in 1945 had lectured to a party of American students on the liner bringing them to observe postwar Europe. He exclaimed to me: "They are so different. They ask questions. They say what they think. They are not afraid to talk." Since I was twenty-one myself, and had never been afraid to talk, I thought he was a little gone in the head. There are few things more delightful than the way in which young Americans all over the country are willing to engage openly and freely in conversation and even friendship with someone perhaps more than twice their age. There is a democracy of manners in America which I would miss terribly if I ever left here.

I have been describing a society that is freeing. But there is no doubt it is also demanding. For if the immigrant feels here that he may invent himself, then is he not in that only being an American already? So much in the Old World is fixed for one: not only one's position but so much of one's life and even one's self. This is what weighs in the first part of Ascoli's remark: "It did not cause me any trouble to become an Italian." But even for an American born here, is it not his "own work" to become an American? This accounts for the one unease I still feel.

With the contrast I am about to draw, it is worth saying, I

know many Americans who agree. It is much easier at first—and it is here that I am thinking of the men—to get to know an American. The welcoming "Hi!," the first names, the ready handshake, the quick generosity. You do not get through these first layers with an Englishman nearly as easily or as quickly. But once through them with an American, you come soon to a dead end, you are not admitted to the core or to any real intimacy. With the Englishman, whereas it is hard to get through the initial reserve, once through those outer layers, all resistance crumbles, and you find that you are sharing a level of extraordinary intimacy.

Julían Marías, the disciple of Ortega y Gasset, who spent much time here in the 1950s and 1960s, observed that although Americans get more mail than any other people in the world, they receive far fewer personal letters. An American friend of mine, Howard Higman, a professor of sociology, makes the point well. A letter from an American is like an itinerary, he says, a letter from an Englishman is like a diary. There is no questioning this, and I have often wondered what it is that Americans fear to expose, even whether they fear that there is nothing at the core to expose at all. But the answer, I believe, is simpler. If there has been so much freedom and informality in which to make oneself, if it really is one's "own work" to be an American, then one is bound to guard jealously a self which must often feel isolated and fragile, far more than in a society where so much of who one is has been determined for one. (For if one has been made by that society, it has made others like oneself, so what is there to fear?) This is the significance of the women's associations on which the English observers at once fixed their attention. The men's associations are far more likely to be centered on some activity—sports, watching football, hunting—anything to avoid having to talk about themselves and bare their souls. This is where one comes to a dead stop. These are the personal letters one misses. Almost all letters from American men are typed, even those from my friends, even those meant to be warmly personal. They might be dictated to a secretary, for the little they dare to say.

There is in all of this one reason why so many American attempts to describe the experience of being an American fall back on myth and metaphor, whereas almost all the English descriptions of what it seems to them to mean to be an American stick to the details and small encounters of everyday life. Americans take too much for granted the details of American life in which may often be found the meaning of the freedom and equality and opportunity which still draw people to it. We all know the wretched side of the life of the immigrants: the rough, menial, even dangerous work; the abysmally low wages; the abject conditions in which they lived, in the notorious dumbbell tenements of New York, for example, honeycombed with tiny rooms. And we know that those wretched conditions, whether in the large cities or in the acres of the Southwest baking under the sun, still exist. Yet there was and is another side. It was not all that long after the Italians began to arrive that, in their communities on the Upper East Side, there were shoulders of meat in the butcher's windows at twelve cents a pound; outside the macaroni shops, under improvised shelters, the macaroni was hung out to dry; along the curbs were the pushcarts with artichokes and asparagus, early melons and tomatoes; and a round of cheese cost twenty-four cents. And although only a third of the Italian immigrants had ever cast a vote in their native country, before the first generation had reached middle age they had politicians courting them; and Fiorello La Guardia was elected to Congress from East Harlem on his second attempt in 1916. As they shopped on their streets, where did their allegiance lie? To Genoa? We can still catch from that picture of their streets the smell of freedom.

As a young officer, George C. Marshall was surprised, when he inspected his troops on landing in France in 1917, at how many of them spoke broken English. But of their stake in America, in its industry, in its freedom, there could be little doubt; this was borne out by the astonishing lack of sedition in America throughout the war. I have tried from my own experience to explain some of the small but revealing reasons why America worked its influence so quickly and so deeply on them. It now seems to be working on some of the new immigrants. In my observation, the East Asians especially (and who would have predicted it?) are responding wholeheartedly to American life—their children are into the Little League almost as soon as they are out of the cradle—as they work their way, often by traditional routes such as running neighborhood stores, into the mainstream. This third wave of immigration is repeating, quite remarkably, many of the characteristics of the first two waves. America is still open, and it will be a tragedy if those who wish it to "think small," who will to keep America as a playground for those already here, have their way, and close America down.

I will give the last words to an American. Daniel Patrick Moynihan wrote in 1978: " . . . while the matter has not received much attention, the United States is quietly but rapidly resuming its role as a nation of first- and second-generation immigrants, almost the only one of its kind in the world, incomparably the largest, and for the first time in our history or any other, a nation drawn from the entire world. The Immigration Act of 1965 altered the shape of American immigration and increased its size. . . . Our immigrants in wholly unprecedented proportions come from Asia, South America, and the Caribbean. In fiscal year 1973 the ten top visa-issuing ports were Manila, Monterrey, Seoul, Tijuana, Santo Domingo, Mexico City, Naples, Guadalajara, Toronto, Kingston. I would expect Bombay to make this top ten list before long. . . . In short, by the end of the century, the United States will be a multi-ethnic nation the like of which even we have never imagined."

In this vision, America is still open. And America is about to be remade by its immigrants—again—as they become enthusiastic Americans. And what will the immigrants write home about? The gadgets, I beg, the gadgets.

If Pooh Were President

A TORY'S RIPOSTE TO REAGANISM

The pretense will be made during the next few months that the presidential election this year is a clash between two political philosophies. But one thing on which almost everyone is agreed is that the liberal philosophy that nourished the Democratic Party a generation or more ago has long since been exhausted. And it has not been replaced by a new one. As Daniel Patrick Moynihan has been saying for several years, "It is a long time since the Democrats had a new idea."

Any notion that the election will be fought over a political philosophy also rests on the illusion that voters will be rendering a verdict on four years of conservative government led by a conservative president. It is an illusion because Reaganism as it has been defined and practiced by its author is not a genuinely conservative philosophy; and neither has the alleged conservative revival in the country yielded anything like a true American conservatism.

Political observation and commentary, like political attitudes in general, do not exist outside some context. I used to be known in Britain as one of the spokesmen of a conservative revival that was supposed to be taking place there, as well as in America, in the 1950s. It was with such a reputation that I first visited the United States in 1965, one of my intentions being to discover evidence of an indigenous conservatism here. It was five months after Lyndon Johnson's clobbering of Barry Goldwater when I arrived. Every political columnist in Georgetown assured me that the Republicans would be out of office for another twenty years. As for conservatives (as distinct from mere Republicans), the political columnists disparaged even my inquiries. Anyone who called himself a conservative was dismissed as some half-crazed prophet who wandered about the deserts of Arizona with no sense that the liberal mainstream set a permanent course the nation must follow.

Soon after my arrival, Irving Kristol[1] took me to lunch with William F. Buckley Jr. at the New York Yacht Club. I was about to embark on a long and slow journey through the South, and asked my two companions the names of conservatives I might visit. They were silent, hemmed and hawed, looked at each other, and were silent again. Surely there must be one name, I protested, and at last Buckley suggested G. Warren Nutter in Charlottesville, who had been an economics adviser and a speechwriter for Goldwater in the 1964 campaign. That was all. It became clear to me that my search for an indigenous American conservatism was going to be extended and even disheartening. Since then I have looked and looked, listened and listened, read and read, and I still cannot find any true American conservatism. I find this regrettable. I have no doubt that a democracy is that much weaker to the extent that it lacks a strong and confident conservative tradition. What passes for conservatism in America now is neither strong nor confident.

The fundamental and persistent weakness of American

1. Irving Kristol (born 1920) is widely regarded as the founder of the American neoconservative movement. A Trotskyite in his early years and graduate of City College, his politics shifted to the right during editorial stints at *Commentary, Encounter* (where he published Fairlie's work), the *Public Interest,* and the *National Interest,* arguing for low taxes and strongly anti-Communist policies.

conservatism is that it is not nourished by any distinct tory spirit. The conservative and the tory may be allies, but they are not the same creatures. Americans may not appreciate how shattering it is to come to their country and find a "conservatism" that has no element of toryism to nourish and humanize and correct it. The conservative can all too easily drift into a morally bankrupt and intellectually shallow defense of those who have it made and those who are on the make if the tory is not there to remind him of what Edward Heath, in denouncing Margaret Thatcher, called "the ugly face of capitalism."[2]

The first mark of the tory is a steady, unvolatile, almost unconscious confidence in the resources and resilience of his society. He is not much disturbed by the "movements" that wash over or through it from time to time. He plants his own saplings; he will not be here to see them when they are grown, but he knows that long after he has gone, and whatever the winds that buffet them, they will take root in the soil of the society and give shade to it. What more can a tory do? More to the point, what more should he do? He can see no reason why those who are the governors of a well ordered society should spend their time reacting to every fad. Why get hot under the collar about the apparent decline of the traditional family? It was never in question that before long people would wish to recover the traditional family, even if altered (and so strengthened) by the assault that was sprung against it. One may say that the English aristocrat has always been the truest tory because he knows that his own family has survived the most eccentric and often reprobate conduct of its members for centuries.

The second mark of the tory is that he despises "trade" and

2. Edward Heath (1916–2005) was a Conservative MP and prime minister of Great Britain from 1970 to 1974. He carried on a long feud with Margaret Thatcher, who did not share his enthusiasm for closer ties with Europe and who ousted him as their party's leader in 1975.

those in it. When John F. Kennedy was president, you could hear tories all over London murmur gruffly over their drinks that if he was put up for their club, he would be blackballed by every member worth his salt. By Jove, sir, how did his father make his money? (It was interesting to consider how their ancestors had acquired their land. "By the battle-ax," one of them said to me, "Not by trade. By the battle-ax.") But the snobbery of the tory about trade means that conservatism is challenged from within itself if it limits its purposes to the defense of moneyed entrepreneurs and businessmen. Stanley Baldwin was a businessman, an ironmaster of the Midlands.[3] But he was speaking as an instinctive tory when he described those who were elected to Parliament in 1918 as "a lot of hard-faced men who look as if they had done very well out of the war"; and it was as an instinctive tory that he so remarkably bound the British classes together through industrial bitterness, the 1926 general strike, and even the depression, creating a sound and united nation to which a born tory, Winston Churchill, could so magnificently appeal in 1940. One has only to ask the American conservative: Has Reagan so united the classes? Has he created so sound a nation? He cannot even carry the nation with him on any venture save conquering a trifling island. Standing tall in Grenada is a scurvy boast for a conservative.

English conservatism primarily was a protest against the Industrial Revolution. The real founders of modern toryism were intellectuals, from Coleridge on, who fed their ideas to politicians, of whom Disraeli was the most spirited; those ideas were kept alive by more recent intellectuals, such as T. S. Eliot—all distrusting and despising trade, all prepared to say with the

3. Stanley Baldwin (1867–1947) was a Conservative MP and, at three different junctures (1923–1924, 1925–1929, 1935–1937), prime minister of Great Britain. After the outbreak of the Second World War, he was criticized for not pursuing rearmament more aggressively.

church, as Eliot did, that capitalism was usury (as they bluntly called it), all believing that capitalism, if unchecked, would destroy community and nation. It is hard to find in American conservatism any reliable tradition that says it is not sufficient for conservatives to defend the moneyed men.

The third mark of the tory is his belief in strong central government. That is the meaning of his support of the Monarchy. (He will always write it with an initial capital letter.) Strong government does not necessarily mean extensive or intrusive government. But of the need for the "political realm" to assert its supremacy over the "economic realm" the tory has not a moment's doubt. He knows that *society* has its own life apart from the central government, but he does not believe that a *nation* has any existence apart from the central government. It is not a society but a nation that goes to war and defends itself against its enemies. The tory does not understand the American conservative who will weaken the claims of the government at home while at the same time urging the people to follow the government in defending the nation abroad.

The fourth mark of the tory is that he capitalizes the People. Disraeli, from the beginning to the end of his career, tried to forge an alliance between the Monarchy and the People against the Whig magnates and their liberal supporters who would have plundered and pulled down both; it was as the self-conscious heir to Disraeli's mantle that in 1940 Churchill drew the Monarchy and the People together into the fighting nation. It must not be forgotten: the appeasers were conservatives, the nonappeasers were tories. Those closest to being tories in America today are those who call themselves (Scoop) Jackson Democrats. But why on earth did none of them cry out in pain when Reagan tried to assume Jackson's mantle and throw it over the Administration's pitiful and even abject foreign ventures? Where is the evidence that Reagan has brought the People of America together so that they will support one extended action by their marines overseas? There is none.

There are two sides to the tory. In all that concerns his society he is unexcited, patient, and not inclined to do very much. This is the Pooh in him. Pooh was a tory. As he often engagingly said when one of his plans went awry, he was a "Bear of Very Little Brain." But then he did not set much store by either plans or brains. In their place, he had wisdom. He knew that the Forest was governed, season after season, by laws he did not understand. Left to himself, he would have done nothing. The Forest would be there when he woke up; even more assuring, he knew that it was there while he was asleep. But he was not left to himself. Most of the other animals in the Forest were anxious and overexcited. Since Pooh was never excited—never—they came to him with their worries; and it was with considerable skepticism, but also with an understanding that they needed to be reassured, that he went in search of the Woozle, and even of Eeyore's tail. As a good tory, Pooh was never surprised to find things where they ought to be. Not until Eeyore found that his tail was missing by looking between his legs did Pooh decide he must do something. On the whole, Pooh was very much like the landed tories of England, whom Walter Bagehot described as "the stupid party." The tory knows that one should not meddle with society; and that if anything goes wrong, it will not go wrong for very long or with much harm done.

But surrounding Pooh were lots of agitating conservatives: Rabbit and Kanga, even Piglet, and especially Tigger. They were all afraid of the Forest. They were like liberals who had been mugged. Tigger was the most agitated. When he saw something unfamiliar, it sent him into a whorl of anxiety and a whirl of activity. He saw a cloth on Pooh's table and at once attacked it, rolling himself up in it until he at last got his head out and asked: "Have I won?" That is exactly how many contributors to *Commentary* write nowadays. Pooh gave the only sensible answer, the answer of a tory: "That's my tablecloth."

Although the tory does not feel exercised about the way his society appears to be going, he looks nonetheless to an active central government to draw out of that society the nation that knows itself and will act as a nation. He relies on society to look after itself, with a little nudging here and there, but does not rely on it to know itself as a nation. A tory might (for the sake of argument) agree that the marketplace enables different private interests to sort themselves out and produce a stable, peaceable, and reasonably decent society; but he does not think that the market can *ever* by itself create and sustain the nation that must defend itself as a nation. A society does not go to war in defense of itself—why should it? it looks after its own interests—it goes to war only in defense of the nation.

And where in modern societies is the nation to be found except in the activity of and allegiance to a strong central government? The *Wall Street Journal* is a highly intelligent—if not so intelligent as it thinks—observer and defender of American society. But I defy anyone to find the American nation in its commentaries. What is more, like many American conservatives, it knows this. From time to time, like Eeyore searching for his tail, it tries to find the nation. It does not find it because it does not accept that the nation exists only in the sustained activity and energy of a strong central government. That is the importance of Irving Kristol's recent proclamation that he is not only a patriot but a nationalist. So he would like to be; and so, one may even say, he tries to be. But no one can be a nationalist from the marketplace. The question the British conservative must in the end always level at the American conservative has also to be put to him: "Where is your Monarch, Mr. Kristol?" For the nation cannot be brought to you, as if it were *Masterpiece Theatre*, by a grant from Mobil Oil.

The British conservative is also ready with another question, although it can be too pat: "Where is your past?" How can one be a conservative unless one allows a special dominion to the past? It is not at all surprising that Kristol, whom I regard as by far the most intelligent and interesting of those who are trying to work out an American conservative philosophy, begins by disowning the past. He may raise his eyebrows and say that he has not done so. But here we come close to a distinction that has to be made between conservatism and Reaganism, and one must ask what meaning can be attached to these words of Kristol's to which he deliberately gives weight. "What is 'neo' ('new') about this conservatism is that it is resolutely free of nostalgia. It, too, claims the future."

That "nostalgia" is one of Kristol's many escape words: the hatch in a submarine or the bay in a spacecraft through which an idea can escape without any harm to the body of ideas left within. One's mind glides over it even as one reads: How right to be "resolutely free of nostalgia." But whenever has a true conservatism been informed by nostalgia? Far from yearning for the past or wishing to recover it or live in it, the conservative cares so much for the past that he wants only to leave it alone. The past is itself, or, as the English conservative philosopher Michael Oakeshott would have said without wincing, the past is herself. Do not touch her. Do not think to rebuke her. Thou art so beautiful—those haunting words of Faust—stay as thou art.

With his disavowal of nostalgia, Kristol seems to shake the past from him, like a dog coming out of a river; and in this he is representative not only of the neoconservatives but of most American conservatives. When he does reach to the past, which he often does to make his argument, it is to plunder it. The past is *usable* to him—an especially American notion—and is interesting for its prescriptions. From the past he will, no less, "claim the future." The idea of any true conservative "claiming the future" is so wrongheaded that one can only suggest that Kristol go back to City College with his fellow Trotskyite students and begin plotting the future again on the back of a greasy frankfurter wrapper.

Kristol's vocabulary is unfailingly instructive and tells us much about American conservatism generally. Having apparently disposed of the past, he then makes an enthralling statement. Taken word by word as an unconscious illustration of the predicament of American conservatives, it is an eye-opener: "Neoconservatism is not merely patriotic—that goes without saying—but also nationalist. Patriotism springs from love of the nation's past, nationalism arises out of hope for the nation's future, distinctive greatness." Patriotism and nationalism need to be distinguished. But Kristol has got it all ass-backward. Patriotism does not spring from "love of the nation's past." Kristol was a staff sergeant during World War II. (He is still the indispensable staff sergeant of the conservative intellectual movement.) Let him recall the photographs in any combat soldier's wallet. They speak of his patriotism, but they do not speak of any love of his nation's past; they are pictures of a farm or a mean street back home, of a backyard, of a dog, or a girl, of parents. The pictures in his wallet are images of the society he loves as it is now, and that he knows (with as little fussing as Pooh) will go on much as before. What soldier was ever willing to fight and die for his nation's past? His patriotism is rooted in the present. But nationalism does spring from a desire to recreate the nation's past and make it live. Let Kristol recall men such as Herder, who sprang on the world a whole new school of history in order to find in the imagined past the hazy notions to fire a new nationalism. Oh! the mists of the past, without which nationalism has no life. Patriotism is satisfied to defend the nation *now*. Nationalism drags in the nation's past to make it speak sense; and that sense, being false, is always destructive.

The American conservative is always confusing nationalism with patriotism in this way. That is why the "superpatriot" in the American conservative sets our teeth on edge. It is also why American conservatism, whether isolationist as in the past or interventionist as it is now, seldom forms a true foreign policy. Nationalism never had and never can have a foreign policy. It is a popular, demagogic notion for domestic consumption. It is always turned inward. It is, quite simply, a vote-getter for demagogues who have nothing else to offer. It has to embrace the past, that past the superpatriot so falsely loves, for it has no love for the present. When we consider why Reagan's foreign policy has left the Stars and Stripes more tattered even than before, we should remember that nationalism cannot tell us where the nation's interests lie. The nation's interests are not its concern, because the nation's present is not its concern.

The brilliance of Reaganism lies in its constant play with the past and the future in order to neglect the present. The rhetoric of Reaganism is a force in itself. It has little to do with conservatism. In fact it is radically, almost violently, hostile to any true conservatism. The apparent simplicity of the rhetoric should not make us deaf to its sincerity and its original if unconscious subtlety.

What does Reagan offer the American people? He offers them progress. Progress is a curious lamp for a conservative to hold before the people. But it is the lamp that Reagan waves. "Progress" was the key word in his homilies for General Electric; the business of General Electric was progress, and the business of America, now as always, is progress. It is this that enables him to clothe with virtue policies that have little other reason than to nourish the great corporations. America will progress to its appointed destiny with a grant from General Electric. Big Business is one huge Foundation for the Progress of America;

and since Americans like so empty a word as "progress," they are only too willing to go on funding the foundation.

But progress to what? What is the "appointed destiny"? Big Business has no idea. Reagan really had no idea. But this is where Reaganism makes its dazzling about-face. No one but Reagan could make such rhetoric out of a U-turn. For America according to Reaganism is to progress toward its past. The fact that it is to be a more idyllic past than ever existed does not corrupt the innocent beauty of the vision. There never was the past of republican virtue and thrift and prudence and neighborliness and self-help to which Reagan invites the American people. So where does he promise to take them? Why, back to the Land of Back.

A vague prevailing mood in the country responds readily to this. The United States is plagued with "back to" movements. Back to Basics. Back to the Family. Back to Babies. Back to Religion. (But not, very clearly, back to God.) Back to Discipline. Back to the Rod. And, of course, Back to the Closet. Back, oh, yes, please, to the Land of Back. That progress, which usually frightens the average conservative, should lead to so green and familiar a pasture, is the wonder. This idea of progress is no more real than the fishes' dream of heaven in Rupert Brooke's poem: "And in that heaven of all their wish, / There shall be no more land, say fish." That is the promise of Reaganism. It works—how could it fail?—in speeches. There is not one of us who does not sigh with nostalgia when Reagan holds out the vision that IBM, Exxon, Xerox, McDonald's, Montgomery Ward, Du Pont, and the rest will make America again a land of contented and peaceable husbandmen, even in the huge cities in which present-day capitalism alone can thrive. America is to progress to its beginning, the beginning it never had. In the future it is to escape from the present to the idyllic past. Magic! It is a magic that has an immediate attraction for Americans.

One way of appreciating the power of Reagan's imagery is to recall Richard Hofstadter's famous quip that America is the one country that, starting from perfection, yet aspires to progress. That is exactly the astonishing union Reaganism contrives in its rhetoric. There is no true relation between that rhetoric and conservatism. For if the conservative does not love his society as it is now, with all its fads and follies, then, one wonders, who will love it, and what does he really love?

The fact that a false picture of the past and a false reading of the present lie at the heart of the vision leads to what is both unconservative and truly damaging in Reaganism. There is nothing all that wrong in itself in a little nostalgia for an idealized past. If the communist is driven to question the present from an imagined and ideal future, the conservative is sometimes driven to question it from an imagined and ideal past. Placing the Golden Age in the past has cost far fewer lives than placing it in the future. Men will not kill to get back to the Land of Back, for which we may be relieved. Yet we must consider that when this reach to an idealized past is made, the aims of public policy become confused. It may even explain why Reaganism cannot persuade Americans to fight. That also is part of the Land of Back: Bring the boys back home. This reveals the crucial fault in both Reaganism and American conservatism. Reaganism has not been able to create the nation that will act out of a society that it places only in the past and the future.

What is so disturbing about Reaganism is that, while it cannot create the nation with the will to defend itself again, it is very busy meddling with the society that a conservative would leave to look after itself.

It is not at all surprising that those who now call themselves conservatives are full of prescriptions for doing something to society. Oakeshott said that what the conservative most abhors are those who bring a recipe book to politics. But from the New

Right to the neoconservatives, American conservatives today have their eyes in recipe books. They will cook up a storm. They will tinker. They will agitate. Let one homosexual, coke-snorting student bum get hold of two food stamps, and the whole apparatus of government is brought into play. The true conservative would not think it was worth rousing public opinion or arming the Justice Department to trap one dopey felon. Yet that is precisely what American conservatives would do in place of developing a policy or public philosophy. Reaganism likes to keep the American people excited about things of very little significance.

This is not the occasion to argue in detail that America is a country with no political philosophy. The failure of every effort in the past thirty years to construct a conservative political philosophy is only the most recent evidence of that fact. But before the pundits begin reading into this year's election a meaning it will not have, one needs to be clear that in November the people will not be rendering a verdict on a conservative presidency—because there has been no conservative occupying the White House—but a judgment on the illusions and seductions of the rare and exotic phenomenon of Reaganism. Will the American people vote again for a mirage? Probably.

In a memorably vivid letter to the editor, Benjamin Hoff, author of The Tao of Pooh, *wrote that he had read Fairlie's essay to Winnie the Pooh, who "didn't understand it." Beyond objecting to certain specific details in the piece—for example, Piglet was the excitable one, not Tigger—Hoff contested its politics. "Quite frankly, the portrayal of happy, generous, compassionate, and fun-loving Pooh Bear as a conservative seems rather desperate, if not outright ridiculous,"* he wrote.*

Migration

I returned to Washington in September, having spent fourteen weeks traveling around the United States in a Chevy van. One unexpected result of my journey is that I think it highly unlikely that I will spend another summer in Washington, and just as probable that I will shake the dust of the capital from my feet for good in fifteen months or so. More insistently than at any time in the past, I have found myself asking what the East Coast has to offer. The answer is now clear: with the exception of New York City, very little. Unless you are interested in celebrity, there is little reason to be on either coast. So: where to live?

There are people who think that if you are no longer married, if your children are grown, and if you are a writer who does not need to be at an office, then you have the luxury of choosing where you wish to live. But it is one of those freedoms that is a perfect bind. What do you want to have around you? Both the family in which I was raised and my own children are scattered. Obligations to other people can keep one in a place; and, of course, there are friends. But friends also scatter. Their jobs and their lives take them elsewhere. I have more close friends in Washington now than in any other place; but I have more friends in different places than I have in Washington.

The New Republic, December 31, 1984. Reprinted by permission from the Estate of Henry Fairlie.

There are so many places "out there" in America that are full of life and interest, because they make things in them. Do you know where your bulletin board is made? No. But you can drive into a tiny town in northeast Indiana, and there they make bulletin boards. How satisfying to make something so useful. I found it exciting to be in the Valley of the Jolly Green Giant, driving south from Minneapolis–St. Paul into Iowa. Ho! Ho! Ho! As my companion and I went from big city to small town and village, I realized how much grittiness and spice is given to life in places that manufacture and produce. To know that Pillsbury is milling flour in Minneapolis, or that they are ranching in the mountains above Helena, Montana, or that they are turning out the hat bodies of the Stetson in Danbury, Connecticut, and finishing the Stetson in all its glory in St. Joseph, Missouri (all places that we visited) makes even the news in the papers seem real. Even in a northeastern town as chronically depressed as Wilkes-Barre, Pennsylvania, people stay; and among the reasons is that manufacturing towns have strong and resilient characters. I've found Washington increasingly unbearable on my return, primarily because it makes absolutely nothing. In New York you can at least see them trundling garments on coat racks along Seventh Avenue.

I was once with an English and an American journalist when one of them asked, "What do we need money for?" The question is searching, but on the spur of the moment I answered: "Books, booze, and a broad." (Years later I found myself explaining awkwardly to someone that I used "broad" only for alliteration.) It is much the same if one asks, "Where do I want to live?" Isaac Bashevis Singer once said that whenever he came to a new place he asked first if there was a good library. I can understand that, and I would insist on being in striking distance of a good library. But thirty miles outside any substantial university town would meet that criterion. So the choice remains wide open. Then there is conversation. A much admired New York poet once said to me, when I was living out West, "Isn't it the height of self-betrayal to live among one's intellectual inferiors?" I was about to answer, "Then how can you bear to live in New York?" But I held my tongue, since I was at his dinner table in his poet's garret on Central Park West.

I hardly read newspapers anymore. This was already fairly true before we set out. I think they are poor reading for a journalist. They are one reason journalists go on saying the same things. But it was a revelation to go for fourteen weeks without ever seeing *The Washington Post,* and only occasionally seeing *The New York Times* for sale in some unlikely small town in northwest Idaho, and to feel no less informed about what a reasonably alert individual needs to know. With *USA Today,* which was available in the smallest places, and a few good magazines—this one, of course; *The Texas Observer* (wherever you live); *Inc.,* which is on the frontier of change in America; *Scientific American; Rolling Stone,* which I devour; *The Times Literary Supplement;* and one or two good quarterlies, which often scoop the papers by three months—I feel I know enough. But the wider point is that conversation broadens itself when it does not revolve around what the papers say. I ban the discussion of politics and journalism from my own table. But it was when I returned to Washington this time that I realized how thin its conversation is, after months of talking to people about events that came out of their own lives, and not out of the Op-Ed pages. When you've met a roaming cowboy in Mankato, Minnesota, who goes by the name of Hooter, and quotes Christopher Marlowe and Thomas Kyd to you, and in answer to a question about his life recites a ballad which he himself has written, it is galling to be asked if you have read George Will's latest column. I don't like living in places where people do the same things I do. I'm interested in what's other than me.

But all of this only points to a deeper dissatisfaction. I find it hard now to be interested in politics. I do not think that America and most of our Western societies engage any longer in political activity. In the age of the media and direct mailing, it is not only Ronald Reagan who has become a puppet. So have virtually all politicians, and most of the American people seem to share my opinion. We toured America in an election year, and only once did anyone mention the election or any of the candidates. That was in the Central Valley of California, when Geraldine Ferraro was being nominated a hundred miles away. (They didn't think much of her.) Americans know that politics is an activity of the past, that the kind of power that changes lives no longer rests with politicians. I used to complain about Washington's obsession with politics. Now the politics they talk about is even less real than before. Conversation here is a lot of journalists talking about journalism. What a capital. Let me out.

Citizen Kennedy

On January 20 it will have been a quarter of a century since the young president stood bareheaded in the cold, and gave an inaugural address of such brilliance and power that Sam Rayburn pronounced it "better than anything Franklin Roosevelt said at his best—it was better than Lincoln." Four of the presidents since then have given six inaugural addresses. We can remember not a word from any of them, nothing of the bearing of the men or the atmosphere of the ceremony. The inaugural address of John F. Kennedy can be quoted by those who were not even born at the time.

"And so, my fellow Americans, ask not what your country can do for you; ask what you can do for your country." There is no one who thinks that those words were said by Richard Nixon or Ronald Reagan, and all efforts to play on them have always failed. Despite their familiarity, they are not shopworn. They were—they still are—the key words of the inaugural. You could put aside everything else about standing on the walls of freedom round the world, and you would still be left with that remarkable summons to the citizens of the Republic.

Ideas in politics must sometimes go underground for a while; the time is not favorable to them. But underground they gather new energy and still work their way into the roots of the nation's life, until the people again feel the need for them. One day some new president will find other words to summon the people

The New Republic, February 3, 1986. Reprinted by permission from the Estate of Henry Fairlie.

from their private pursuits to remember their obligations to the Union, the Republic, the *Res Publica*—the state.

It is astonishing to read again the almost liturgical language in which Kennedy fashioned, sentence by sentence, his call to the American people. He began at once with a series of the rhetorical antitheses he got from Theodore Sorensen, who wrote most of his major speeches: "We observe today not a victory of party, but a celebration of freedom, symbolizing an end as well as a beginning, signifying renewal as well as change." Of course if was exactly "a victory of party" that was being celebrated, but every new American president has to disown politics at his inauguration. In that opening sentence, past, present, and future were brought together to proclaim a universal mission: " . . . the same revolutionary beliefs for which our forebears fought are still at issue around the globe." The mission had been made universal in time and space.

"Let the word go forth" (whose spine does not tingle still at the archaism, the almost Old Testament archaism?) "from this time and place, to a new generation of Americans born in this century" (like JFK), "tempered by war" (the Second World War had not yet passed into history), "disciplined by a hard and bitter peace" (the Cold War was made to seem like an occasion for national regeneration), "proud of our ancient heritage" (the mission was given the authority of the past), "and unwilling to witness or permit the slow undoing of those human rights to which this nation has always been committed, and to which we are committed today, at home and around the world" (the whole, wide world).

There was one decision that was all-important, an understandable but revealing and radical mistake. Working on the early drafts of the speech at Palm Beach, Kennedy was dissatisfied with each attempt to outline a domestic program. On January 16, when work on the final draft began, he decided to make no mention of domestic questions. Not only was foreign affairs his dominant interest; as a politician he always trod warily among the interests that have to be reconciled on domestic policy. But in a last-minute addition to the speech, he added that human rights must be defended as well "at home." This was as far as he would go in meeting the criticism that he was avoiding the issue of civil rights. The address would have seemed a great deal less martial if he had leavened it with some real attention to people's concerns at home.

Already universal, the mission was now made boundless: "Let every nation know, whether it wishes us well or ill, that we shall pay any price, bear any burden, meet any hardship, support any friend, oppose any foe, in order to assure the survival and the success of liberty. This much we pledge—and more." What more could be pledged?

You cannot just take snippets for a book of quotations from this speech. It was knit together with every word reinforcing, expanding every other. So it went on: "the graves of young Americans . . . around the globe"; "a grand and global alliance"; "maximum danger"; "long twilight struggle"; "patient in tribulation"; "strength and sacrifice." By then who could resist the final call: "And so, my fellow Americans . . . "?

The language, the elevated sense of purpose, the incitement to a limitless mission, still seem as dangerous and misplaced in a democracy in peacetime as they have always seemed to me. And yet—and yet—how we need something of that voice now. I still do not like the reckless wording, the implications, of the "ask not . . . " sentence. And yet it calls us with a summons that America and the West pine to hear again, after Nixon, Ford, Carter, Reagan. John Kennedy and Lyndon Johnson were the last two presidents who in their inaugurations addressed the American people as if they were citizens.

It is rather an old-fashioned word: "citizen." When you hear it now, you think of classes in civics; or your mind reaches back to the Funeral Oration of Pericles, or to the Romans who did more to elevate the idea of citizenship than any other people, or to the Founding Fathers, or to Lincoln, or to the New Deal— and the Second World War. You don't hear the word "citizen" and then think of Grenada.

What passes for conservatism now in America, in the administration or outside it, has all but dispensed with the idea of citizenship. No political leader can expect the American people —or the British, French, or German people—to sacrifice their lives and their treasures overseas if they are asked to sacrifice little of their private greed and pleasures at home. You are not going to get a people to fight for the freedom of Indians in the Punjab if they've been told they may forget the plight of the Indians on the Pine Ridge reservation. There is a direct, unequivocal relationship between the Americans of the New Deal and the Americans who then returned to Europe to march over the whitened bones of their fathers. The citizen is public; he cannot be addressed as private.

Behind every overseas enterprise of a democracy, there must be a sense of compassion: "These people must be saved—even with our own lives." Democracies will not for long go to war for less. But what if the springs of compassion are dried up at home? What if the citizens have been told they need feel no compassion for their fellow citizens? If they have been told that if they make enough money it will trickle down and help the whole society? Then why not let it trickle down and help all those people abroad? See how much money the American people would contribute to a Christmas appeal for the *contras*! And so, you fellow Americans, buy your condominium and your Volvo— that's your war effort.

Norman Podhoretz wrote a column the other day, and I

agreed wholeheartedly with its general drift: that people have been given far too many excuses to escape the responsibility for their own lives. But then at the end there came an attack on the idea of compassion: we are too compassionate of others, of their failings, of ourselves, of our own failings. It seemed, as I read it, wholly gratuitous to introduce this harsh, unlovely note. But it reflected a need in these former Democrats and liberals not just to correct the mistakes of their former allies, but to pull down the whole temple of concern for others they built over the years. Is it really necessary to reject civic consciousness, of which compassion for one's less fortunate fellow citizens is the ultimate binding cement, to be a conservative or neoconservative?

The educating fact about John Kennedy is that, although throughout his presidency he tried to avoid the domestic questions that would have brought him political difficulties, his own sense of mission, as defined in the inaugural address, again and again forced him to act, and usually to act to the right end. There was also his sense of the majesty of the office, and that is a contribution to the idea of citizenship as well, for although no one can be very happy about Robert Kennedy's use of the Department of Justice, there was no way that John Kennedy could have appointed a John Mitchell as attorney general.

Perhaps only a schoolboy's education makes me echo the Roman insistence on the three great civic virtues: *dignitas, gravitas, pietas.* But Kennedy's inaugural address, even though too elevated, reminded us of those virtues; and to a great extent so did his presidency, with all its mistakes. In contrast, the current administration has drained, drop by drop, almost all *dignitas* and *gravitas* and *pietas* from the public discourse in America. With the idea of citizenship all but submerged in appeals to private pursuits, private satisfactions, the private sector, the most Reagan could hope to lead against a real enemy would be a herd of the Gadarene swine.

The Democratic impulse needed correction: no one now sensibly denies that. It has not only been corrected—it has been over-corrected. The Union needs to be put again before the States. The public sector needs to be brought back refreshed to direct the private sector. The citizen needs to be called out of his worries about how to live on $85,000 a year.

Will any Democrat before 1986 be unafraid enough, not to use the language of John Fitzgerald Kennedy 25 years ago, but to find in it the inspiration to create his own summons to the citizen that is appropriate to the last 12 years of the 20th century? I sadly doubt it. But in the next two years will one please try? If the American is not public, what's left of the Republic?

The Idiocy of Urban Life

On December 8, 1986, the New Republic *published a cover story titled "The Idiocy of Rural Life." Fairlie responded with this essay several weeks later.*

Between about 3 a.m. and 6 a.m. the life of the city is civil. Occasionally the lone footsteps of someone walking to or from work echo along the sidewalk. All work that has to be done at those hours is useful—in bakeries, for example. Even the newspaper presses stop turning forests into lies. Now and then a car comes out of the silence and cruises easily through the blinking traffic lights. The natural inhabitants of the city come out from damp basements and cellars. With their pink ears and paws, sleek, well-groomed, their whiskers combed, rats are true city dwellers. Urban life, during the hours when they reign, is urbane.

These rats are social creatures, as you can tell if you look out on the city street during an insomniac night. But after 6 a.m., the two-legged, daytime creatures of the city begin to stir; and it is they, not the rats, who bring the rat race. You might think that human beings congregate in large cities because they are gregarious. The opposite is true. Urban life today is aggressively individualistic and atomized. Cities are not social places.

The lunacy of modern city life lies first in the fact that most city dwellers who can do so try to live outside the city bound-

The New Republic, January 5, 1987, originally titled "The Idiocy of Urban Life: Or the Cow's Revenge." Reprinted by permission from the Estate of Henry Fairlie.

aries. So the two-legged creatures have created suburbs, exurbs, and finally rururbs (rurbs to some). Disdaining rural life, they try to create simulations of it. No effort is spared to let city dwellers imagine they are living anywhere but in a city: patches of grass in the more modest suburbs, broader spreads in the richer ones further out; prim new trees planted along the streets; at the foot of the larger back yards, a pretense to bosky woodlands. Black & Decker thrives partly on this basic do-it-yourself rural impulse in urban life; and with the declining demand for the great brutes of farm tractors, John Deere has turned to the undignified business of making dinky toy tractors for the suburbanites to ride like Roman charioteers as they mow their lawns.

In the city itself gentrification means two tubs of geraniums outside the front door of a town house that has been prettified to look like a country cottage. The homes, restaurants, and even offices of city dwellers are planted thick with vegetation. Some executives have window boxes inside their high-rise offices; secretaries, among their other chores, must now be horticulturists. Commercials on television, aimed primarily at city dwellers, have more themes of the countryside than of urban life. Cars are never seen in a traffic jam, but whiz through bucolic scenery. Lovers are never in tenements, but drift through sylvan glades. Cigarettes come from Marlboro Country. Merrill Lynch is a bull. Coors is not manufactured in a computerized brewery, but taken from mountain streams.

The professional people buy second homes in the country as soon as they can afford them, and as early as possible on Friday head out of the city they have created. The New York intellectuals and artists quaintly say they are "going to the country" for the weekend or summer, but in fact they have created a little Manhattan-by-the-Sea around the Hamptons, spreading over the Long Island potato fields whose earlier solitude was presumably the reason why they first went there. City dwellers take the city with them to the country, for they will not live without its pamperings. The main streets of America's small towns, which used to have hardware and dry goods stores, are now strips of boutiques. Old-fashioned barbers become unisex hairdressing salons. The brown rats stay in the cities because of the filth the humans leave during the day. The rats clean it up at night. Soon the countryside will be just as nourishing to them, as the city dwellers take their filth with them.

The recent dispersal of the urban middle-class population is only the latest development in this now established lunatic pattern. People who work in Cleveland live as far out as lovely Geauga and Ashtabula counties in northeast Ohio, perhaps 30 or 50 miles away. A bank manager in Chardon, which used to be a gracious market town in Geauga, once explained to me how the city people who come to live there want about five acres of land. "But they want the five acres for themselves alone, and not for others who come to follow their example, though no one is going to supply the services—electricity, gas, sewerage, water— for a few people living on their five acres. So the place fills up, and soon they've rebuilt the urban life they said they were escaping. What is more, they don't like paying for those services, since the rich come out to escape the high city taxes." They also force up the price of land and old houses, so that real estate is put beyond the reach of farmers and others who must work there.

In the old industrial cities, people lived near their places of work. The mill hands lived around the cotton mill, and the mill owner lived close at hand, in the big house on the hill, looking down on the chimney stacks belching out the smoke that was the evidence they were producing and giving employment. The steelworkers and the steel magnate lived close to the steel mill. The German brewer Miller lived next to his brewery in Milwaukee. The city churches had congregations that were representative of both the resident population and the local working population. It wasn't so much that work gave meaning to life as that it created a community that extended into and enriched the residential community, and sustained a solidarity among the workers. It was the automakers, especially the ever-revolutionary Henry Ford, who realized that their own product enabled them to build factories far from the dispersed homes of the workers, and not unconsciously they appreciated that a dispersed work force would be docile.

Work still gives meaning to rural life, the family, and churches. But in the city today work and home, family and church, are separated. What the office workers do for a living is not part of their home life. At the same time they maintain the pointless frenzy of their work hours in their hours off. They rush from the office to jog, to the gym or the YMCA pool, to work at their play with the same joylessness. In the suburbs there is only an artificial community life—look at the notice board of community activities in a new satellite town like Reston, outside Washington. They breathlessly exhort the resident to a variety of boring activities—amateur theatricals, earnest lectures by officers of the United Nations Association, sing-songs—a Tupperware community culture as artificial as the "lake" in the supposed center of the town. These upright citizens of Reston were amazed one day when they found that their bored children were as hooked on drugs as those in any ghetto.

Even though the offices of today's businesses in the city are themselves moving out to the suburbs, this does not necessarily bring the workers back closer to their workplace. It merely means that to the rush-hour traffic into the city there is now added a rush-hour traffic out to the suburbs in the morning, and back around and across the city in the evening. As the farmer walks down to his farm in the morning, the city dweller is dressing for the first idiocy of his day, which he not only accepts but even seeks—the journey to work.

This takes two forms: solitary confinement in one's own car, or the discomfort of extreme overcrowding on public transport. Both produce angst. There are no more grim faces than those of the single drivers we pedestrians can glimpse at the stoplights during the rush hour. It is hard to know why they are so impatient in the morning to get to their useless and wearisome employments; but then in the evening, when one would have thought they would be relaxed, they are even more frenetic. Prisoners in boxes on wheels, they do not dare wonder why they do it. If they take to public transit, there may still be the ritual of the wife driving the breadwinner to the subway station, and meeting him in the evening. Life in the suburbs and exurbs has become a bondage to the hours of journeying.

The car, of course, is not a vehicle suitable to the city. The problems of traffic in the city, over which urban planners have wracked their brains for years, could be simply eliminated if private cars were banned, or if a swinging tax were levied on those who drive into the city alone. The dollar toll in New York should be raised to five dollars—each way. There should be a toll on all the bridges crossing the Potomac from Virginia, and at every point where the rush hour drivers cross the District line from Maryland. The urban dwellers in Virginia and Maryland make sure that their jurisdictions obstruct any legitimate way the District might force the suburban daytime users of the city to pay for its manifold services. But ten dollars a day to cross into Washington, in addition to parking fees, would soon cut down the urban idiocy of bringing a small room to work and parking it in precious space for eight hours.

On the bus or subway each morning and evening other urban dwellers endure the indignity of being crushed into unwelcome proximity with strangers whom they have no wish to communicate with except in terms of abuse, rancor, and sometimes violent hostility. The wonder is not that there is an occasional shooting on public transit, but that shootings are not daily occurrences. The crushing of people together on the subway can have unintended results. One of my memories is of being on a London tube at rush hour in my younger days, pressed against a young woman who was with her boyfriend. To my surprise, though not unwelcome, her hand slipped into mine. It squeezed. Mine squeezed back. Her expression when they got out at Leicester Square, and she found she'd been holding my hand, and even had begun pulling me off the train, has not been easy to forget in 35 years. But generally even eye contact on public transport is treated as an act of aggression or at least harassment.

This primary urban activity of getting to and from work has other curious features. As every Englishman visiting America for the first time remarks, the smell of deodorants on a crowded bus or subway in the morning is overpowering. Even the stale smell of the human body would be preferable. It must account for the glazed looks—perhaps all deodorants contain a gas introduced by the employers to numb the urban office workers to the fatuity of their labors.

But whether they have come by car or public transit, the urban office workers must continue their journey even after they have gotten to the city. They then must travel in one of the banks of elevators that often run the height of three city blocks or more. Once again they are herded into confined spaces. City people are so used to moving in herds that they even fight to cram themselves into the elevators, as they do into buses or subway cars, as if it mattered that they might get to their pointless occupations a minute later. The odd thing about the elevators themselves is that there are no fares for distances often longer than those between two bus stops. Office elevators are public transit, free to anyone who needs to use them—but there's no such thing as a free elevator ride, as the president will tell you. Banks of elevators occupy large areas of valuable city land on every floor. This and the cost of running and maintaining them is written into the rents paid by the employers. If the urban workers had not been reduced to a docile herd, they would demand that the employers who expect them to get to work subsidize all the public transport into the city, while leaving those who bring their rooms on wheels to pay for them themselves.

In the modern office building in the city there are windows that don't open. This is perhaps the most symbolic lunacy of all. Outdoors is something you can look at through glass but not touch or hear. These windows are a scandal because they endanger the lives of office workers in case of fire. But no less grievous, even on the fairest spring or fall day the workers cannot put their heads outside. The employers do not mind this, may have even conspired with the developers to dream up such an infliction, because the call of spring or fall would distract their employees. Thus it's not surprising that the urban worker has no knowledge of the seasons. He is aware simply that in some months there is air conditioning, and in others through the same vents comes fetid central heating. Even outside at home in their suburbs the city dwellers may know that sometimes it's hot, and sometimes cold, but no true sense of the rhythms of the seasons is to be had from a lawn in the back yard and a few spindly trees struggling to survive.

City dwellers can now eat the vegetables of their choice at almost any time of the year—always with the proviso that they will never taste a fresh vegetable, even though the best supermarkets have various ways to touch them up. Anyone who has not eaten peas picked that morning has never tasted a pea. The simple fact is that some frozen vegetables (frozen within hours of being picked) are fresher than the alleged fresh vegetables on the produce counter of the supermarkets. The suburbanite again struggles to simulate the blessings of rural life by maintaining a vegetable patch in the back yard. The main consequence of this melancholy pursuit comes in high summer, when office workers bring in their homegrown tomatoes to share with their colleagues, ill-colored, lump-faced objects with scars all over them, since they have not been staked correctly.

The city dweller reels from unreality to unreality through each day, always trying to recover the rural life that has been surrendered for the city lights. (City life, it is worth noticing, has produced almost no proverbs. How could it when proverbs—a rolling stone gathers no moss, and so on—are a distillation from a sane existence?) No city dweller, even in the suburbs, knows the wonder of a pitch-dark country lane at night. Nor does he naturally get any exercise from his work. When jogging and other childish pursuits began to exercise the unused bodies of city dwellers, two sensible doctors (a breed that has almost died with the general practitioner) said that city workers could get their exercise better in more natural ways. They could begin by walking upstairs to their office floors instead of using the elevators.

Every European points out that Americans are the most round-shouldered people in the world. Few of them carry themselves with an upright stance, although a correct stance and gait is the first precondition of letting your lungs breathe naturally and deeply. Electric typewriters cut down the amount of physical exertion needed to hit the keys; the buttons on a word processor need even less effort, as you can tell from the posture of those who use them. They might as well be in armchairs. They rush out to jog or otherwise Fonda-ize their leisure to try to repair the damage done during the day.

Dieting is an urban obsession. Country dwellers eat what they please, and work it off in useful physical employments, and in the open air, cold or hot, rainy or sunny. Mailmen are the healthiest city workers. When was your mailman last ill for a day? If one reads the huge menus that formed a normal diet in the 19th century, you realize that even the city dwellers could dispatch these gargantuan repasts because they still shared many of the benefits of rural life. (Disraeli records a meal at the house of one lordly figure that was composed of nine meat or game entrees. The butler asked after the eighth, "Snipe or pheasant, my lord?") They rode horseback to work or to Parliament even in the coldest weather, and nothing jolts and enlivens the liver more than riding. Homes were cold in the winter, except in the immediate vicinity of the hearth or stove. Cold has a way of eating up excess fat. No wonder dieting is necessary in a cosseted life in which the body is forced to do no natural heavy work.

Everything in urban life is an effort either to simulate rural life or to compensate for its loss by artificial means. The greatest robbery from the country in recent years has of course been Levi's, which any self-respecting farmer or farm worker is almost ashamed to wear nowadays. It was when Saks Fifth Avenue began advocating designer jeans years ago that the ultimate urban parody of rural life was reached. The chic foods of the city have to be called health foods, which would seem a tautology in the country. And insofar as there used to be entertainments in the city that enticed, these can now be enjoyed more than sufficiently on vcrs and stereos.

It is from this day-to-day existence of unreality, pretense, and idiocy that the city people, slumping along their streets even when scurrying, never looking up at their buildings, far less the sky, have the insolence to disdain and mock the useful and rewarding life of the country people who support them. Now go out and carry home a Douglas fir, call it a Christmas tree, and enjoy 12 days of contact with nature. Of course city dwellers don't know it once had roots.

Merry FAXmas

If TNR were to choose a Man or Woman of the Year for its cover, my nomination for 1988 would be the five nuns of the Discalced Carmelites of the Most Blessed Virgin Mary of Mount Carmel in Morris Township, New Jersey, who this fall barricaded themselves in their monastery in protest against the introduction of modern comforts to their cloistered life. The worldly distractions against which they revolted, all introduced by Mother Teresa Hewitt since she took over the monastery a year ago, include "television, newspapers, radio, snacks, and a high-tech lighting system in the chapel," according to the Catholic journal *Crisis.* These nuns are the sanest people of whom I have read all year, joyful models for us in this season of universal gorging and gouging. They are simply saying that they do not wish to clutter their lives. I never stroll through a shopping mall without observing that the display of goods includes almost none of the necessities of life. Shoes, we may think, are necessary; but then, of course, the *Discalced* Carmelites go unshod. The gross national product in America now feeds a gross national appetite for the conspicuous consumption of vanities. The "curse of plenty" against which Churchill warned is now a disease and daily distraction. The nuns are speaking to us. Perhaps it is the society as a whole that needs to take a vow of poverty.

The New Republic, January 2, 1989. Reprinted by permission from the Estate of Henry Fairlie.

In the last two decades one product that has come to be conspicuously and ravenously consumed is paper, and no city has a more voracious maw for it than Washington. The *Washington Post* the other day ran a story on "New Age Printing," the booming demand for "quick printing" and copying of many varieties. One local printer of 40 years' standing said: "Washington's appetite for paper is the hungriest I've seen." The electronic and other technological advances that were expected to create a paperless society have instead made it easier to commit words to print. This office is not alone in now having a nerve center that houses three gadgets: a copier; the printer for the word processors; and what is called a FAX, the silliest toy for adults yet invented. No nun would believe how much paper these machines spew forth in a day. It is no coincidence that the noise made by these machines is a chatter; the FAX even begins to chatter to itself in the middle of the night. On a much larger scale this is going on all over Washington. Why should the nuns not close their ears to the chatter that distracts us? As they might point out, things were said much more clearly when Moses had to carve the Ten Commandments on tablets of stone. In place of the printout machine and the FAX, in the new year, let us substitute slabs of granite and a chisel.

To supply our paper, forests must die. Yet in all the chatter around us we scarcely notice that Weyerhauser, the tree-slaughtering company, claims in its commercials to be "The Tree-Growing Company." In no Weyerhauser ad do you see a tree fall. Moreover, Weyerhauser appears also to be The Eagle Preservation Company and The Bambi Protection Company. We are surrounded by lies, and in the chatter do not notice them. GMAC calls itself "The Official Sponsor of the American Dream." Who appointed it the *official* sponsor? And how elevated is the Dream it finances? Without television, newspaper, and radio, the nuns will hear the tidings of comfort and joy this Christmas. We will be deafened to them by the hectoring disinformation of the ads of the merchandisers.

In a savage line in his poem "Bess," about an elderly woman who always helped her neighbors and is dying of cancer, William Stafford contrasts the significance of this local happening with "the grotesque fake importance of great national events" that usually seize the headlines. The words should be placed on the desks of every editor, anchorman, and columnist. It is no wonder that I noticed, when I traveled 13,000 miles by road around the country in 1984, that again and again ordinary Americans switched on the local news, then kept it on for the network news—with the sound turned off! Why should they, any more than the nuns, be subjected to the chatter? But the event that has seized the headlines this Christmas is not fake. The earthquake in Armenia makes national and ideological differences look trifling. It is also a reminder that, in however tragic a form, the Christ child was born to be the Prince of Peace. It is all the more sad, therefore, that not even for a few days could the Armenian protest leaders forgo the opportunity to press their political demands. The chatter of politics in the world today leads more and more to rage.

Since the problem has never occurred to me before, I have spent much of 1988 trying to discover why we say "Ooops!" when we almost bump into each other, or catch ourselves in some minor error. I calculate that I hear "Ooops!" 20 or 30 times a day, not least because the corridor in this office has a sharp L-turn, where I am constantly bumping into attractive young ladies. We each say "Ooops!" I have consulted every full dictionary. None helps.

I have also called the press offices of various embassies, and found that in their countries people say something like "Ooops!" except for a rather snooty, firm French denial that they would ever use the Franglais "Ooops!" I will personally award a bottle of vintage port of a fine year to any reader who can explain when "Ooops!" entered the language, and why we say "Ooops!" and not "Aaarps!" or "Uuups!"

The best news out of Washington in 1988 is that the Redskins are sunk. Nothing excites the Christmas spirit more than the sight of the proud and mighty being humbled. They join their humbled sporting cousins the Baltimore Orioles, the American League East cellar-dwellers just purchased for $70 million by a New York investor who has made his fortune by shifting around paper in lieu of money. Too bad the Orioles' new owner couldn't have spared some change for the New York Historical Society. The *New York Times* recently carried yet another story about the Society's efforts to scrape together a few million to save it from insolvency, rescue some of its damaged archives and other treasures, and expand its role. When one estimates the numbers of enormously rich people and corporations who operate in New York, it is a shaming Christmas thought that they cannot adequately support the Historical Society of the most historical city in the United States, out of which they have gouged their millions. Baseball or history, FAX or facts? We know which our culture chooses. The five nuns chose better.

In a follow-up Diarist a month after this column ran, Fairlie wrote, "My admiration for the readers of TNR has only been fortified by the dedication, solemnity, and etymological fancifulness with which they have answered my plea for an explanation of why we say 'Oops!'" Though he received more than fifty responses from all parts of the country, he awarded the bottle of port to a reader from Charlottesville, Virginia, who claimed that the word was derived from an invocation of the god Pan used to avert the evil eye—unless, that is, cockney soldiers in India derived it from "upla," the Hindi word for cow dung.

Greedy Geezers

Thirty percent of the annual federal budget now goes to expenditures on people over the age of 65. Forty years from now, if the present array of programs and benefits is maintained, almost two-thirds of the budget will go to supporting and cosseting the old. Something is wrong with a society that is willing to drain itself to foster such an unproductive section of its population, one that does not even promise (as children do) one day to be productive.

It is always difficult to question the programs for the aging because of an understandable if increasingly misdirected sympathy for them. In addition to the widespread feeling that they have earned their reward here on earth (and need not wait until they get to heaven, as the old used to expect), there is our contemporary guilt about them—and our fear. Americans still do not accept aging, dying, and death from old age itself as part of living. Of course there are the needy, the infirm, the helpless, for whom society should care. But when the old people's lobbies rally their considerable resources for a ferocious fight to protect Medicare, or to oppose a cut in the cost-of-living adjustments (COLAs) to Social Security, they are not speaking only for the needy. They are arguing for the perpetuation of a massive entitlements system for anyone and everyone over 65.

Glance through the advertisements in *Modern Maturity,* the fat, glossy magazine published by the American Association of

The New Republic, March 28, 1988, originally titled "Talkin' 'Bout My Generation." Reprinted by permission from the Estate of Henry Fairlie.

Retired Persons—one of America's most powerful lobbies. You can be tempted by the Florida country clubs: "RETIRE IN STYLE TO FORT MYERS, FLORIDA!! . . . the New Pine Lakes Country Club. Imagine . . . acres of lakes, 18-hold golf course, tennis, heated pool, a lakeside jacuzzi, 24-hour manned security, and an unbelievable clubhouse!" Not far away the Del Tura Country Club "features Florida's finest ($3.5 million) executive golf course and clubhouse complex." Or you can buy your own ranch on the Forbes Wagon Creek Ranch in the Sangre de Cristo mountains. If all this palls, you can take a Holland America Line Alaska Cruise, with "gourmet meals, sparkling entertainment, first-class service, swimming pools, tennis courts, casinos, and million-dollar art collections." But turn the pages and, perhaps most remarkable of all, the AARP's own Travel Service offers cruises or tours to Alaska, "North to the Future." From all of this, go back to the sheaf of question-and-answer sheets setting out the AARP's arguments for almost every proposed government expenditure on the old. Something jars.

The old people's lobbying groups have proliferated in recent years. The Leadership Council of Aging Organizations (surely they do not mean "aging organizations"; if they do, one could suggest some candidates) lists 29 such groups, starting, alphabetically, with the American Association for International Aging. They range from Catholic Golden Age to the scholarly sounding Gerontology Society of America, to the once slightly notorious Gray Panthers (senior citizen urban guerrillas), to the National Association of State Units on Aging, to the United Auto Workers/Retired Members. Anyone who knows the first thing about office rentals in Washington must be impressed by the addresses of some of these groups—not least on K Street, the capital's upscale strip for the suites of the powerful industrial and commercial lobbyists.

These groups are strong because no one, especially in election years—and it is always election year in America—dares to say a word that might offend the supposedly meek, ailing, frail, and deserving gray heads. The old have been set beside motherhood and apple pie. Yet meekness is hardly an attribute of the old in their new incarnation. Their hero, Representative Claude Pepper, is not an amiable soul caring for the downtrodden old. He is a shrewd, ambitious politician who, as the *Almanac for American Politics* puts it, was "floundering about, looking for a major cause." As a member and then chairman of the Select Committee on the Aging, he found one that provided a "good match of convictions and position," especially for a congressman who represents the 18th District of Florida (most of the city of Miami, all of Miami Beach, Bal Harbor, and Key Biscayne), where 30 percent of the adults are 65 and over. It can be said confidently that a substantial majority of those, as in the rest of Florida, do not need such extensive benefits or so many free services.

Not surprisingly, over the past 30 years the elderly's standard of living has improved faster than that of younger people. Quite apart from the significant increase in Social Security benefits and their protection from erosion by inflation, the Supplemental Security Income in effect guarantees them a minimum income; national health insurance is provided through Medicare; and special tax privileges protect their assets in retirement. They even receive discounts on movie and bus tickets, and much more. All of these entitlements are available to the elderly regardless of need. And while claiming that their own benefits are beyond challenge, locally the old organize to oppose tax hikes to pay for school bonds and other desirable social policies.

The history of the Older Americans Act is instructive. This simple bill authorizing funds to state agencies for a few supportive and nutritional services was passed on the heels of Medicare in 1965. When Congress extended it for another four years in 1987 (a preface to the election), the services were generously expanded. The bill is still primarily addressed to the needy old, but within it are explicit assumptions that show how its provisions can be expanded. Take the definition of "elder abuse." When we hear of "child abuse," we think specifically of certain intolerable offenses: beatings and sexual molestations. However, in many state laws the definition of "elder abuse" is so wide as to include forms of neglect that may not be neglect at all—merely leaving the old to do for themselves what they wish to do, however slowly. This is only "abuse" in the eyes of the social workers and old people's organizations, who must justify their activities and funding.

My own age gives me some standing in this matter. As I approach the arbitrary line of 65, which of course I do not consider aged, my first savoring of growing old seems to promise a time of great richness, contemplation, and absorbing interest. One not only has the years ahead, but begins to recapture the whole of one's life, in ways for which even one's middle years are unequipped. But most obviously it is less costly; one simply does not need so much. One's children are grown up and earning; one's grandchildren provide pleasure without much responsibility; mortgages are often paid off; and one need scarcely add to one's wardrobe. One is more content with simple fare in everything. It is less urgent to look for friends; one already has them, and new ones, often the young, keep turning up. In growing old, one has a stocked attic in which to rummage, and the still passing show and pageant of human life to observe, not only at a more leisurely pace, but with the convincing satisfaction and interest of having lived through many of the changes, even from their beginnings, that have brought us from there to here.

The elderly among whom I was raised did not withdraw. They may have retired from their jobs, but then they usually stayed where they were, assuming the responsibilities of a grandparent, and advising and encouraging the other young people they knew in the neighborhood. They also naturally assumed, not least in the working class and mainstream middle class, positions of leadership in the organizations, including the churches, that hold society together, so taking some of the pressure off the middle-aged and producers. They brought to them the wisdom of experience, and an unruffled, almost bustling, way of dealing with a crisis or emergency, because they had been through so many before. If I look back amazed at the time my elders found for me, then I also realize that they were not altogether selfless. I brought them news, kept them in touch, just as they brought me the otherwise inaccessible news from the immediate past. If this two-way transmission ceases, both the young and the elderly suffer.

But suppose the old, encouraged by federal programs, siphon themselves off to places where they congregate only with other aging people. A few years ago, when I traveled around the country for five months with a companion almost a third of my age as my driver, I bought a 338-page book called *Sunbelt Retirement: The Complete State Guide to Retiring in the South and West of the United States.* Partly guided by it, I went to see some of the retirement communities, resorts, call them what one wishes. Some of them, of course, are for the rich. La Jolla, just north of San Diego, had a population of 30,000 when I was there; it also had 400 doctors. One doctor for every 75 people who anyhow are about to be called to Abraham's bosom—cite that ratio in any inner city or small town in rural America, or even in the suburbs, where the middle-aged are terrified of the possible cost of medical care for their families. And how many of those doctors catering to the old are psychiatrists, therapists, and cosmeticians? (When I was in the hospital not long ago, the nurses told me that the medical care for many elderly patients was really cosmetic, to disguise the natural process of aging.) If one needs a psychiatrist by the time one is 65, one should take the quick way out—make a swallow dive from a high bridge to the tarmac, and go to meet the Great Therapist in the Sky.

Yet it is not the rich communities that are most alarming. The vast industry of "Sunbelt Retirement" is not built on the rich. It is built on federal programs for the elderly. (And of course even those doctors in La Jolla are sustained largely by Medicare.) Most of the communities composed solely of the old are for the retired mainstream Middle Americans from the Northeast and Midwest. These are not people who have accumulated exorbitant personal assets. As soon as I reached Arizona, I realized that the Southwest is living off, and ripping off, the very "government in Washington" that it always criticizes for taxing people too much for giveaway programs to the undeserving. Huge federal subsidies to the retirement industry have replaced the military establishments, defense industries, water subsidies, and the rest that have hitherto sustained the West.

All the way from the Pacific to the Atlantic you can see the old lined up in banks, feeding into their accounts the checks from a range of federal agencies. The pensions and other benefits from the Veterans Administration alone are not only generous but cumulatively indefensible, since the average age of today's 27 million living veterans is 62. Every month government benefits to 91 percent of those over the age of 65 total $13.6 billion; the $50 billion per year spent on medical care for the old when Reagan took office is expected to be four times as large 12 years from now. Senator Daniel Patrick Moynihan has dryly observed that the United States may be "the first society in history in which a person is more likely to be poor if young rather than old." Moynihan's point applies even to children, 20 percent of whom live in poverty, compared with 14 percent of the elderly. It is not something to be proud of. This coddling is not how the elderly are meant or should expect to live.

The pampered ones, increasingly numerous, are rather pathetic to observe, some riding around in golf carts even on the streets, instead of taking an invigorating walk—what used to be called a "constitutional." These are not the infirm, only the naturally aging. There are no young where they live, no children, no bawling infants, no working, productive men or women. They are set apart, no longer of a piece with any larger society, with no obligations. Everything is provided. For the first time in their lives, in effect, they have servants. In vast Sun City outside Phoenix, which you reach by driving through the barrios, the legal and illegal Mexican immigrants attend to the needs of these white elders. Although they are tanned and imagine they are active, following their balls on the championship course in their carts, they in fact move as if in a mindless soft-shoe shuffle.

Of course there are millions of old people who do not live like this. Although the median income for people over 65 is now $22,000—a high figure for those who have few large purchases to make—there are still the third of the elderly blacks who live on less than $5,300. *That* is need. But the prominence of the resorts draws attention to the changed expectations of old age, among the elderly themselves, ourselves, and the society as a whole. And as in other areas, when such new expectations get lodged they take root, burgeon, and are hard to uproot, especially if they are stimulated and supported by programs that develop their own entrenched life. For it is a question not only of government, but as the gerontologist Carroll Estes has said, of "the aging establishment . . . the congeries of programs, organizations, bureaucracies, . . . providers, industries, and professionals that serve the old in one capacity or another." Even if an organization like the National Council of Senior Citizens concentrates on assisting the needy and helpless, it is trapped into supporting the fat in the entitlement programs that goes to those who are not the deserving poor.

The mischief must be halted and reversed, and not least in the interest of the elderly. For one thing, there is likely to be a revolt of the working members of society when the huge baby-boom generation reaches retirement age. And as the population comes to include ever-growing numbers of young Mexicans, Central Americans, South Americans, and Asians, they too are likely to rebel, especially since their own (nuclear *and* extended) families assume so many of the traditional responsibilities of caring for the old, even in their new environment. Why should they work to indulge the white elders so generously? The old might heed another of Moynihan's predictions: that quite early in the new century the American people will be markedly brown, Spanish-speaking, young, and Catholic.

Old age must be redefined, with the majority of benefits going only to the needy. We probably will have to make stern decisions. With the increasing number of people living beyond 85, we may even have to decide that today's costly medical technologies, such as transplants, should not be provided to truly elderly people. Early retirement, especially to a self-centered and soft existence, must be discouraged. Perhaps above all, we must shake off the peculiar notion, of only recent growth, that old age is a time in which people are entitled to be rewarded for no more than performing the accepted tasks of life, or fighting in the Second World War, as many of today's elderly bleat; that if they raise a family and contribute to society by working, then when they cease to be productive they have a right to live off the still-producing like the grasshopper in the fable; that because their needs diminish, their expectations are entitled to rise.

The old people's organizations sometimes work along these lines, as in resisting mandatory early retirement. Some have started and encouraged programs to stimulate the elderly to become productive again and remain an organic part of their society, such as working in schools as volunteers, or in special programs out of school; and of course old people are precisely those who should be well equipped to counter the basic illiteracy of even affluent children in the suburbs, the ignorance of any cultural heritage, and the decay of manners. But these efforts are marginal and sporadic, and are as nothing to the energy the lobby musters to protect the benefits for an entire class.

Meanwhile, by failing to define old age in a more limited way, by discouraging the elderly from remaining in their society, we are building a system of care that has one critical flaw. The sweeping claim of entitlements is the bubble in the whole glass house of federal assistance to the old that will eventually shatter it.

Brief Whining Moments

THE COLLAPSE OF ORATORY

So far in the presidential campaign this year neither candidate nor his running mate has made a speech that was worth hearing or, by any standard other than the meanest calculations of political advantage, worth delivering. What is more, we do not expect to hear anything resembling a memorable speech before the election is over. If voter turnout is lower in 1988 than even in other recent elections, this oratorical void will be one reason. After months of wearisome campaigning, the differences between the candidates and the parties are more blurred than at the beginning. The American people themselves are registering, in opinion surveys, comments to reporters, and simply in what one hears going about one's day—the mood one can pick up almost by osmosis—their dismay and appalled anxiety at the quality of the political debate that is being staged for them this year.

If the decline of campaign oratory was lamented in TNR before the last presidential campaign ("The Decline of Oratory," May 28, 1984), it is not repetitive to raise the cry again. Already we have evidence that there is today even less likelihood that any candidate will deliver a speech that is coherent, sustains an argument through more than two brief paragraphs, connects one theme forcefully to another; displays courage, inspires, promises leadership; or simply is honest.

The New Republic, October 10, 1988. Reprinted by permission from the Estate of Henry Fairlie.

The standard by which we are now to judge the campaign speeches was demonstrated at the two national conventions. Going by the instant reactions of the TV anchormen and all but a few of the print journalists in the following days, one would have thought they had listened spellbound to Demosthenes in Atlanta and Pericles in New Orleans—or Webster, or Calhoun, or Lincoln, or Theodore Roosevelt, or Wilson—or, to be done with it, even Adlai Stevenson. "His splendid acceptance speech," David Broder wrote of George Bush's performance, as if he was purring at one of the Gridiron dinners he enjoys so much. And Broder was not the most extravagant. But where, from Bush's—or rather, Peggy Noonan's—first sentence to his last, was the splendor? What single phrase is even now memorable? No other than Broder himself, only a few weeks later, devoted a column to criticizing the vapidity of both Bush and his opponent.

Even when one speech is supposed to address a single theme, to enlighten us and perhaps to convey an impression of strength and toughness in the candidate, the extent of oratory's decay is still visible. On September 9 a reporter for the *New York Times* who had been following Michael Dukakis wrote of "a day of muscular oratory." One combs his report for the evidence. At last one discovers this Dukakis quote: "How strong do American forces need to be? Strong enough to defend America's interests. Strong enough to meet our treaty commitments. Strong enough to crack down on terrorists, with force if necessary." Some muscle! Some oratory! Nothing in that flatulent paragraph or in the rest of the speech enlightens us about Dukakis's specific intentions. As the reporter notes, the net effect of this muscular oratory was to keep Dukakis's foreign policy aide "scrambling throughout the day to explain what he meant."

The very existence of a new profession of political consultants responsible for "spin control" after the candidates have spoken attests to their incapacity to speak intelligibly or forcefully, much less to say what they mean. At the Democratic convention, one of the divisions of the party's media operations was actually called "Spin-Control Coordination." A handbook advised its staff, according to the *Columbia Journalism Review*, to "track location of top Democratic pundits and operatives to work to coordinate their availability to print and broadcast media." Of course press officers and others in the past have tried to explain (away) the occasional indiscretion or indistinct verbiage of politicians. But when these spin-control experts—campaign consultants are always experts—are added to the vast teams of speechwriters—also experts—it is no wonder that the majority of people no longer believes that their politicians are addressing them directly.

Was it ever much better? It was, even quite recently, until the arrival of television. But let us take a stump speech given by Woodrow Wilson during his first presidential campaign in Lincoln, Nebraska, on October 5, 1912. Like Dukakis, Wilson was relatively unknown, his only apparent credentials a career as a university professor and as governor of New Jersey. And like Dukakis, he faced a Republican challenger whose party had occupied the White House for the past eight years. Moreover, not only was Wilson up against the incumbent William Howard Taft, he was himself threatened by the formidable Theodore Roosevelt, the Bull Moose candidate supported by most of the Progressives.

Nebraska was a strongly Progressive state, and Wilson chose as his subject the then politically charged issue of monopoly. He began by directly confronting Roosevelt by name, providing an incisive analysis of TR's position in seven fairly long paragraphs. Saying that "I am not in this campaign engaged in doubting any man's motives"—a claim Bush cannot make today—he accused the monopolists of being not "a body of deliberate enemies, maybe, but a body of mistaken men," and added that the "only

hope of a program of human uplift" from the Republican Party
and its Bull Moose rump "is that the monopolists will cooper-
ate." Then he closed in on Roosevelt:

> And what I want to point out to you is that Mr.
> Roosevelt subscribes to the judgment of these mis-
> taken men as to the influences which should govern
> America. That is the serious part of it. Mr. Roose-
> velt's judgment has been captured. Mr. Roosevelt's
> idea of the way in which the industries of this coun-
> try should be controlled has been captured.

Wilson was in fact making a deadly political attack—stripping
TR of his claim to independence; he had been captured—but
the words, manner, and tone of the whole passage relied on
connected cerebral argument to stimulate and persuade his Nebraska audience. Bush deals with his opponent only by innuendo charged with spite, and Dukakis parries so feebly that he
can hardly bring himself to use his opponent's name—with the
exception of the pathetic "Where was George" refrain.

Wilson's attack on Roosevelt was itself only a prelude to
the unfolding of his views on monopolists and the trusts, the
changes they were causing in the lives of ordinary Americans,
and their far too great influence at the elbow of government on a
wide range of policies: tariffs, banking, conservation, and so on.
On conservation he was taking on the issue Roosevelt had made
his own, indeed, introduced to the center of political concern.
Did Wilson waffle?

> What is our fear about conservation? The hands
> that will be stretched out to monopolize our forests,
> to pre-empt the use of our great power-producing
> streams, the hands that will be stretched into the
> bowels of the earth to take possession of the great

riches that lie hidden in Alaska and elsewhere in the incomparable domain of the United States, are the hands of monopoly. . . .

And so to the rhetorical conclusion to which he has built: "The question of conservation is a great deal bigger than the question of saving our forests and our mineral resources and our waters. It is as big as the life and happiness and strength and elasticity and hope of our people." It is the word "elasticity" that springs the full force of the passage, the unexpected word that provokes us to think and make new connections, that energizes us; the unexpected word we never hear in this campaign. Both Bush and Dukakis are trying to grab the issue of conservation, but neither has confronted it with the directness of Wilson. On September 2 Bush described himself laughably as "a Theodore Roosevelt conservationist," because he cannot claim to be a conservationist in his own right. Bush does not point to the commercial interests that have dumped in Boston Harbor for decades. Neither does he even hint at how he will deal with yet more powerful interests that will be at the elbow of government on the issue of the environment.

After hearing Wilson's speech—a speech he delivered on a relatively insignificant occasion—we do not need to ask a second time if this man would be a strong president. Neither do we have the slightest difficulty in grasping the character of the man—come from Princeton and New Jersey to Nebraska—or what we now curiously call an "identity." An identity is what is established in a birth certificate, driver's license, identity card, or, indeed, a fingerprint. But today pundits worry whether the candidates have successfully established their "identities."

It was Bush and not Dukakis who was said to have identified himself most successfully in his convention speech. He said he regards the presidency as "an incomparable opportunity for 'gentle persuasion.'" That was not the kind of leadership Wilson was offering—or John Kennedy, or (to look abroad) Margaret Thatcher, or any worthwhile candidate; and neither is it the kind of leadership the presidency exists to provide. The art of "gentle persuasion" is a skill, and a useful one; but it is not the edge of leadership. Bush said, "I want a kinder, gentler nation," which is sweet, but it doesn't tell us much about the man or what policies he will pursue and with what command. Then Bush identified himself by his "ordinariness." He and his wife in Texas lived "in a little shotgun house, one room for the three of us . . . had six children . . . moved from the shotgun to a duplex apartment to a house . . . " It was pap. But Bush tried to make a virtue of it, and the media applauded him for his boast that he cannot speak. "I may not be the most eloquent. . . . I may sometimes be a little awkward. . . . I am a quiet man. . . . I'll try to hold my charisma in check." Just plain folks for president.

So what has happened? If the blame for the further decline of American political oratory can be assigned to any one factor, it is to television. Certainly television has wrecked political conventions; that has been obvious for some time. It was in 1972 that people could still be aghast at the scripted convention of Richard Nixon, with everything ordered for the cameras. But the once lively and even brawling Democrats—whose 1972 convention got so out of hand that George McGovern didn't deliver his acceptance speech until the wee hours—followed the Republican lead this year, with predictable mediocrity and yawns. Conventions used to be events where the unexpected happened. Television does not permit that. Conventions are now literally scripted for prime-time entertainment. And this year, after orchestrating the life right out of them, television executives have the gall to say that conventions may have become too dull to merit live coverage.

But beyond the death of political conventions is the continuing influence of the television reporters, anchormen, and commentators who have forced politicians to speak in "bites" of 30 seconds for 90-second slots. We are now nearing the end of eight years in which a president who does not really lead by his speeches has been praised for being a "great communicator." The euphemism is necessary because he does not make speeches. The irony points to the uncomfortable truth that the communications industry—the media—recognized a package of its own manufacture and labeled it Great Communicator. It is not out of political conviction that the media has given Reagan so easy a ride. The relationship is one of symbiosis. Anchormen read scripts; politicians read scripts. Anchormen talk in bites; politicians talk in bites. Anchormen speak over pictures; politicians speak over pictures. Anchormen don't have to say anything; politicians don't have to say anything. "Good Morning America" is a television program; "It's morning in America" is a politician's slogan. Politicians merge into Brokaw, Jennings, Rather, and they merge into the politicians they have chosen. They are all, in the end, great communicators, while saying as little as possible.

In this electoral season, one other convention speech was praised. That of Jesse Jackson. I do not share the virulent fear of and hostility to Jackson of some people. In fact, I wonder why they think he is so important. Perhaps because he's such good media fodder. But his speech at the convention was not much of a speech. What was moving in it was the occasion: a black within striking distance of the presidency, and the elderly black faces in the audience that reflected how far they had come and how far yet to go. A demagogue is not someone who commands his audience; he is someone who surrenders to it. And in Jackson's oratory there was no such command. He gave what was expected, all he is capable of, schmoozed the media, and left nothing at all unchanged. Even the delivery was false. Carrying the oratory of Martin Luther King Jr. were the true cadences of the Southern pulpit. The repetition of words and constructions were not meant to elicit only an "Amen" from the audience; they were vehicles to carry the audience forward to another plane, one to which they had never expected to be taken. To join people, that was King's aim. Read his speech before the Lincoln Memorial on that still unrepeated day. Read how he makes people see farther than themselves. "I have a dream"— yes, we all remember that. "Let freedom ring"—yes, we remember that. But then watch how King took the dream, and made freedom ring:

> So let freedom ring from the prodigious hilltops of New Hampshire. Let freedom ring from the mighty mountains of New York. Let freedom ring from the heightening Alleghenies of Pennsylvania. Let freedom ring from the snowcapped Rockies of Colorado. Let freedom ring from the curvaceous peaks of California.

So far he has not mentioned one Southern state:

> But not only that; let freedom ring from Stone Mountain of Georgia. Let freedom ring from Lookout Mountain of Tennessee. Let freedom ring from every hill and molehill of Mississippi. From every mountainside, let freedom ring.

Not a syllable now rings any less true. There was in that oratory the substance of a man; and given that, no less than in Wilson, there was a substance of argument that preceded the rise to full eloquence. Was Jackson anywhere near that in Atlanta?

Oratory is not a matter of artistry. It must come from a single source. But election campaigns are now more out of the hands of the people than ever they were in the days of the smoke-filled rooms. A vast community of professional and well-fattened advisers and consultants now create their puppets, and what holds the community together is an uninformed media, talking to the speechwriter and not the speech-giver, who direct our attention only to the strings they pull. Leadership doesn't have a chance.

Pen Ultimate

"My, my!" Winston Churchill exclaimed shortly after the war, when an American said that he and his wife always got up to breakfast together. "My wife and I tried two or three times in the last forty years to have breakfast together, but it didn't work." Clementine Churchill found other ways to communicate with her husband during his busy days, not least by letter. Not only did the two of them write often lengthy letters to each other when they were apart, but Clementine wrote to him even when they were both at home. Her letters were frequently sharp corrections, and the man who was to the world the image of fearlessness reacted like Rumpole, who referred to his wife as "she who must be obeyed."

They were at home when she wrote a letter scoffing at him for planning to wear his Royal Air Force uniform to a purely civil occasion in France. He went in a suit. He was in Oslo when she wrote telling him to write to Queen Wilhelmina of the Netherlands, who had just entertained him in The Hague: "*Please* write quickly 'in your own paw' before memory fades." He sat down in Oslo and wrote the queen. They were at home in 1949 when Churchill was proposing to continue on from an engagement at MIT to holiday at Lord Beaverbrook's home in Jamaica. Clementine wrote, not once but twice:

Vogue, April 1989, originally titled "Pen Ultimate: Henry Fairlie on the Immediacy and Intimacy of the Old-Fashioned Letter." Reprinted by permission from the Estate of Henry Fairlie.

My Darling:

I am so unhappy over Jamaica. . . . But as I said in my letter yesterday (which I tore up perhaps before you had time to assimilate it), I feel that for you, at this moment of doubt and discouragement among our followers . . . [it] would seem cynical and an insult to the Party. . . . You do only just as much as will keep you in Power. But that much is not enough in these hard anxious times.

If he insisted on going to Jamaica, she said, she could not accompany him, "feeling as I do." You've guessed—Churchill sat down and wrote to Beaverbrook that he must forgo the pleasures of Montego Bay: "I do not feel I ought to be away so long."

In his memoirs, *The Vantage Point,* Lyndon Johnson publishes several letters and memoranda from Lady Bird, including a lengthy one of May 14, 1964, in her own hand on sheets torn from a stenographer's notebook, discussing whether he should remain in the presidential campaign. In the first section, called "If you do get out," she imagined the consequences, including the possibilities: "You may look around for a scapegoat. I do not want to be it. You may drink too much for lack of a higher calling." In the second, "If you do *not* get out," she included a possibility: "You may die earlier than you would otherwise." (He did.) The third section, "Stay in," is encouraging and consoling.

To many people these days it seems peculiar that wives and husbands should write to each other when they are living under the same roof. But for Clementine Churchill, Lady Bird Johnson, and other wives similarly placed, what chance would they have of influencing their busy husbands if they interrupted them when their minds were on other matters, and spoke to them only hurriedly? Moreover, these letters, even when they were sharp with advice and correction, also carried warmth and support—"I love you always. Bird"—as did any letters from the husbands, not least Churchill's hand-drawn, signature pig.

Julián Marías, a disciple of Ortega y Gasset, who spent time lecturing in America, published a journal of his visits, *America in the Fifties and Sixties,* that is one of the most observant commentaries on everyday life in the United States. Americans, he said, receive more mail than any other people in the world, and fewer personal letters. In the same vein, an American sociologist I know says that a letter from an American friend is seldom more than an itinerary (it states that he will be in Boulder, Colorado, the following Thursday on the way to Aspen, and asks if they may meet for lunch), whereas a letter from an English friend is like a diary (he says he will be in town the following Thursday, and then, in explanation, describes the present state of his marriage, his need to get away from the children, or his current digestive disorders).

The decline in American letter writing is one of the impoverishments of our lives. Letters need not be long, but they should be snatches of autobiography, taken from the day, week, month, or however long since one last wrote. They should digress, rely on anecdote and vignette, and, of course, offer a dash of gossip about mutual friends. They should have most of the qualities of good conversation, and even have one advantage over conversations: one can return to them later. "The electric telephone," as a septuagenarian friend of mine still calls it, is useful only for itineraries, or for editors to badger writers who are behind their deadline.

Letters should be handwritten, but even if one resorts to a typewriter—but not, God forbid, a word processor—at least the envelope should be handwritten. Because it is with the envelope that the pleasure begins. One takes one's mail out of the box, throws away the junk, puts aside the typewritten letters, and is left with the handwritings one can recognize, sometimes even after not hearing from someone for many years, as has happened to me several times. Before one opens the envelope, there is the relish of anticipation.

No fewer than three readings are usually necessary for a good letter. This is especially true since, humanly enough, we tend to read a letter quickly first to find what we want to hear. If I receive a letter from a friend with whom I have had a spat or even more serious row, or to whom I have been negligent in my own letter writing, I gaze first at the envelope, perhaps even pouring a Scotch, summoning the courage to open it. When I unfold the pages, I turn at once to the final paragraph and the signing-off. If the letter ends with a reasonably adequate expression of continuing affection, I feel emboldened to start at the beginning, though I may skip the passages of protest and reproof. The more general point here is that the charms of a good letter are often hidden, because they glance as good conversation does; and the miracle is that, without the presence of the face, the glances are just as easy to catch.

But the real value of the letter is that one can return to it even years later. Who has not come across an old letter while sifting through his papers, or gone to a file of them to extract only one, and instead sat down to several hours of pleasure to read those from long ago? They are records of a friendship, its growth and continuity. There is no substitute for them.

Of course, letter writing takes time. People today think that they are too busy to set aside hours for letter writing. Yet the Victorians (and others) who did so were among the busiest people who lived, wrote, and acted in public life. In the anthology *Letters in American History,* there is not one letter from the famous we would like to be without; yet these were all the most active people of their times. Besides, not only are letters engaging to write, because one is conversing with an absent friend (who can't interrupt!), but one is likely to be rewarded with a letter in return.

One of the hazards of letter writing, of course, is that people then begin to expect them. Once when I had neglected one of my daughters for some time, she wrote to me: "The telephone is a cop-out." I had only to read that to know she was her father's daughter. In the 1960s I wrote a letter to my hippie son, chiding him for most of his behavior and appearance. It ran to ninety-one pages of yellow pad. His reply defending his choices, though not so long, was substantial. He ended: "Still, I am the only boy at school who gets a ninety-page letter from my dad telling me to get my hair cut."

Such are the rewards, unpredictable but always to be found, of letter writing. They are nourishment. "Don't call me," I say. "Write me a letter."

Spurious George

On the 250th anniversary of his birth, I called George Washington "the greatest man who ever lived." I did not then know that William IV, the son of George III, used precisely those words about him, and what is more, refused to qualify them after Washington died. Of other contemporary judgments, perhaps that of Abigail Adams, never easily taken in by anyone, not even her husband, is the most sufficient: "Take his character together, and we shall not look on his like again." Of today's salutes, none is better than that of his biographer, James Thomas Flexner: "The gentlest of history's great captains, one of the heroes of the human race." The sheer greatness of the man may seem to make the contrast with the 41st, 40th, 39th, 38th . . . presidents unfair. We would be foolish to expect (or even wish) every president to be a Washington. But however embarrassing the contrast, it is legitimate to examine the qualities of the first president, "his character together," which we may then justifiably take as a model in judging the presidents we elect, notably the one most recently elected.

Washington was continually in the field of action, where men usually show themselves at their worst. Set against him an Alexander, a Caesar, a Napoleon, a Lenin, and this one man, brilliant though many of the other Founding Fathers were, shines. He was the leader of a revolution both in war and peace, as general and statesman, who never (unlike most generals) cost

The New Republic, May 8, 1989. Reprinted by permission from the Estate of Henry Fairlie.

by his actions one life more than was necessary. He was of commanding stature among his contemporaries. He was surrounded by temptations to overreach his power, for which he could many times have found justifications, as the Napoleons did, yet through a ceaselessly strenuous life in testing times he remained rooted in his shining humanity. That is why he is so approachable. We may contemplate him in wonder and gratitude, but not in awe. He is as we should try to be as citizens of a democracy, and as our presidents should at least try to be as his successors.

In picking out some of the qualities that enabled Washington to define the office of president, and in fact to bring the Constitution alive from the paper on which it was written, it is inevitable that one should overlook other qualities that others might choose to emphasize. The man was so various in his endowments that omission is almost dictated. Yet first among his qualities, surely, was his vision of the country. As striking as anything about him was that his eyes, for inspiration, were never turned east to Europe, unlike those of most of his contemporaries of his class. He only once left these shores, going to the West Indies on a matter of urgent family concern. He always looked to the west, from the moment he surveyed the Ohio Valley for Lord Fairfax, and beyond it to the vast continent he could imagine without seeing, and the mighty but beneficent nation that might be built there. We do not think of Washington as a great writer or even an eloquent orator. Yet his descriptions of the land he saw as a young surveyor rise to eloquence—majesty, if one likes—not least in the concrete detail of observation from which he drew and painted his picture of the promise of the beauty, fertility, grace, and sweetness of the land he saw. The emphatic lesson for our own time is that we always know from where Washington came—the land he knew and loved.

We in our time have not known from where Nixon, Ford,

Carter, Reagan, and now George Bush came. Nixon was—is—a kind of displaced person in his own country, whether in California or New York City: hence his consternation at the first sign of rebellion in the people, his suspicion of his fellow countrymen, his distrust and fear of rivals and even of colleagues, his lack of confidence in the democratic process. Carter was less from the South than from Annapolis, less a peanut farmer than a Navy engineer, less religious than falsely biblical: disembodied. Reagan had a vision of America, but it was a construct; the images were mythical, of a supposed and idealized American golden age—an Eden, even—to which we were to return. George Bush is no more Kennebunkport, Maine, than Midland, Texas, no more Down East than Lone Star. It is their lack of true roots in a local place that accounts for the poverty of their national vision, as in Bush's inaugural address, so that they seem to be servants only to the special interests that promote their careers. In his first hundred days Bush is, as he always has been, a butler to the interests he serves, dry cleaner to a democracy.

Another of Washington's qualities as a statesman was that he did not think it his or any government's business to check on the private lives or morals of his countrymen. In many ways a model of personal decorum, with some engaging lapses of the heart and more regularly with the bottle, he left the people generally to pursue their often unruly lives, while governing them in necessary things with his wise and austere authority. The idea of the "virtuous citizenry" that some conservatives now like to say underpinned the republican experiment is simply not borne out by any historical evidence or even by any commonsense expectations. Much went on in the homes of rich and poor alike to make one raise one's eyebrows, however primly these people walked to church on Sundays. The virtuous citizen existed only in his capacity as a citizen, exercising his freedoms, without the prying of government, and accepting his obligations to the political order that guaranteed them. Recent presidents demean their own office as well as the people by thinking it their duty to preach of "family values," or the duty of their wives (imagine Martha Washington doing it!) to instruct us, "Just say No." On drugs, crime, education, ethics in government, Bush always resorts to kind and gentle pleas for individual moral regeneration, in the absence of any willingness to confront tough policy choices, especially economic remedies, that might have some effect. Washington sought the hard solutions.

In an unruly time, at the birth of the nation, Washington could tolerate unruliness. When this then-experimental federal structure was endangered, Washington put his foot down, magisterially as usual, not only himself but through men like Marshall on the Supreme Court. But otherwise he understood as well as Jefferson that there must in a democracy be a "whiff of a little rebellion in the air." He could live with the untidiness of a democracy and a free people. (He had to live and march with a ragtag and bobtail of an army, constantly deserting for the summer to attend to the harvest at home.) In contrast with today's presidents, he understood the remark of the 18th-century American conservative Fisher Ames (paraphrased into modern vocabulary): the autocratic monarchies were like great ships that sailed majestically on, until they struck a rock and sank forever, whereas democracy is like a raft—it never sinks but, damn it, your feet are always in the water. Washington in his whole two terms did not distract himself, his administration, or the people by exhibiting puppies so that his presidency might be patted.

It was not only the people and the states who were unruly. No president, at least until the days preceding the Civil War, held together so many talented, factious, scheming colleagues. His eventual disdain for Jefferson (of which Jefferson in his vanity seems to have been unaware to the end), as near to bitterness as Washington could come, was provoked (justifiably) by the incapacity of Jefferson to be simply loyal. Otherwise Washington put up with and kept in harness a ministry of some of the most ambitious and brilliant men ever to compose a Cabinet, in any nation in any age. That set the standard that Bush, like his immediate predecessors, refuses to try to meet: a fully mature man as president who could act as a statesman while allowing his colleagues to gallop sometimes in all directions. What Washington realized was that if you wish to govern well an energetic people, you must expect the people, unruly themselves, to throw up energetic and unruly leaders. They all tell you something you need to hear. The last president with this gift was of course FDR.

It is false to judge a politician by his reading. (Jefferson read too much too glibly, and often spoke and wrote too much too glibly.) Yet it is important to know that our politicians understand what literature and ideas are. Go to Mount Vernon and look at Washington's library. Or read his letters, full of obviously informed references to some classical author, drawing an example that should be followed or a warning that should be foreseen. As with all the Founding Fathers, Washington belonged to, he respected, he was *cultured* in, the heritage of Western civilization, its literature, its thought, and its history, to which the new nation was the heir.

It is now exactly 200 years since George Washington was installed as the first President of the United States, and we remember him still for "his character together." History will doubtless not be so kind to George Bush. Yet the question we have to ask about Bush's first hundred days, and about his immediate predecessors, is not what is so dismaying to one's soul about them, but what is wrong with our soul that we expect and demand no better in our leaders.

Perrier on the Rocks

For a weekend, the news was big. Nothing more could happen in Moscow, since Dan Rather and Peter Jennings had left. But Ted Koppel, Tom Brokaw, and Rather all turned up in South Africa, and such is the power of the anchors, Nelson Mandela was at once released. Blacks in American cities as in South Africa danced in the streets. But the big news these days all seems to come from abroad. Nothing as significant and electrifying ever happens in America. No issue here arouses any passions. Wrong. On Saturday, February 10, a news story sent frissons, then shock waves, through the cohorts, as demographers call them, of the nation's young elites. Perrier Group of America Inc. announced that it had recalled 72 million of its addictive green bottles after the discovery of benzene in some samples.

By Sunday, as Maureen Dowd reported on the front page of the *New York Times,* the American middle and upper-middle classes were rent into mourners and gloaters. "An entire class of people," said James Buckley, a Republican consultant, "have just had their weekend ruined." Worse news sank in. The smug bottles would not reappear in America for possibly three months. Then the final blow fell. Source Perrier S. A. in France announced that it was indefinitely closing down production from its magical underground spring in Vergèze. Wendy Wasserstein

The New Republic, March 5, 1990, originally titled "Water Down: Perrier on the Rocks." Reprinted by permission from the Estate of Henry Fairlie.

said, "We'll all have to go back to scotch," although it was not clear in print whether she was grieving or relieved.

Ms. Wasserstein should never have given it up. Scotch whisky (from the Scots Gaelic *uisge beatha,* meaning literally "the water of life") is made from nutritious whole grains, mainly wheat, and the clear water that splashes down the burns of the heather braes of my native glens. The distinctive taste of the whiskeys is not acquired from any artificial additive, but from the quantity of peat (from the same glens) used in the curing, the manner of distilling, and the kind of casks employed for maturing them. So pure is the product that the shepherds and lairds in each glen that boasts its own malt (unblended) scotch say that, if one *must* barbarously add water, it should be only from the burns of the glen in which it was made. No scotch has ever been found to be contaminated. The God of Presbyterians, and He is a jealous God, would not countenance it.

The abandonment of such a wholesome and convivial liquor for a suspect Gallic product, cleverly marketed at up to $3.50 a supercilious bottle, is the height of youthful frivolity and depth of abject surrender to the peer pressures of "lifestyle." I am not by nature a gloater. He who gloats will not laugh last. But when everything one innocently enjoys has for two decades been scorned, condemned, and subject to punitive taxation; when one has been banished to the back of commercial flights and is now further harassed and drilled if one seeks lawful passage on them, while indulgent Perrier parents bring on unruly American infants who are not fit to be in a confined public space, then even a worm, after long persecution, may be allowed to smack its lips— if a worm has lips—at the discomfiture of its oppressors which, as long foretold by the prophets, the jealous God in his wroth has now visited upon their hubris.

But "tak a cup o' kindness yet," as Rabbie Burns said: I have the interests of Ms. Wasserstein at heart. At $3.50 the little green bottle is a rip-off of the first water. (So are the prices at health food stores.) If the dinks (Double Income No Kids) must drink mineral water, plenty of American springs provide just as good for much less. They buy the bottle and the label. As a bartender once said to me of the bimbos and their blow-dry companions who order Perrier on the rocks, they want their pure French mineral water to be poured into a glass of ice cubes frozen from Potomac water! The gullibility of today's young professionals in their fretting over their bodily well-being is remarkable. Thus they will pay through the mouth, literally, for what one could once normally have expected to be provided free: a glass of water on one's table in a restaurant.

It was no wonder that the manager of the Palm Restaurant in Washington could be seen gloomily taking Perrier off each table. In Los Angeles, Perrier "hasn't been hip for a while," according to the manager of Hugo's Restaurant. He said: "We serve Ram-Losa instead because it's a smaller bottle with less water for the same price, so we make even more money than with Perrier." What is more, I have long shared the suspicion of many that no small, previously undiscovered spring can cease-lessly produce a Niagara of water sufficient to fill, at all times, 72 million bottles for the North American market alone. Do the young professionals care to inquire what they are paying for? No. The bottle is status, the label is assurance, the content is French. They can cease to fret. *Merde!* Since when have the French been the paragons of purity in their lives?

But the fretting during the weekend was fearful to hear. A resident of—natch!—North Side Chicago whimpered: "First they tell us mother's milk causes cancer. Then they tell us that oat bran doesn't reduce cholesterol. Now they tell us Perrier contains benzene. What are we supposed to do?" Does he not have a mind of his own? Live by the "experts," you will perish by the "experts." Whatever happened to the sufficient injunction of my Scottish mother and elders: "A little of what you fancy does you good"? With that one is released from the distractions of the body anxious.

Epictetus, the Phrygian Stoic philosopher, wrote: "It is a sign of [a nature not finely tempered] to make, for instance, a great fuss about" exercise, eating, drinking, walking, riding. "All these things ought to be done *merely by the way*. . . ." (Italics added.) Matthew Arnold commented: "This is admirable." So it is, and I commend it to Ms. Wasserstein, who I believe is redeemable. She should take "a wee dram"—an elastic Scottish measure—in the name of Rabbie Burns, who took many, enabling him to contribute a formidable three-and-a-half pages of well-loved lines to the *Oxford Dictionary of Quotations*.

An Evening with Hooter

We headed south late one afternoon, having no idea where we would spend the night, more or less following the course of the Minnesota River through the Valley of the Jolly Green Giant to Le Sueur. The Green Giant Company is the only one of the canning and fast-freezing firms, drawing its vegetables from the truck farming in the area, which has its headquarters in Minnesota. I admire the Jolly Green Giant for that. Ho! Ho! Ho!

So we came to Mankato, an immediately inviting town, but also, at a first glance as strangers, a puzzling one. We needed to get our bearings. Among empty streets on a drizzly early evening we found a neighbourhood corner bar, which had the added curiosity that it was called the Shamrock.

Inside all was warmth: at the tables was the buzz of locals after work; in the corner, a small bar with three or four of them and a very welcoming bartender. In fact, they were all welcoming. This lack of surliness or any suspicion in these smaller towns of America is worth just a passing salute. Perhaps it is because Ruth is with me, with her open, ready, American "Hi!" to almost anyone and everyone, but how quickly we cease to be strangers.

I think the reader deserves to be told that, yes, people do have a certain curiosity about this rather stodgy Scot in his tweed

Excerpt from unpublished manuscript of "Journey into America." Henry Fairlie Papers, MS 296, Special Collections Department, University of Colorado at Boulder Libraries. Reprinted by permission from the Estate of Henry Fairlie.

jacket and this lively and curly-headed New Mexican, going round the country together and arriving in their towns. We can see some people trying to work out our relationship. But very soon they seem to put their questions out of their minds, and surely there has been some welcome freeing of manners in recent years which makes us just accepted as two quite friendly people, who happen to be of different ages and sexes. I cannot help feeling that some time in the past twenty years or so a breath of fresh air swept a lot of sly prurience out of Main Street.

My inquiry as to where we might find somewhere pleasant to stay in the area was thrown open by the bartender to the customers, whose explanations of what might (and could not) be found in and around Mankato would not have pleased its Chamber of Commerce.

We still did not know where we would end up, but no matter, the conversation had been made general, and it was not difficult to piece together, from the lively exchanges they had with each other about their own town, appealing to Ruth as if she were an arbitrator and would decide which of them we could believe, a picture of this important little place of about 30,000 people. ("Didn't it drop a little in the last census?" "No, Bob, they just forgot to count you.")

Apart from a woman lawyer who came over from a table where she was sitting with a friend to join us—I am not sure why she did so—I am fairly confident that none of them had gone past high school and some not as far as that. Yet they had a variety of jobs—white-collar of a kind, mainly clerical, some supervisory—and a lively interest in their city. We had struck another of the smaller towns where a lot happens that we know nothing about.

Mankato after the Second World War had only half the number of people that it has today, and had a fair claim to be taken as a fairly representative, moderate-sized Main Street, U.S.A., like many other places in Minnesota and the Midwest. After all, we are in the state where Sinclair Lewis was born at Sauk Centre, on which he modelled Gopher Prairie in *Main Street*. In Mankato we were given a quite vivid picture of how Main Street can and will (more and more) change.

Forty years ago as now it was the regional centre for an agricultural area of dairying and grain; then as now it does some food processing, including Minnesota's own business of flour milling; then as now it has some durable goods industry, especially in agricultural implements; then as now, it does some brewing; then as now, it has some oil refining. Altogether it was and is busy with more activity than one might expect in a town of its size and numbers.

Nothing much might have changed, and it certainly would not have doubled its population, if it had not had something else: Mankato State Teachers' College, which in 1957 was rechristened Mankato State College, a very large institution which is fairly widely celebrated for the training it gives in various fields of education.

The reader should not by now be surprised that Mankato, with that asset, increased its population by almost a third in the 1970s, just as other cities with state universities and colleges in Minnesota, such as Moorhead and St. Cloud, also grew by much the same percentage. Once again we had driven unwittingly into yet another example of this remarkable dispersal of people and new industry to small cities with state colleges.

But we had not heard before Mankato such a variety of locals, most at some stage of middle age, talking so personally of how it has changed and how it has stayed the same. As long as it kept its agriculture and its food processing, as long as it kept some of its old manufacturing, it could take willingly the new industries and service companies and institutions: that was the emphasis that came through. Mankato must keep those.

It was one of the worries of Mike Spellacy in his office on Front Street at the State Department of Economic Security. The demand for employees had momentarily levelled off but was still rising, but what made him anxious was that the jobs Mankato lost were blue-collar ones, and the jobs which were replacing them were not blue-collar. What I felt among all the lively, even bantering, exchange was a distinct fear that the new industries and service sector would not have so much interest in keeping the agriculture, the food processing, and other small but useful plants.

It is these that give character: they did not quite put it like that, but that was what they were saying. If they went, then Main Street, at last, would also go. Producing food, making things: cities, especially small towns, get their feel from that.

A man with a weathered face, a quarterback's hands that could be wrapped round a ball to throw it, a cowboy hat, cowboy vest, cowboy boots, had come in through the back door, taken a stool at the other side of the little bar, tried to make head or tail of the conversation, and of these two strangers in town, was largely ignored by the others who knew him, in spite of the noisiness of his interjections, and took to watching the local television news which, as usual, was turned on but with the sound down.

Some of the others had left one by one to go home to supper, when the report that the Minnesota Twins had lost again the night before produced from the aging cowboy, his hat pushed to the back of his head, an uproarious outburst of self-advertisement. The Twins were boys. That's what they were playing with, that's why they lost: a team of boys. He had offered himself for a trial at the beginning of the season, but they had this damn silly rule about age. They didn't even give him a try. "They could have had Hooter! Hooter was game for a trial! With Hooter they would not lose! But look at them—a team of boys—when Hooter was ready."

Of uncertain age, somewhere about fifty—he was vain enough to trim or add a decade, whichever he thought would impress you most—he was handsome in the way that comes mainly from believing that you are handsome, ebullient, cocky, trying ineffectively (and until later, inoffensively) to be raunchy; with a quick, blunt humour—he would not count a rapier as a weapon fit for a man—wholly engaging, wanting to be in on things, two strangers in town; irritating the more staid of the locals, especially the woman lawyer, who unnecessarily told me not to take my impression of Mankato from him, which only made me want to hear more from him; devil-may-care, in-for-a-penny-in-for-a-pound, in every word and movement, he opened up:

"Well, Sir, you may kid the others that you're a writer, but I'm something of a writer myself, and Hooter knows that you're not really a writer unless you have a publisher. There's people all over America who call themselves writers, but they don't have publishers"—an unexpectedly shrewd observation, I thought.

"I have a publisher."

"What one."

"Harper & Row."

"Whoa there, Englishman, Harper & Row—Harper & Row's big apples." He turned to the bartender to inform him and the rest of the bar: "Harper & Row's big apples. Give him a drink from Hooter. Yes, Sir, I'll be happy to join you." He sat on the other side of Ruth: "You're a mighty pretty lady."

The moments when he managed to disengage his attention from Ruth were full of surprises. He seemed ready—to prove his literary credentials—to launch into a recital of one of Shakespeare's soliloquies (in fact, he chose a sonnet), and then:

"Shakespeare's all right, but I like Marlowe more—and Kyd, too."

You really do not expect an urban cowboy in the Shamrock bar at Mankato, south central Minnesota, to start talking about two Elizabethan dramatists, one of them quite out of the way. Can you kid about Kyd?

"Studied English literature at college. Loved it. Especially the Elizabethans . . ."

"Isn't he something?" the bartender laughed to me. "I told you you'd have your hands full."

Hooter's rather impressive way of talking to me about Christopher Marlowe while his hands made their own barely disguised approaches to the "mighty pretty lady" made me think that it was a question rather of how full his hands would be before the sun went down.

He was an engineer, a construction engineer: "make things, make machines, make small plants. Metal, always work with metal—Hooter's a great engineer. Travel a bit until I find someone who wants something built, then I stay there, finish the job, and if there's no more work in town, I move on."

"How long have you been in Mankato?"

"This time? Since February. Will soon be moving on."

Women? Why, of course, women. But they always want him to settle down. "They like Hooter because he's free and easy, and takes them places, and then they want Hooter to settle down. . . . I like London. . . . Took my bride there. She was a Swede, met her in Sweden, took her to London for a honeymoon, stayed at the Stafford Hotel."

Now, the Stafford is a rather exclusive, not self-advertising, hotel off St. James's Street. It is not a hotel whose name one might pick up from a newspaper. When he had talked of Marlowe and Kyd, a few questions, a line or two quoted laughingly back at each other, confirmed that he really knew their work. Now a few questions about London—"You must have got used to the vagaries of the No. 11 bus route." "The No. 11 bus—that's the one that runs in convoys. You wait for one for half an hour, and then five come together"—again proved that it was not all fancy.

You were always about to put him down as one of the most consummate bullshitters of all time, enjoyable but a bullshitter, but every time you tested one of his claims you found that he could fill in the details that supported it.

He solved one of our problems. Where should we stay the night? Everyone else had dithered, and made no useful suggestion. "New Ulm," said Hooter. "That's the place for you. The Holiday Inn there. Don't turn up your nose. Trust Hooter. Anyone can trust Hooter. It's no ordinary Holiday Inn. You'll see. New Ulm is no ordinary place. You can't ignore the Germans, can you? Yes, you should call."

Having skilfully got rid of me to the telephone, he turned more intently to the mighty pretty lady.

He then solved another problem:

"You're two precious people. You're pre-e-e-cious. You won't believe it unless Hooter takes you there, but the best restaurant in America is in the middle of a cornfield a few miles from here. Hooter wants you two precious people to be his guests at dinner."

Neither of us had any hesitation in accepting.

When talking about his life, he again and again broke into a verse he had written. They were ballads, based on his life. "I've tried plays. I've tried novels. I write these ballads. I don't have Harper & Row, of course. . . ."

Recited with verve (and certainly with conviction) in his Texas accent, the ballads needed only a guitar, and you might have been on a cattle drive, as some lonely cowboy in the evening sang a sad, quietly sardonic, lament over some woman left behind. He had one written down on a piece of ruled paper in his wallet. He gave it to us, and signed it.

He was as pleased as punch that one of Hooter's ballads might be in "a book published by Harper & Row." (I could not help wondering if he would have been so impressed if I had been writing for Praeger.) I think his ballad deserves to be printed:

> (Hooter's ballad is mislaid—*Not Lost.* I'll find it to insert here.)[1]

There you are Hooter, wherever your travels have taken you: your ballad in print.

He mimicked my English accent so well that I wondered if his own Texas accent might not be mimicry. At one point he looked past Ruth at me, and said to her: "Look at him in his tweed jacket—could you find anything more English than that? How did a pretty lady like you get mixed up with Tweedy"—and Tweedy I remained for the evening.

At last the time came to go to the restaurant. I had switched from beer to scotch; not to be outdone, he switched to bourbon. I downed one scotch. "Look how fast Tweedy drinks," he said to Ruth. "He was just served that scotch"; not to be outdone, he downed his bourbon. There was one problem he had to solve. He clearly thought that for me to be in the company of Ruth, and for him to be unaccompanied by *any* "mighty pretty lady," would make dinner a little unbalanced. He scanned the room. The woman lawyer had returned to her table and her woman friend. Hooter had clearly decided that the woman lawyer was not mighty pretty enough. This did not stop him from going across to lay siege to her friend. I would like to have heard his ten minutes' effort to persuade her to join us. He came back a little rueful. Rejected. Hooter rejected. Well, you can't win 'em all. Anyhow, she was probably a "tight-assed, preacher lady."

We went out to go to the restaurant in our van. It had been

---

1. Despite Fairlie's assurance, which appears in a handwritten note on its own page in the manuscript, the ballad has not been found.

gloomy in the drizzle when we had arrived. Ruth had left the lights on. The battery was dead. Hooter was out of the parking lot in a flash, came back in five minutes in the 1960s pick-up in which he roamed the country, and with some dispatch jump-started the van. It was late by now, but it was midsummer. A watery sun was slanting over the rolling, green but sodden land. We did indeed turn into a cornfield about ten miles out of town; and there tucked away above a stream to which a pasture sloped was a wonderfully elegant restaurant. Hooter strode in in his hat, vest and boots, refused the first table we were offered, and secured the best table in the restaurant by the window overlooking the stream.

It was made clear the moment the menus were placed in front of us that we would hurt his feelings if we ordered anything but the best and the most expensive. The wine—why, of course, the best in the house: one bottle, two bottles, three bottles. Three courses—why not more? Liqueurs, cognacs. And then when the check was brought, after about three hours of royal feasting and almost as royal talk, he threw down a tip of noble generosity on top of a bill which must have been heading to the $200 mark. A demur from us at his generosity produced only a shrug and a smile: "Easy come, easy go: that's how it is with Hooter."

It sounded like, not only a way of life, but a philosophy.

Except when he felt it necessary to exercise his raunchiness, there was something courtly, almost old-world, in his manner to us and to most people. As for his hospitality, "You're pre-e-e-cious," and imitating his Texas drawl, Ruth laughed back, after the twentieth "you're pre-e-e-cious," "And you're pre-e-e-cious, too." "You've given Hooter his best evening for months, you two precious people, when he was feeling a bit down—blue." He was blue—genuinely, it seemed—about one more woman, who had wanted him to settle down, left him.

He insisted that we should go his hotel for a nightcap. It was really a rather rundown rooming-house-of-a-hotel, with a vast saloon with pool tables on the first floor. It was full of exactly the kind of men (mostly) of all ages you would expect to find in a saloon below a rooming-house-of-a-hotel, but undeterred by either their intoxication or their clear ignorance of and indifference to the world of publishing, Hooter kept on introducing us with the commendation that I was "writing a book for Harper & Row." I don't know if he expected the denizens of his rooming house to be electrified by this information. They showed a steady lack of emotion in response.

The time had come to try to pull ourselves away—he was reluctant to let us leave—and obviously realizing that time was running out, he made the most direct approach a man's hand can make to a "mighty pretty lady" sitting on a bar stool. Open—undisguised—frontal: straight up the thigh. Ruth firmly placed the hand back by his own side, and for a moment he looked chastised, then again the good-humoured shrug: You can't win 'em all.

"He's going to wake in the morning," I said when we left, "and realize he's down about $250." But one could be certain of one thing: Hooter would not for a second regret it. This was partly because there was not a stingy fibre in his body. He knew what he was doing. We were strangers in town who broke the monotony of the weeks for him, as he did for us. He could also talk about things which he did not usually have the chance to talk about. The man who had kicked off the evening with Marlowe and Kyd—it was the only time all the way round America that someone quoted from *The Duchess of Malfi*—could talk about his own life and life in general with pointed observations; and about his engineering—he was clearly skilled, and regarded himself as a superior craftsman, showing us the construction he was then working on—and about wildlife in Minnesota and the Southwest. He was a wanderer, obviously enough, but not a drifter—and there is a world of difference. He was not, emphatically he was not, a bum.

Two years before, my son had hitchhiked across America to Los Angeles, and then up the West Coast, through Canada and the Yukon, to Alaska with his girl friend. In a long letter he described to me the people who had given them hitches: "all friendly, hospitable, talkative, open, and all seeming to be living to the full some very personal myth of America. . . . Louise, the South Dakota farmer's wife, Steve the Idaho lumberjack, Rick the cocaine dealer. . . . " His gallery of portraits seemed endless. Hooter would have fitted into his gallery.

No country needs many Hooters; but America certainly needs some. In this craven corporate world that grows round us like a coral reef, cell added to cell, you come away from an evening with Hooter believing unsentimentally and with no illusions that he is the salt of America. He still uses the freedom of America, of American space and time, in ways that most of us do not dare.

I told him that a friend had said to me once that I am "half very domestic, half a gypsy," and it is a description, with some qualification, I accept. Hooter liked it, echoed it, adopted it.

"Where will you be when our book comes out? I'll send you a copy. After that dinner, you deserve one."

"Oh, I don't know. I think it's time I tried Oklahoma again. Haven't been there for a long time. But I'll be back in Mankato some year. Send it here: I'll get it some year. Where Hooter's been, they don't forget Hooter."

And there is no boast in that.

I fully expect to be travelling in America some day, and from the far end of the bar, his cowboy hat pushed to the back of his head, will come the shout: "It's Tweedy—and where's your mighty pretty lady?"

THE HARLOT'S PREROGATIVE
Writers and the Press

Some years ago, when he was Prime Minister of Great Britain, Stanley Baldwin was being viciously attacked by the press barons, and at last counterattacked with one scorching remark, which is said to have been supplied to him by his cousin, Rudyard Kipling. The press lords, he said, were claiming "power without responsibility, the prerogative of the harlot through the ages." The American press is today claiming the harlot's prerogative.
—*"The Harlot's Prerogative,"* The New Republic, *1977*

Necessary Weapons

Parliament has risen for the summer recess and the Chamber of the House of Commons is left, with its ghosts, to the parties of school children and curious New Englanders. In other words, this column, which began with the opening of Parliament last November, has now completed its first Parliamentary year. If my view of the general political situation has not become apparent during these nine months, then the failure has been so great that it can scarcely be rectified by a hurried summing-up in twelve hundred words. It seems to me to be far more useful to devote the space this week to a comment on the object of political journalism; and it may be additionally useful because both the content and the manner of my weekly remarks have been severely criticised from time to time. I think it is too often forgotten that the object of political journalism is political action—whether it is a leading article in *The Times* or an ounce of raillery by Cassandra of the *Daily Mirror*[1]—and I hope in the next few hundred words to convince my critics that there are certain weapons which the political journalist is obliged to use in order to provoke action.

The origins of British political journalism are to be found in the great British political pamphleteers of the seventeenth and eighteenth centuries. It was during the Civil War that they

Spectator, July 29, 1955, originally titled "Political Commentary."

1. "Cassandra" was the pen name of the vitriolic Irish journalist Bill Connor, who wrote a wide-ranging column for the *Daily Mirror*, at this time the most-read daily newspaper in Britain.

first became an important influence, but, having established themselves then, they did not surrender their influence until they were replaced by the press. Milton's *Areopagitica* and the anti-Cromwell tract *Killing No Murder*, William Walwyn the Leveller and Gerrard Winstanley the Digger, Defoe's *The Shortest Way with Dissenters* and Swift's *Modest Proposal:* these should be the models for political journalists today.[2] But if Swift's proposal for relieving Irish poverty by using Irish children as meat for the rich were published today it would be regarded as shocking. Cassandra would call him "an eager bespatterer" and the *British Weekly* would dismiss him as "a nasty clod." Wilkes[3] today would be constantly arraigned before the Press Council—in his own way he only had to run the gauntlet of the House of Commons—and Defoe would be banned from the BBC. The reason seems to me to be obvious. The Establishment has now

2. *Areopagitica* was a 1644 pamphlet by John Milton (1608–1674) using religious arguments to press for free speech during the English Civil War. *Killing No Murder* was an anonymous 1657 pamphlet advocating the assassination of Oliver Cromwell. William Walwyn was a seventeenth-century radical opponent of corruption in Parliament and agitator for civil rights. Gerrard Winstanley (1609–1676) was the leader of the Diggers, a seventeenth-century egalitarian group that, in 1648, began cultivating public land and giving away food to followers. In 1702, Daniel Defoe (1660?–1731) anonymously published *The Shortest Way with Dissenters*, a satiric pamphlet that purported to be a High-Church Anglican zealot's call for religious dissenters to be banished and their leaders hanged; discovered as its author in 1703, Defoe was pilloried and imprisoned. In 1729, Jonathan Swift (1667–1745) published *A Modest Proposal for preventing the children of poor people in Ireland, from being a burden on their parents or country, and for making them beneficial to the publick*, a satire on the cruelty of landlords that advocated eating Irish children.

3. John Wilkes (1725–1797) was a radical journalist and reform-minded MP who was repeatedly barred from taking his seat in Parliament, even though the voters of Middlesex kept electing him to occupy it.

extended itself far beyond Crown, Church, and Parliament. It now includes—amongst other institutions—the press.

The press today is largely owned by people who are high-ranking members of the Establishment. Whatever the differences between individual papers, there is one resemblance between them which is far more important. They all wish to preserve the "moderate" Conservatives and the "moderate" Socialists. They are all cast in the "front-bench" frame of mind. But the press is intended to have the freedom and independence which once belonged to back-benchers. The whole point about "moderate" Conservatives and "moderate" Socialists is that they are both primarily interested in maintaining the *status quo,* in shoring up the Establishment. None of them wishes anything uncomfortable to happen or be done. This is all very well, but I recall a comment which the *Manchester Guardian* made during the 1950 election campaign. It pointed out that Mr. Attlee was being constantly praised for the quietness of his campaign, for pushing round the country in his little four-seater, with his wife at the wheel, making quiet, sensible speeches wherever he stopped. But, asked the *Manchester Guardian,* is there any reason for believing that a quiet, sensible campaign gets as near the truth as the more rumbustious, tear-away, scandal-ridden campaigns of the past? It did not answer the question, but it posed it with a *num,* expecting the answer "No."

The truth is that politics does not exist apart from opposition, the opposition of interests and ideas. To try to find the *via media,* which is the task to which the *Observer,* notably, but the entire British press, in general, has devoted itself, is to try to obscure the depth and reality of the conflicts which underlie politics. Politics demands the opposition of a strong antithesis to a strong thesis, and out of the conflict will emerge a satisfactory synthesis. The synthesis cannot be found by trying to unearth the lowest common denominator. Today, though I frequently and sometimes fundamentally disagree with their views and policies, I recognise only two journals (apart from the *Spectator*, of course) which are devoted to the *serious* discussion of political issues: *Punch* and *Tribune*.[4] One is Right-wing anarchist, the other is Left-wing leveller. But both have pitted themselves against the prevailing climate, which is encouraged, above all, by the BBC's presentation of political issues, which reduces all political discussion to the level of parlour games. Both of them have, from time to time, been accused of bad taste and unfairness, but neither has ever done anything which is not fully in the tradition of British political journalism.

That tradition is an honourable one. It concerns itself with personalities, because it knows that politics is in the hands of persons. Nothing I, or *Punch*, or *Tribune*, have written about any political personality has ever been as vicious as what Byron or Shelley wrote about Castlereagh.[5] If one happens to believe that it is necessary for the good of the country to remove some public figure from his pedestal then one must hit hard, and the greater the idol that he is—the heavier his feet of clay—the harder one has to hit. It is all immensely shocking if the victim happens to be one's own idol. How enraged I used to get when I read the attacks of the *Daily Mirror* on Sir Winston Churchill! But the shocking is salutary, and it is especially salutary when we have almost ceased to be capable of being shocked. I wonder how

4. *Punch*, the satiric weekly founded in 1841 and discontinued in 2002, was edited in these years by Malcolm Muggeridge, whom Fairlie credited with instigating a mood of wicked protest; Fairlie wrote for it frequently. Founded in 1937, the socialist weekly *Tribune* in these years supported the left-leaning, Bevanite wing of the Labour Party.

5. Robert Stewart, better known as Viscount Castlereagh (1769–1822), served as foreign secretary during the Congress of Vienna. After Castlereagh committed suicide, Byron wrote: "Posterity will ne'er survey / A nobler grave than this: / Here lie the bones of Castlereagh: / Stop, traveler, and piss!"

many of my readers have at this stage any idea of the fundamental issue I am talking about. It is freedom. Political discussion and political journalism require freedom, and freedom's main enemy in Britain today is not censorship by government, but censorship imposed by an atmosphere of moderation and good taste which stifles—and is intended to stifle.

Press Against Politics

At one point between about 3:30 and 4:00 a.m. on the morning of November 3, the voice of Walter Cronkite changed. After hours—and weeks—and months— of talking about Jimmy Carter as a candidate, he suddenly found himself using the words, "the President-elect." There may be no way of hushing the voice of Walter Cronkite, but there is no doubt that his voice becomes hushed by itself in the presence of immanent power. If one can imagine the late Cardinal Cushing at the manger of the infant Jesus—a picture that does require a considerable exercise of imagination—one has some idea of Walter Cronkite in the presence of sudden majesty.

It is only because Walter Cronkite in his ineffable glibness seems to me to summarize the faults of American journalism—print as well as television—that I use him as my object lesson. It is the American journalist's coverage of this election that is my subject.

I need to present one credential before arguing my point. Back in early spring I was the after-dinner speaker at a seminar in Washington, DC. The other speakers at the seminar had included some of the more prominent managers of all the candidates of both parties who were then in the primary races. At the end of my talk, I said that I thought that it was the duty of a political journalist to go out on a limb, to commit his own judgment without the aid of polls or computers; and so I went

The New Republic, November 13, 1976. Reprinted by permission from the Estate of Henry Fairlie.

out on a limb. I said that Ford would defeat Reagan in the primaries, that Carter would defeat all his Democratic rivals, and that in the election Carter would defeat Ford.

There were low whistles from some of the audience; and the managers of Ronald Reagan and Henry Jackson pounced on me after my speech. I was out on my limb, and I will admit that in the intervening eight months there have been moments when I thought that it was being sawn off from under me. It was not really until Walter Cronkite was ready to give his unctuous blessing to the born-again king from Georgia that I could feel satisfied that my long-ago prediction was virginally immaculate.

I do not tell that story to boast; but to suggest that the American press and television news programs were this year guilty of the primary sin of American journalism: lack of commitment. When I say that a political journalist should go out on a limb, I mean that he should commit, not only his judgment, but his faith. He should himself make a choice, and from that commitment develop his own perceptions.

It does not matter whether he is Democrat or Republican—liberal or conservative, for Joe McCarthy or Gene McCarthy—he is worthless unless he cares enough to allow his passion to inform his judgment, his beliefs to discipline his observation. The political journalist ought to be the first into the ballot box; even if he loses. His judgment is useless unless it is regulated by passion. His real task is to uncover for other voters the glimpse of heaven which lies behind their mundane concerns. He cannot be objective. He must lay his hands on the child before it is enthroned in power.

Or withold his hands.

Of all the American columnists and commentators in this year's election, only one stands out as a man of dredging conviction and therefore truth. George Will is some kind of American conservative. He would prefer to have a genuine Republican party in office than a genuine Democratic party. Yet he never moved all year, either in print or on television, from an intellectually impassioned contempt for Gerald Ford. No matter how much of an ass Jimmy Carter sometimes made himself look, no matter how often the Democratic party was still obviously the party which he distrusted, George Will stuck to his own bitter truth about the inadequacy of Gerald Ford.

His advocacy therefore became its own form of accurate observation. What he was saying was that, in the end, by however small a margin of conviction, one simply could not take Gerald Ford for "four more years." If at any point during the election I had read a single sentence of his which suggested that he could stomach Gerald Ford, I would have had my own doubts about the ultimate success of Jimmy Carter. He was telling me something about the attitudes of a conservative mind in this election.

It is this lack of intellectually impassioned conviction that makes another kind of American conservative—James Jackson Kilpatrick—worthless to the point of professional fraudulence.[1] He appears to be very conservative, very right wing; he certainly would have preferred a Reagan to a Ford, if he prefers anything that does not dissolve when touched. But once Ford had defeated Reagan, he was still gung-ho for the Republican party. To be "gung-ho," according to Webster's, is to be "extremely or overly zealous or enthusiastic." That is exactly what happens to the kind of intellectually unimpassioned political journalism that James Jackson Kilpatrick represents. He reaches for the lowest common denominator of political motive in those for whom he so grossly appears to speak. There is no conservatism in his journalism because he reaches always to what is most

1. James J. Kilpatrick (born 1920) was at this time a columnist for the *Washington Star* and the conservative half of the *60 Minutes* debate segment "Point-Counterpoint."

immediate and vulgar. If he met a saint, he would imagine that he or she was on his level.

And this affects his judgment. To coin a phrase—and it seems to me to be a phrase that is worth the coining—the real duty of the political journalist is to supply *moral information* from a coherent intellectual position: to supply it to the politicians on the one hand, and to the voters on the other. From a supposed conservative like James Jackson Kilpatrick there comes no moral information at all. There is something terrifyingly wrong in a political journalism that insists on making a sow's ear out of a silk purse.

There is even a perverted kind of worth in the conservative journalism of Robert Novak and Rowland Evans.[2] Sheer malevolence of spirit must have some original value. There is something to be said for a column that allows one to settle over one's breakfast and say, even before one has read it, "Let's see how mean and small we can make the world look today." In fact, there is a kind of moral information in Evans and Novak. As we start to read their revelations of the shoddy—they would have reported the Virgin Birth by saying that in a secret meeting between Joseph and Mary in a Holiday Inn at Nazareth, Joseph had paid a Teamster to make Mary pregnant—we know that we are reading about everything in the political world which is unglorious, unmajestic, unlovely; and therefore turn to meet the day and find that it is not as ugly as they steadily assure us it will be.

What is more, in the moral information which they supply, there is again the kind of information that makes possible a prediction. As I said to a friend about 10 days before the election, "Once Evans and Novak are reduced to scurrying round

2. Robert Novak (born 1931) and Rowland Evans (1921–2001) were the longtime coauthors of "Inside Report," a widely read syndicated column on the backroom machinations of politics, with a conservative point of view.

California to find the evidence that Carter cannot win, one knows that Ford is certain to lose." The real value of their column is not so much that one knows in their hearts they are right, but that they are right in spite of themselves, somewhere down in their bowels.

But it has not been the conservative journalists who have most distorted this year's campaign; it has been the rest. The lack of moral information has been most evident in those who are supposed to be most liberally minded and anxiously concerned. It is not the talents or the worth of the following journalists that I am questioning, but the use to which they put their talents and their worth, their failure to supply moral information either to the candidates or the voters.

The fact is that once Mary McGrory[3] found that there was no candidate this year over which she could break her heart, she stopped using her head.

The fact is that when Joseph Kraft[4] at last came out with a whimper of an endorsement of Jimmy Carter, it was after eight months of almost consistent undermining of Carter's claims to any honesty or decency or intelligence at all. But a slippery endorsement of a candidate whom one has spent one's time making look slippery is perhaps some kind of moral information about the journalist's own perceptions.

The fact is that David Broder,[5] who was once an acutely modest

3. Mary McGrory (1918–2004) was the longtime reporter and much-admired columnist for the *Washington Star* and later the *Washington Post*. Her coverage of Watergate won her a Pulitzer and a spot on Richard Nixon's "Enemies" list.

4. Joseph Kraft (1924–1986) covered politics for the *Washington Post*, the *New York Times*, and *Harper's*. His column was widely syndicated.

5. David S. Broder (born 1929) is national political correspondent and a columnist at the *Washington Post*, which he joined in 1966. He is widely regarded as the unofficial dean of the Washington press corps.

reporter of events, has become an immodest distributor of cynical opinions. He is like a monk who, when he at last has the courage to disrobe himself, finds that his energies have atrophied.

The fact is that James Reston[6] writes now like a sports columnist on the slope of Olympus. When he gets around to telling us why we should—or should not—vote for Jimmy Carter it is as convincing as the National Zoo telling us why it bought a Bactrian breeding camel with no testicles.

The fact is that when Tom Wicker,[7] at last and yet again, bares his soul and says that Carter should be supported, he makes his soul seem so superior to that of the candidates and the voters that one wonders why he does not just say that America is just one great Attica, and he is its warden.

The fact is that Anthony Lewis,[8] after yapping at American society, its politics and politicians, year in and year out, suddenly on the day after the election found nothing less than "amazing grace" in Jimmy Carter's victory, a "special wonder" in Gerald Ford's concession, and a "deep poignance" in the whole process. As a colleague remarked, "It's enough to make one sick."

And so one could go on, through the "best and the brightest" of the journalists; and on television it is even worse than in print. The absence of moral information from the Cronkites, the Chancellors and the Reasoners—from the Brinkleys, the Sevareids, and the Smiths—is not only alarming, it is degrading. There comes no word from them to suggest that democracy is

6. James Reston (1909–1995), a longtime columnist for the *New York Times* and two-time winner of the Pulitzer Prize, was regarded as one of the best-connected and most influential journalists in American politics.

7. Tom Wicker (born 1926) was a reporter, Washington correspondent, and political columnist for the *New York Times* from 1960 until his retirement in 1991.

8. Anthony Lewis (born 1927) wrote "Abroad at Home," a left-leaning political column for the *New York Times,* from 1969–2001.

the accumulation of the moral aspirations and decisions of vexed but hopeful individuals, and that their task is to reinforce the process with their own intellectual commitment.

Everything about an election is reduced by them to so miserly an estimate of human motives that there can be no sense of the sheer hopefulness of a free people when they vote. Individuals are translated into units: that is all that they now know how to measure, humans as units measured by categories.

Since the journalists whom I am criticizing are among the best journalists we have, it seems to me necessary for us to confront what they will not confront in their situation: that it is not ultimately their own fault, that they are the nerveless victims of a system that is inescapably corrupting. If one really feared democracy, if one really feared the people, one would not waste time discrediting a Democrat as against a Republican, a liberal as against a conservative; one would simply discredit them all, candidates and voters. One would impute base motives to the politicians, and mundane motives to the people. One would teach them to despise themselves; one would instruct them to have contempt for the political process; one would make something—anything—look superior to the political motive: art, movies, sports, pornography, nature. It does not matter what the distraction, as long as it distracts; and always the purpose is the same, to leave the economic realm in command over all others, to explain all human impulse, as it is expressed in the political process, in terms of nothing more than the "acquisitive instinct."

There is no way in which the newspapers and television can ultimately escape from the fact that they are in bondage to an economic view of human aspiration against which they have no defense once the supremacy of the political realm has been surrendered. The individual journalists whom I have mentioned may be at fault, but they are among the best; and their primary fault is not to recognize or acknowledge that their—my—

whole profession is trapped in a diminishing concept of human aspiration.

From the funeral oration of Pericles to the profoundly moving and graceful words of Jimmy Carter's acknowledgement of victory on the morning of November 3, the one realm in our existence which has released us to contend with the tyrannies of every other realm that matters to us—not least the economic realm of mere survival—has been the world of politics. It is not in an art gallery, not in a church, not on a stock exchange, not even in bed, that man is whole. It is in the ballot box.

To make my point, I would like to be allowed to be personal. My thesis in *The Kennedy Promise* has very often been misused. In fact, in its editorial on election day this year, the *Washington Star* quoted from my "wisdom" in that book to make it seem that I was arguing that the world of politics cannot really achieve very much. That was not my point. I criticized the politics of John Kennedy and, to a lesser extent, of Robert Kennedy, not because I think that politics should arouse no expectations, but because I think that they aroused the wrong expectations. I thought that I was defending the world of politics against the Kennedys' misuse of it.

That is surely why I said in my conclusion that politics is not just the art of the possible, as is so often slyly said, and certainly is not the art of the impossible, as the Kennedys tried to practice it; but that it is *the art of the necessary*. There are necessary things to be done which only politics can do.

We have no other defense now against the dominance of the economic realm than the determination of the political world to assert itself. The task of the political journalist—and of the newspapers or television companies which employ him—is to strengthen that assertion. He may criticize an individual politician; he has no right to diminish the political function. He has no more right to do so than an art critic, in criticizing an individual artist, has the right to diminish the function of art, or a music critic, in criticizing an individual composer, has the right to diminish the function of music.

Frank Mankiewicz[9] is among the more experienced, more intelligent, more decent, more hoping men who are active in the political world. A few days before this year's election he said that the press and television had made it seem that no candidate ever advocated anything for any other reason than that it would win him votes. He is right. If Jimmy Carter said in Pittsburgh that he wished to reduce unemployment, the television reporter automatically said, "Jimmy Carter made another pitch for the blue-collar vote in the big cities which he needs to carry"; and it was the same if Gerald Ford made a speech about taxation. Of course the politician is aware of the voters: that is one of the purposes of democracy, that the voters should tell the politicians what they want and need and hope. But it is equally true that most politicians are believing and honest men. Carter believes something, Ford believes something; each true to himself.

In fact, it may well be true that our politicians are today among the few who really believe anything at all. I have not reported politics for 31 years in 26 countries to imagine that politicians are innocent and guileless. But equally I have not reported politics for all those years in all those countries without being certain that politicians as such, however many individuals amongst them are venal or stupid, are the most hopeful messengers of a society's will to improve.

Against that will to improve, which is felt as much by the genuine conservative as by the genuine liberal, there today stand

9. Frank Mankiewicz (born 1924), who served as press secretary to Robert F. Kennedy and campaign manager for George McGovern, wrote a political column and in 1977 became chairman of National Public Radio.

many urgings to inaction. The strongest was once established religion; the strongest today is the economic realm.

This realm does not have to "buy" individual newspapers or journalists, television companies and reporters. It no longer has to work through the blackmail of threatening to withdraw its advertising. In fact, it now generously contributes its advertising: life is brought to us "by a grant from Mobil Oil." Its seduction is more sophisticated. It encourages the elevation of every other realm of life above that of politics, so that we are encouraged to believe that no one is more base than the politician, and that it is only from mundane motives that free men go to the polls. The economic realm can afford to let people believe in gods and gurus, in art and play, because these are ultimately not threatening to it; in fact it can manipulate them. Over its review of the Rauschenberg exhibition that opened in Washington in election week, *The Washington Post* put the rather brilliant headline "Goofy and Grand." It is an enticing summary of everything in Rauschenberg that makes his work a pleasure to look at. But the bother is that it *is* goofy, as well as grand; and that is why even the world of art, without the defense of politics, is a world of culture which the economic realm can manipulate. It can render it harmless, as art has indeed been rendered harmless.

The one thing that the economic realm knows about the political world is that it is not goofy. So its only defense against politics is to make it seem less than grand. This is the corruption to which political journalism is at the moment subject. Political journalists have been seduced into believing that politics is probably if not necessarily ignoble.

The moral information which has been lacking in the coverage of this year's election is the conviction that the political world is inherently good. It is as if every journalist is afraid that he might be caught in believing in something or in somebody.

Yet on the whole, the political world in the past 200 years has accomplished a great deal of good for a vast number of people. There is more for it to do: the art of the necessary is always in need of redefinition. People whom we did not think of as poor yesterday seem to us to be poor today, because we have redefined our idea of poverty; we have raised the threshold, by the energy of our politics.

What is wrong with Walter Cronkite's laying on of hands, once he is told who has won, is that he is laying his hands on power and not on politics. Jimmy Carter is open to every nit-picking slur until suddenly he has power; and that obeisance to power is just as much a rejection of the political world as the nit-picking at the mere candidate before he has achieved it.

Politics is not primarily about power. It is about the will to power: the will to use the resources of the political world to subdue the other realms when they become overweening. To make my own position clear, there are all kinds of things about Jimmy Carter that make my stomach turn with apprehension. One must remain alert to every cunning and temptation in him, as in all great politicians. But from the beginning he has looked like a great politician, a man who has learned from his own background and his own time; and the one thing that the political world needs today is a great politician to restore its claims to supremacy.

"The pollsters will never go out on a limb," said Jimmy Carter when he realized that he had won, using the phrase with which I began. It is an important remark because if he had ever heeded the polls more than his own judgment, he would never have started on his improbable journey. However many skills, however much ruthlessness, contributed to his victory, they were much less important than his own willingness to go out on a limb, with the deep conviction, as trustworthy as it may be in a priest or an artist of their own worlds, that the political world is there to be used to alter our perceptions and our condition.

If political journalists do not also believe as much, they should get jobs as fashion writers, or movie critics; or abandon journalism altogether and be satisfied to be interior decorators. If revolution is not a picnic, the politics of a free country is not a boutique. The political world today needs an imagery of grandeur equal to its own measure: to excite that imagery may well prove to be Jimmy Carter's most lasting contribution to our times. He should be encouraged to attempt it.

Magnates, Mischief, and Mass Circulation

Piers Brendon, in *The Life and Death of the Press Barons* (Atheneum), defines a press baron "by his extravagant display of journalistic independence. What distinguished [him] from a mere conductor of newspapers . . . was his will to freedom. He was determined to run his life and his journals with as little interference as possible from outside—from politicians, commercial interests, advertisers, from his own kind, sometimes even from his readers, from popular opinion itself." The press barons might be driven by a "ruthless quest for wealth, power and independence. But whatever their motives, their refusal to endure restraints on journalistic freedom was a real boon."

Chapter by chapter, Brendon crosses and recrosses the Atlantic, looking at the newspaper owners in the United States and Britain. His thesis is that they gave newspapers an unusual period of independence between two, possibly more natural, periods of subservience. Newspapers before the press barons, living on nothing more substantial than their wits, sold themselves to political parties, while newspapers today are subservient to the accountants of large corporations, who all too often look on their newspapers only as peripheral and rather risky investments. Brendon argues that in between these two periods the press barons, with their personal wealth and their exuberance, gave the press a brief reign of independence and even a kind of

Grand Street, Autumn 1983. Reprinted by permission from the Estate of Henry Fairlie.

glory. Agree with Brendon or not, his thesis makes his rogues' gallery very much more rewarding than the mere collection of anecdotes his book could well have been.

And what rogues most of them were! Let it not be thought I am accusing any press baron of being a "criminal" or a "swindler." I am satisfied with the third definition in the *OED:* "One of a mischievous disposition"; with just the hint that in their mischief they went to the limits, and sometimes beyond, of what the law, fair play, or even ordinary human decency, would permit to more mannerly and less uninhibited men. From my own experience of some of them—actual, self-made Lords—they acted on a simple principle: if you wish to play in the Big League, you had better not whimper when the game gets rough.

When I was employed by Lord Rothermere to write for his *Daily Mail,* I received the inevitable bid for my services from Lord Beaverbrook.[1] It all went exactly as I had heard it described by others so often before. First there was the lunch in his penthouse in St. James's: the marvelously engaging conversation, rich with anecdotes of the great of half a century, as he pulled them down with impish malice to show what mortals they were; the rapid-fire questions thrown in abruptly to catch me off guard and test me—always one was aware of being tested; and then the traditional offer over the dessert: "I don't know what the *Mail* is paying you. But whatever it is, I'll double it." I had three small mouths to feed at the time, and anyhow I had been bewitched by the legendary (and real) charm. I murmured that I thought I

1. Esmond Harmsworth, 2nd Viscount Rothermere (1898– 1978) was the conservative proprietor of the *Daily Mail,* which he inherited from his father. Max Aitken, 1st Baron Beaverbrook (1879–1964) owned the *Evening Standard* and *Daily Express,* founded the *Sunday Express,* and was one of the most powerful press barons of Fleet Street. Canadian-born, he served as Tory MP for Ashton-Under-Lyne and was part of Churchill's war cabinet.

would like to write for him. "Go and see Pickering"—then editor of the *Daily Express*—"right now. I'll have called him before you get there." I didn't quite like that. It seemed too naked a statement that his editors had no freedom. It was being made amply clear, in other words, that I would be working directly for him—till he tired of me!

I went to see Pickering. "Yes, Henry, I've heard from the Beaver," he said. "Of course I'd like to have you here, but if you will listen to my advice, I sincerely hope—for your own sake—that you won't come." I was surprised at the number of Beaverbrook journalists who said the same during the next couple of days as I sought advice. But my moment of decision came while I was alone, pondering the temptation, and I remembered one of the things that Beaverbrook had said to me. He had just cut open a pear, and I had done the same. They seemed to me two of the juiciest pears that had ever graced the table of a nobleman. Beaverbrook called the butler: "These pears aren't ripe. Take them away," and my luscious pear was whisked from me, without my permission, and with no other fruit put in its place. "Ever been to America?" the imp asked. I confessed that I had not yet been, but wanted to go very much. "I would take you to America," he said, and then added: "I could show you worlds you've never seen." As I sat alone two evenings later, his words came back to me. Where had I heard something like them before? I remembered and took down the Bible. Matthew 4:8–10:

> Again, the devil taketh him up into an exceeding high mountain, and showeth him all the kingdoms of the world, and the glory of them;
>
> And saith unto him, All these things will I give thee, if thou wilt fall down and worship me.
>
> Then saith Jesus unto him, Get thee hence, Satan.

I thought that the devil—I mean, Beaverbrook—had gone to his home in the south of France, and sent him a telegram through the *Daily Express* office: "Imperative I talk to you before I sign contract." But the next day one of his top henchmen found me in a Fleet Street pub, and said: "The Beaver wants to see you at five o'clock this evening—yes, he's in London." So I returned to St. James's. He sat down on a couch next to me: "What's the trouble?" I said: "I can't sign. I think you would kill my work." He paused a second or two, and then he said: "Heard that before. Heard it often: that I kill writers. Well, let's go through them one by one"; and starting far back, with Arnold Bennett, he mentioned without pause about twenty more names of his top writers and editors over the years, adding after each of their names: "Tested him. He was weak. . . . Tested him, he was weak." He made only one exception: Michael Foot, who, though a left-wing Socialist, had nonetheless been a very good editor of the *Evening Standard:* "Michael Foot. Tested him. Found him strong. . . . It's not I who kill them, Fairlie, it's they who are weak. As for you, would I kill the goose that lays the golden egg? Would I do that?" I looked down at my lap, raised my head, and said to him: "Yes, I think you would do just that." (I had taken along a written letter of guarantees of independence that I wanted him to sign. He had refused.) I rose and said: "I thank you for your offer. It's very flattering, and I appreciate it. But, you see, I don't think I'm any stronger than all the others."

Several years later, at the time of the leadership crisis in the Conservative Party in 1964, I was for various reasons not doing any journalism. I felt it was a pity. I then knew Conservative Party politics inside out. One of Beaverbrook's men again tracked me down one evening in a Fleet Street pub, and took me aside: "The Beaver wants you to cover the Conservative crisis for the *Express*." "On what terms?" I asked. "Your terms," he answered. "As a free lance. Just cover the story, as long as it lasts." Half an hour later I was throwing down my coat in the *Express* office, and turned in the first of a series of front-page stories—scoops, some of them—which earned me a bit of money and a fair amount of grudging congratulations from my colleagues on other papers.

The story seems to me worth telling because so much of Beaverbrook is in it. The fascination of the man to anyone who met him. The belief that he could buy what and whom he wanted. The challenge to you to prove that you were not weak, that you could play in the Big League with him. And the waiting for years after my refusal, to pick the right moment when I wished with all my heart to be covering a great political story, offering me the opportunity on terms of mutual respect. Most of my news stories on the crisis came from my own knowledge and digging, but for about four months I had Beaverbrook again and again on the telephone; deeply embroiled in what he liked most, a good political fight to the death; feeding me information of his own, which only he could have gathered; the imp's glee at some politician's discomfiture, audible to me even over the telephone; and finally the almost total lack of interference in my actual writing of each story. I could not but admire the old man. Alive and throbbing with the excitement of politics, alive above all with precisely that characteristic of the press baron on which Brendon lays his emphasis: the glorious (I use the word deliberately) independence of party and of politicians—I was never once asked to suppress a story or weaken an adjective out of fear of hurting the feelings of a politician whom the Beaver might know. His newspaper—the story: those came first. But it needs to be emphasized that if I had been a member of his staff, if I had been bound to him over the years, I do not believe that the relationship would have been so exhilarating. It was not long afterward that the famous banquet was given in his honor, only a couple of weeks or so before he died. I looked round the vast assembly of all those whose lives he had touched, and I looked at the now frail and wizened old man, who exerted himself for one last act of self-assertion, getting out of his wheelchair to walk slowly and unsteadily to the head table, while the whole political and literary society of London stood and applauded him all the way. How could one not feel that one was watching the passing of the press barons?

Brendon is good on Beaverbrook: "sought advice voraciously and took it abstemiously"; the daily excitement of a newspaper which to him "became quite intoxicating when mixed with mischief and served without restraint"; even the little ditty that he would sing over the telephone to his editors, "Sow the seeds of discontent, Sow the seeds of discontent." Brendon is also good on the difference between the Harmsworth brothers: Lord Northcliffe,[2] the megalomaniacal newspaper genius; and Lord Rothermere, the dull financial genius who built the *Mail* group's commercial prosperity. But he does not deal with the 2nd Viscount Rothermere, who owned the *Daily Mail* when I worked for it; and here another story is worth telling.

During the 1959 general election, when I was writing a political column for the *Mail*, a very Conservative newspaper, I not only attacked Harold Macmillan, who was the Conservative Prime Minister, and supported Hugh Gaitskell, the leader of the Labour Party, but I fatally carried my hopes into prophecy, predicting that Gaitskell would win. In the event, Macmillan doubled his majority.

A couple of weeks later, the editor, William Hardcastle, told me that I was invited to dinner by Rothermere at his home in the

2. Alfred Harmsworth (1865–1922), 1st Viscount Northcliffe, built an empire of more than one hundred newspapers, magazines, and other publications, including the *Daily Mail*, which he founded, the *Observer*, and the *Times*.

shadow of St. James's Palace: just Rothermere, Hardcastle, and myself. After polite cocktails, the conversation was turned at dinner to my (obviously to Rothermere) rather radical and outlandish views. I could not stand the man—meaninglessly civil, mediocre, arrogant, full of sly menace. I cut loose, and not only repeated my objections to Macmillan's election slogan, "You've Never Had It So Good," but attacked the *Mail*'s support of Fascism under his father. As I spoke, I became aware of a tapping on the table; it was Rothermere, rapping his fork on the rich polished mahogany, as if I were a schoolboy to be corrected and intimidated. With that, I shut up; the dinner was soon over; Hardcastle and I left. "I cannot say, Henry," said Bill, as we strolled along Pall Mall, "that you strengthened your position." A couple of days later, he called me to his office: "Henry," he said, "you're being sent to Africa." "For how long?" I asked. "For as long as you like. Go where you like. Write what you like. I have a feeling, Henry, you're being told—*get lost.*" Actually, since it was the year when Macmillan was "giving away" Africa, it was a fascinating assignment. But Beaverbrook would never have reacted as Rothermere did to my election columns. Beaverbrook's papers were conservative, indeed, but Rothermere's were *party* newspapers: a world of difference, illustrating Brendon's thesis.

It is difficult to convey the richness of characters, stories, and judgment that Brendon compresses with apparent effortlessness into this splendidly written book. There is James Gordon Bennett Sr when he began the *Herald:* "Nothing can prevent . . . success but God Almighty, and he happens to be entirely on my side." (An interesting number of press barons seem to have believed that. W. T. Stead of the *Pall Mall Gazette* called God his "Senior Partner.") The altogether outrageous Bennett stands at the beginning of Brendon's story, and with some justice since he went on to write in his paper: "Get out of my way, ye drivelling editors and drivelling politicians," which is a fair Declaration of Independence. There is Joseph Pulitzer growing demented with "a pathological aversion to noise," which grew so terrifying that finally "he constructed a completely sound-proof annex to his mansion on New York's East Seventy-third Street. Known as 'The Vault,' it was connected to the main house by a passage hung on ball-bearings to prevent vibration. It had padded doors, cork floors, double walls and triple-glazed windows." But not until "the ventilation chimney had been hung with thousands of silken threads to absorb every resonance, did Pulitzer attain quiet." How Pulitzer, blind and half-crazed, morbidly suspicious and irritable, "rose from the depths of yellow journalism and set himself up as the conscience of America" is a story that Brendon sketches well but that needs a master ironist.

Then there is William Randolph Hearst, of whom Charlie Chaplin said: "Rockefeller felt the usual burden of money; Pierpont Morgan was imbued with the power of it; but Hearst spent millions nonchalantly, as though it were weekly pocket money." To him at first, as one of his foreign correspondents said, journalism was "an enchanted playground in which giants and dragons were to be slain simply for the fun of the thing; a Never-Never Land with pirates and Indians and fairies; a wonderful, wonderful rainbow, with uncounted gold at the other end of it." And with Hearst was the pathetic Marion Davies, by her own admission a "silly, giggly idiot," whose idea of bliss was to drown in a tub of gin, but who at least had the wit to say of her relationship with Hearst: "Hearst come, Hearst served." Then there are the McCormicks, and the Pattersons, and Edward Wyllis Scripps, who founded thirty-two newspapers altogether, and held shares in fifteen others, exercising his detailed management from his desert retreat, "Miramar," outside San Diego, where his editors found him, "a hulking, bearded figure in a skull-cap (he was terrified of catching cold), rough clothes and rawhide boots," smoking forty cigars and drinking a gallon of whiskey each day.

Are we ready after such a profusion of extraordinary characters to come to Rupert Murdoch, who on a global scale, says Brendon, "has perhaps achieved the greatest spread of newspaper power in history"? How can we fit this tycoon into the gallery of rogues? Is he to be measured against them, and if so, how does he stand the comparison?

From all the stories in Murdoch's papers that Brendon might have chosen as characteristic, he repeats from the *San Antonio News* one defying parody:

> A divorced epileptic, who told police she was buried alive in a bathtub full of wet cement and later hanged upside down in the nude, left San Antonio for good this week-end. The tiny, half-blind woman, suffering from diabetes, recounted for the *News* a bizzare story filled with rape, torture and starvation.

What a lead! What else could one throw in? Perhaps a tiny, half-blind, leprous pervert? But, no, at that Murdoch's papers, with their very individual, elusive standards of propriety, would draw a line.

All the same, Brendon is disappointing on Murdoch. He passes over too quickly Murdoch's political use of his papers. Murdoch's promotion of Edward Koch, first successfully as mayor, and then disastrously as governor (although that happened, presumably, as Brendon's book was going to press), is a cautionary tale, a fable with several morals: about the limits of the political influence of the press, about the role of a city newspaper, about the always uncertain role of the outsider who tries to play in the same league as the Establishment—any Establishment. It is especially a cautionary tale about confusing circulation with influence over the readers. Murdoch's political use of his papers is perhaps most important in his role as proprietor of *The Times* of London. Brendon is extremely sketchy about *The Times* under Murdoch—and one notices that he sometimes writes for Murdoch's *Sunday Times.*

When Murdoch bought *The Times* and appointed Harold Evans to be the editor, Evans asked me to contribute a weekly column from Washington. I was aware from time to time, talking over the telephone to London, that I was being gently guided—or, rather, deflected from pursuing too freely my rather unconservative views and interpretations. I knew that this did not represent how Evans, left to himself, would have liked things to be. He believed that *The Times* should, as an independent newspaper, find space for several different attitudes. The smallest hints over the phone made me realize that Evans, quite justifiably, was trying to protect his flanks, as he maneuvered to avoid a head-on collision with Murdoch. The collision, of course, came; out went Evans and, along with others of those he had appointed, out went my column. The whole story was complicated. Evans was *not* altogether in the right; Murdoch was *not* altogether in the wrong. Evans was, for one thing, a spendthrift editor. At a time when *The Times* was losing millions a year, its survival at stake from day to day, he not only tolerated but seemed also to encourage a profligate expenditure by some (favored) members of the editorial staff. Perhaps such expenses are only a drop in the bucket, compared with the millions that *The Times* still loses, but it was a corroding example. Evans also did not handle—either ruthlessly enough or appreciatively enough: one or the other would have done—the traditionalists on the editorial staff. In short, he gave too many hostages to fortune and, as the struggle with Murdoch for his independence as an editor deepened, he found himself more and more isolated, until all that Murdoch had to do was saw off the branch.

Yet Murdoch is the fitting climax to Brendon's thesis. His opening sentence to the chapter on Murdoch is precisely worded: "Certainly nothing has been able to halt the spectacular expansion of Rupert Murdoch's *international press corporation.*" (My italics.) We are in a world very different from that of the old press barons. Brendon is left only to wonder inconclusively what course Murdoch's career will now follow. "It largely depends on whether he becomes, as seems probable, an entrepreneur fully engaged in directing companies, raising loans and organizing takeovers, or whether he remains primarily what his upbringing made him, a newspaperman." But how much freedom to choose does Murdoch really have, when he is "heavily preoccupied with defending and expanding an empire which is always stretched to its financial limits"? The conglomerates that increasingly control the press on both sides of the Atlantic have their own drives. "When [the Lonrho corporation] acquired the *Observer* in 1981, it behaved as though it were simply adding to its growth by a single economic unit"; and in one of his few limp statements, Brendon says: "The watchdog of the people is in danger of becoming the lapdog of international commerce."

Brendon is quite right to fix on the diversification of the "communications corporations" outside the field of newspapers as the most important recent development and one of still immeasurable consequences. But as he himself hints here and there, one began to notice a shift of power back in the 1950s, even in what were still then the press barons' own fiefdoms. I once complained to a great old reporter on the *Daily Mail* that too often, when I went to discuss an idea (even for that night's paper) with Bill Hardcastle as the editor, too often there was a buzz from the fifth floor—where the managers and accountants were—and Hardcastle always had to drop our discussion and go at once upstairs. The old reporter said to me: "When the editor starts going up to the fifth floor, instead of the fifth floor coming down to the editor, the newspaper *as a newspaper* is lost." Brendon curiously does not touch the *Washington Post,* a paper made in the last fifty years by three "press barons" by his definition: Eugene Meyer, Philip Graham, his son-in-law, and Katharine Graham, his daughter. It can be convincingly demonstrated—it has been done best by Ben Bagdikian—that a crucial structural change in the *Post* company in recent years has altered and damaged the character of the paper. I put it thus in an article in the *New Republic* ("Profit Without Honor," May 7, 1977): "There is a sense in which Kay Graham, since she converted the *Post* into a public company, is hardly a free agent any longer, is herself subject to the faceless managers who run the corporate system. And this is true also, of course, of the proprietorship of the *New York Times.* It is the main reason why the editorial floor has in a lifetime been surrendered to the managerial floor."

The fascination of Rupert Murdoch is, as Brendon suggests, that he's the most vivid, most successful, of the present-day captive controllers of the press. Brendon says that they are "at once too captive and too free," too free because of the gigantic resources that a conglomerate can command; so that, whereas the old press barons "were, in one sense, responsible to their readers," because they could not make their newspapers successful if there were not enough readers, the diversified corporations today "can sustain newspapers which have circulations in thousands and losses in millions." Well, they can sustain products that *look* like newspapers. Newspapers used to be for wrapping fish and chips in; newspapers now are for wrapping another conglomerate product in. The underlying dissatisfaction that we all feel today at reading *The Times* or the *Observer,* the *New York Times* or the *Washington Post,* is that, for all the often striking talent they still employ, we sense throughout the unease of the top journalistic staff at producing a product for the extraneous motives of the conglomerate as it shifts investments around, explores tax loopholes, and seeks to attract capital from the "vast pension funds, unit trusts and other such institutions," which have come to dominate the British and American stock markets.

The development has gone further in Britain, where three conglomerates—Reed International, Trafalgar House, and News International (Murdoch's corporation)—own ten of the seventeen national newspapers, representing almost 75 percent of the daily and some 90 percent the Sunday circulation. But Brendon's own telling account of what has happened to the *Los Angeles Times* since Otis Chandler turned the Times-Mirror Company into a huge conglomeration of commercial interests is warning enough of the way things are going. "Thinking corporately, managing through a team, writing by committee, the *Times* today identifies itself with the great industrial and financial institutions of America. . . . The flagrant lies of a press baron like General Otis were easy enough to detect, even had there not been competitors enough to expose them. The subtle ways in which Otis Chandler's *Times* distorts the truth are more difficult to spot and there are fewer independent newspapers to do the spotting." No journalist can today be happy or confident about the future of his profession. If anything, I feel more gloomy even than Piers Brendon.

How Journalists Get Rich

In the eighteen years since I first visited Washington, I have seen two major changes. The first I noticed after I had been away for three years and returned on the eve of Thanksgiving Day in 1975. I was struck by how altered the life of the city seemed, and wrote a piece for the *Washington Post*, which proclaimed in its headline: "Washington—A Capital at Last!"

By this I meant the much more varied social and cultural life that was finding expression all over the place; and I attributed it to the way Washington seemed to have become a magnet drawing young people of very different interests from all over the nation. Young artists, writers, poets, actors, musicians, and of course students—all of them much more vivid than the deadly products of the law schools making their way to the Hill in their three-piece suits—were enlivening the city in a hundred small but impressive ways.

The second major change has occurred since then. It was beginning a long time before, but has accelerated since Watergate, and the transformation has now more or less been accomplished. The change is that Washington today is less a political city and more a media city.

Though we talk easily of "the media" now, the term is recent. In its present meaning, the word is not in Webster's *Third New International Dictionary* (1966), the last complete revision of that work. It certainly did not exist when I first knew Washington. If

The Washingtonian, August 1983. Reprinted by permission from the Estate of Henry Fairlie.

my thesis about the city is to be found plausible, we must remember that the media are a new growth, not just an extension of something that went before.

The growth has had two effects on the city.

First, the primary activity of Washington is no longer the government of the country through its political institutions; it is now the sustaining of the illusion of government through the media and in obedience to the media's needs and demands.

Second, the most certain avenue to celebrity and considerable wealth is not now in the institutions of government along Pennsylvania Avenue, between 1st Street, Southeast, and 17th Street, Northwest. It is through the intricate networks of the media.

The people in the media dictate the terms. The people in the media make the killing. Even more than the three A's—attorneys, accountants, associations—that feed off the federal government, rapacious members of the media feed off every form of political activity. Abusing, if not manipulating, the protections of the First Amendment, prattling about the "public right to know," they use this city to enhance their reputations and push their incomes, first to six, and then even to seven figures.

The people of the media are today the wheelers and dealers. Point to any others so skillful at using the machinery of Washington, and so protected from any public challenge or scrutiny.

Gibbon noticed the "cloud of critics" who suddenly descended on Rome, heralding its decline and fall even as they dined off peacocks' tongues. They tore ravenously at the heart of the decomposing empire. Carlyle noticed the swarms of pestiferous lawyers who came to Paris during the French Revolution to push their schemes and advance their careers. Washington has long been used to them.

But the more dangerous insects who infest Washington today are the media: locusts who strip bare all that is green and healthy, as they chomp at it with untiring jaws; those insatiable jaws that are never lost for a word, on the screen or on the platform, and occasionally, when they can spare a moment for their old trade, in print. For these, Washington labors, and provides.

During the plagues of locusts in the Great Plains in 1874–77, one swarm contained 124 billion of the insects. Not quite so many have settled on Washington, but the numbers are still startling. According to the American Newspaper Publishers Association, Washington is the working home for 3,389 correspondents and editors, the largest concentration of journalists in the world.

The ANPA takes this figure from *Hudson's Washington News Media Contact Directory* (1983), and it is said to include every American and foreign journalist in newspapers, magazines, news services, newsletters, radio, and television. One may accept it as the basic figure, but it is certainly a severe underestimate.

The newsletters are like an army of proles. From the 1,800 trade associations in Washington that publish one or more newsletter each, from the commercial newsletters, and not least from the public-interest groups that have multiplied like rabbits, they spread into every corner of the political and business life of the city, not least in the evening when they feed and drink free.

They are important for two reasons. Their sheer numbers give the impression that the media have depth. The countless newsletters make it seem as if the media stars are backed by a great engine of information, and that is their second importance. For the media live by manufacturing their own information, and then serving it up as news, and the newsletters play a crucial role in sustaining the illusion that the media know what is going on. Why are newspapers, newsmagazines, and television news programs all so similar? They are more and more carbon copies of each other, trekking over the same ground in a very small range. They milk the same sources, and the newsletters are one of the udders.

There are also organizations like the American Enterprise Institute, which is its own media hive. Ben Wattenberg[1] of AEI needs Washington as a clown needs a three-ring circus. Ralph Nader and his organization must also be regarded as a media creature. As a rough guess, I would suggest that the number of people in the media in Washington now is about 30,000—including freelance writers like myself.

The media compete in size with the political community—the 100 senators, the 435 representatives, and their staffs. This explosive growth in the media community has taken place simultaneously with the similar inflation of the legal community. In such numbers, both are parasitic. No capital can long remain true to itself with two plagues whose common symptoms are cynicism and cant.

How does the transformation of Washington into a media city debilitate the profession? How does it debilitate the political life of the capital? How does it debilitate the public? The answers are interlocked.

The starting point is that the media are not just an extension of journalism. That is why the term had to be invented. The media trade not in substance, but in celebrity. The celebrity at the top is bought, and sells himself, for large sums. He is not selling any work. He is selling only himself.

There is now a well-worn path to this celebrity, and to the fortune it promises. No professional body ever examines the ethics of this yellow brick road.

First, you set up as a columnist. Like most first steps, this is the difficult one. But it can be done with a little application, especially when the *Washington Post* is profligate in allowing its space to be used as the launching pad to the talk shows on

1. Ben J. Wattenberg (born 1933) is a neoconservative columnist and longtime senior fellow at the American Enterprise Institute.

television. The *Post*'s op-ed page has become a joke to all serious journalists. Its main purpose has become to provide the foundation for careers that seek greater rewards outside the newspaper.

It now feeds to *Agronsky & Company:* George Will, Carl Rowan, James J. Kilpatrick, sometimes Joseph Kraft, and occasionally Hobart Rowen. It also feeds Robert Novak to *The McLaughlin Group;* George Will, again (and sometimes the executive editor of the *Post,* Benjamin Bradlee), to *This Week with David Brinkley;* and sundry others who rotate irregularly on the other political programs.

The effect of this on the profession is obvious. Fewer and fewer young journalists are willing to be and to remain just good reporters. A true and experienced reporter such as Helen Dewar of the *Post* is not made a television star. It is not the reporters—not even the foreign correspondents covering major and long-running stories—who get lifted to this celebrity; and we as readers begin to overlook them.

The young journalist wants to be a columnist. What is more, because the purpose of the column is to carry him on to television, he wants his column on the op-ed page. Richard Cohen has one of the best spots for a column in the *Post,* running down the left-hand column of the front page of the Metro section. Moreover, although I disagree with almost everything he ever says, it's a good column. He's a master of its length and form.

But Richard Cohen feels frustrated. He gets invited to do tidbits on television, and from television he gets invited to give baby lectures to organizations that do not pay much. When asked about his lecturing, he said wistfully: "I'm the warm-up for Frank Sinatra."

Poor Richard! There are just not enough lecture engagements at $7,000 a throw. He wants to be Frank Sinatra, but he won't make it from the Metro section. Yet not so long ago the city-page columnist was one of the proudest members of the profession.

Those who make it to television are an incestuous group; in fact, all Washington media at this level are incestuous. When the cameras showed us Bradlee and Brinkley and their crowd in their royal enclosure at the Super Bowl this year, they were like Roman emperors who had grown fat off the city whose team was now putting on a circus for them in the Coliseum. But which of us even then would have predicted that within a few months Bradlee would display his and Sally Quinn's sense of professional propriety by buying a $2 million-plus Georgetown house?

Using a column as the way into television can be practiced in magazines as well as newspapers. Hugh Sidey long ago translated his unsightful insights from *Time* to *Agronsky & Company*; Morton Kondracke has broken in from the *New Republic*, which shows that you can make a silk purse out of a sow's ear; and Jack Germond has made it from his several bases, including *The Washingtonian*.

The television networks rarely allow their own correspondents to express their opinions on a political talk show. The TV correspondents and anchor people are eunuchs of their profession. The studs are purchased from newspapers and magazines —for the names of these journals are the only credentials they have—and the papers never seem to examine the propriety of the deals being made.

But television is only a step to the real goal, the lecture circuit. There is the big money for utterances that require a minimum of thought or creative work. The fundamental principle of the lecture circuit is simple: to make much the same speech to organizations that wish to hear much the same thing. The system would break down if the lecturers suddenly made new speeches with original opinions.

George Will addressing the National Soft Drink Association, David Brinkley addressing the Mohawk Executive Forum or the

National Pork Producers Council, James J. Kilpatrick addressing the Potato Chip/Snack Food Association—they really do
not have to think very hard in deciding what it is that their high-
paying audiences wish to hear, and what kind of undangerous
speeches will keep them on the lecture agents' lists.

"To Our Association and Corporation Friends": Thus opens
a characteristic brochure of Conference Speakers International,
which has its offices in the Foundry, 1055 Jefferson Street in
Georgetown. Another agency, Washington Speakers Bureau, in
Alexandria, recently celebrated its second anniversary with a
gathering of clients and speakers. "As we said then," it remarks
in a brochure, "we are very grateful for the reception we have
received from the association and corporate communities." So
there is defined the kind of people who will pay.

You will search these agencies' brochures in vain for any suggestion that they will book their speakers to address a local
church group, or a citizens' group at a public library in Prince
George's County.

In the Conference Speakers International's list of speakers,
the second-largest category is Media Journalists/Correspon-
dents, and a mixed bag of media people turn up in the largest
category, Entertainment/Specialty Attractions. The Washington Speakers Bureau says that the National Association of
Chain Drug Stores last spring "asked us to provide" six speakers,
of whom three (Barbara Walters, William Safire, and Howard
K. Smith) were media people.

The lecture circuit today is a continuous road show in which the
star performers are the media creatures, each of them projected by
television, their essential instrument of self-advertisement.

Thus we have the newspapers tolerating columnists who use
their space to get on television, and television then tolerating the
use of its political programs as a way onto the lecture circuit. Is

there no editor or producer who will clean the stables of these pious self-advertisers and self-seekers? Is there not one who is aware that in such performers there is a conflict of interest?

Now and then someone tries to find out how much the media stars are paid on the lecture circuit. (Most of them were coy when asked.) It is enough to suggest the range: say, about $12,500 for an appearance by Art Buchwald, $12,000 for William Safire, $7,000 to $10,000 for George Will, and $5,000 to $7,000 for the general run. These sums have raised most media stars to millionaires and even multimillionaires.

The damage to the profession is visible and serious. The actual writing, which ought to be the center of any journalist's career, must and does suffer.

The main deficiency of American journalism is the lack of good, experienced journalists who will write at length, if need be, for those journals and reviews of opinion that do not command large circulations, and cannot pay large fees. I often hear American journalists, including some of these media stars, praise *The Spectator* of London. Well, then, look at the English journalists, of wide experience, great style, and public reputation, who contribute to write for it; and I know that it pays even less than the *New Repulic*'s ten cents a word.

It gives me no pleasure to say that George Will's columns, which promised so much seven years ago, have significantly deteriorated, in quality of writing, in force of ideas, in range of interest, since he began to devote so much time first to television, and then to the lecture circuit. Lecturing from 80 to 100 times a year is a time-consuming, intellectually debilitating exercise.

The common criticism that one hears made of his journalism now, often said more in sorrow than in anger, is that it has become predictable; and this surely points to his surrender of time to being a performer.

The repetitiveness and predictability of most of the columns on the op-ed page of the *Washington Post* are directly related to their unimportance in the eyes of their authors. They are hackwork, which, if their authors were not media stars, any self-respecting editor would drop. Some of these columns have lately been cut even further in length: In other words, they have become mere adjuncts to the paper's main interest in them, that they are written by media names.

There can be nothing more corroding than to give much the same lecture to much the same kind of audiences, to receive much the same applause at much the same points. The lecturer comes to believe the applause; he comes to believe that he is talking sense.

That is the influence on the profession. Before long, these performers find it hard to distinguish the lines of propriety. From addressing the trade associations and corporations, it is a small step to being a paid consultant to them. There is every reason for believing that some well-known journalists take substantial and even regular fees as consultants to corporations and trade associations. Occasionally we see the tip of what must be a very large iceberg.

The position in which George Will now finds himself as a result of the role he played in preparing Ronald Reagan for his television debate is not just one unfortunate lapse. It is the inevitable result—although on a dramatic scale—of a new media ethic that permits journalists to earn fame and fortune outside their strict profession. In the old days, a journalist caught in that situation would have been immediately fired.

Yet this is the same George Will who, when I was first introduced to him in 1976, said that he saw no reason, and in fact thought it rather dangerous, for a political journalist to get close to politicians.

This last point is one that I made in a book, *The Kennedy*

Promise: my shock, when I first came here, at watching the top political journalists grovel for dinner invitations to the tables of Robert McNamara or McGeorge Bundy, and watching also their groveling to have the politicians in their own homes.

That is not a fit relationship. I had just come from England, where the Conservative government had been under severe attack. The chairman of the Conservative party had said in a speech: "I would not invite a British journalist to my country house for the weekend." (He excluded American journalists from this proscription; but then American correspondents in England behave like poodles in country houses.) I answered in *The Spectator,* "I would not invite a British politician to my town house for the evening," and I believe that is the relationship that should exist.

Take not a crust of bread from a politician. Take not a cab fare from a corporation.

The effect on Washington is that, trading in celebrity, the media trade also in the wealth surrounding the celebrity. The very profession that should be the acid, relentless critic of the affluence and cynicism of Washington is now the most ostentatiously affluent and cynical profession in the city.

For God's sake, why fudge words? This is deeply corrupting of what is meant to be the political capital of the nation, the symbol of its democratic faith.

I once watched a party of high school students being escorted around the newsroom of the *Post.* One heard only one whisper, "Where are they?" They craned to see only two people, Woodward and Bernstein.

It was hard to see Woodward for a time. Incarcerated in a special glass cage in the middle of the news room, like a panda at the zoo, he surrounded himself with a tropical jungle of exotic plants. This only increased the interest. Just as the children exclaim, "Ooh!" when one of them detects the panda, lying curled up in a corner, so they exclaimed, "Ooh!" when they at last spotted Woodward, chewing a bean sprout, and no doubt ruminating on the brilliance of the Janet Cooke story, which the *Post* was, under his direction and with his extravagant praise, about to run.

It did not all begin with Woodward and Bernstein. But the *Post*'s successes in Watergate were not nearly as significant as it imagines. By pretending that Woodward and Bernstein's reporting was much more than just an ordinary day's work in journalism, the *Post* displayed an extraordinary lack of self-respect and provided a strong impetus to the transformation of journalists into media figures.

The *Post* smells of affluence. The *Post* gives no sense that it is run or written by people who know the ordinary life of the city. We are talking here of an old-fashioned notion called class. The simple fact is that the media have removed themselves from all contact in their daily lives with the ordinary middle-class life and tastes of the community.

The media increasingly see politics and government as a source of celebrity and entertainment. The media are a circus; they present politics and government as a circus.

Enough has been written in recent years of the despair of many politicians at the way in which the media now choose the issues and will even choose the candidates. A straw poll in New Hampshire, more than a year before the national conventions, is solely an invention of the media.

The media settle on the White House and Congress to strip them like locusts, for the purpose of advancing themselves on television and the lecture circuit, and year by year they complain at the debility of the political system. They are like doctors who drain the blood from a patient, and then on *Agronsky & Company* pronounce him as dying of anemia.

In all of this, I am talking less of personal motive, even in the stars, than of a collective motive that now dictates the media's standards. Those standards have become corrupt.

There is too much going on in New York for even its powerful media to dominate the city. London and Paris are capitals with a thousand stars in all kinds of professions. But in Washington there are not enough other sources of life to enable the city to resist the influence of the one profession that has at its command the main avenues of communication.

And not only the main avenues of communication to the public and to the lecture audiences, but the avenues of communication to the heart of the democratic political system.

Thus the media in Washington dictate the terms; the media in Washington make the killing. Unwilling to restrain their greed, they are asking for an outside rein.

A Radical and a Patriot

RANDOLPH BOURNE

The pandemic of influenza that swept across the world at the end of 1918 killed some 25 million people. Willard Straight, the founder and owner of *The New Republic,* died in Paris. On December 19, a brilliant and impoverished young writer, formerly a frequent contributor to *The New Republic* but then bitterly at odds with it, was bothered by a cold, and moved into the apartment of the woman he was soon to marry, on the third floor of 18 West 8th Street, New York. Three days later, gasping for breath, balking at the oxygen, he asked for an eggnog. When it was brought to him, he deliberately praised its pale yellow color; and a few minutes later he died. Not all that many years ago, if one had told that story in any reasonably literate circle, everyone would have known who it was. Randolph Bourne, dead at 32.

In a tribute that the magazine published after his death, Floyd Dell called him "one of the strong and triumphant personalities of our generation." A year later, introducing a small collection of his essays, Van Wyck Brooks acclaimed him as "the flying wedge of the younger generation itself. . . ; not the critic merely, but the leader." Writing in 1932 in his novel *1919,* John Dos Passos said that Bourne had "put a pebble in his sling/and hit Goliath square in the forehead with it." Max Lerner in the early 1940s called him "one of the men of moral and intellectual stature of

The New Republic, February 28, 1983, originally titled "A Radical and a Patriot." Reprinted by permission from the Estate of Henry Fairlie.

our century." Alfred Kazin in *On Native Grounds,* published in 1942, said that "in no one of his generation did 'the promise of American life' shine so radiantly as in Randolph Bourne." But then the legend began to fade and the reputation with it. A renewed interest in his work was shown in the 1960s by those searching for a radical tradition that was native to America. Two new collections of his essays were published, and a new and full, if unsatisfactory, biography. But this revived interest did not really catch fire. When the most comprehensive selection of his writings to date was published in 1977, with a preface by Christopher Lasch, it was not generally noticed, although Olaf Hansen, the European intellectual who made the selection, said in his introduction that Bourne was "one of the eminent figures of his time." We are faced with some interesting questions. What was the influence on his own generation? Why did his reputation fade? Most important, why should we read him now?

The bare facts of his life, although remarkable, may be given quickly. He was born in 1886. It was, as he said, "a terribly messy birth." His face was badly deformed by a bungled forceps delivery. The umbilical cord was coiled round his left ear, leaving it permanently damaged and misshapen. As if this were not enough, he contracted spinal tuberculosis at the age of four, which dwarfed him, and made him look like a "grotesque hunchback." Ellery Sedgwick, then the editor of *The Atlantic Monthly,* said of their first meeting in 1911 that in appearance Bourne was "without a redeeming feature," and that "I could not bring myself to ask him to stay to lunch." Writing to Mary Messer in 1913, Bourne described himself as a man

> cruelly blasted by the powers that brought him into the world, in a way that makes him both impossible to be desired and yet—cruel irony that wise Montaigne knew about—doubly endowed with desire.

Due to the improvidence and, it seems, the indifference of his father, he had to make his own way to the university, and he did not go to Columbia until, at the age of twenty-three, he received a scholarship. His academic performance was so good that he graduated a year early, and Columbia then awarded him the Gilder Fellowship for a year's travel in Europe. He had already made something of a name for himself, as a writer and as a spokesman of his generation, by his numerous contributions to *The Atlantic*. When he returned from Europe—he was there when the war began—*The New Republic* was just beginning. It was to be his main source of income for the next two-and-a-half years—he wrote seventy-five essays for it in that time—until he broke sharply with it on the issue of America's entry into the war. From 1916 until his death two years later, he also contributed thirty-two essays to *The Dial;* and during its brief life, seven important essays to *Seven Arts*. Given the range and length, quality and substance, of most of the pieces, it was an astonishing performance—in only four years.

By his own intellectual generation, after he died, he was elected a martyr; and in these simple facts of his life there lay, indeed, the stuff of which legends are made. The conquering of his hideous deformities, and of his early frustrations and bitterness; the spokesman but also the critic of his generation of rebellious youth who, perhaps, best clarified their impulses and aspirations; the young man who turned his back on Europe, discarding it like a worn-out coat, to proclaim "the promise of American life," to interpret it and try to energize it anew—and then. . . . Then, the lonely, unflinching opposition to America's entry into the war; the desertion of almost the entire generation that he had led; the sacrifice of his career, the wracking poverty he endured. (His own apartment was not even properly heated when he caught influenza.) When the armistice at last came, he was ready, his friends tell us, to sing the songs of America again. But he died. Of his writing and example during the war, *The Nation* said in 1920 that he had left "the cleanest picture of ourselves when we were not ourselves." It is still one of the cleanest pictures of ourselves.

Let us begin at the end, with his opposition to the war. On the central issue his position was rather awkward. He was not a pacifist. He did not deny that war might sometimes be justified; he avoided saying that World War I was an absolute evil. In an article in *The Dial* in September 1917, which does not appear in the collections of his writings, he explicitly detaches himself in his first paragraph from the evangelism of the conscientious objector. As he put it in *Seven Arts* at the same time, "We can be apathetic with a good conscience." Because of his handicaps, he would not be drafted. This placed him in an uncomfortable position, which privately he did not altogether face. There is something unsatisfactory in his advice: "Let us compel the war to break in on us. . . . When we are broken in on, we can yield to the inexorable. Those who are conscripted will have been broken in on. If they do not want to be martyrs, they will have to be victims." This is scarcely a ringing call to oppose the war. If he had been drafted, would he have gone? We cannot tell.

But it was not really the war in itself that interested him; at no time did he consider the occasions that led to the war. He was least satisfactory when he argued in "The Collapse of American Strategy" (August 1917) that America should have remained neutral so that it could continue to be the arbiter. So what did interest him? "There is work to be done to prevent this war of ours"—not Germany's, mind you—"from passing into popular mythology as a holy crusade." He was one of the very few intellectuals in 1917 who did not buy the notion that America was entering the war for selfless reasons to make the world safe for democracy. "There must be some irreconcilables left who will not even accept the war with walrus tears." But that gives only a hint of his insight or his impulse.

In his opposition to the war, he was cutting far deeper. One can disagree with him about the war—as I do—and still be thankful for the position he took. He was shocked by an unsigned editorial in *The New Republic* on April 14, 1917, which contained a remarkable passage at which one still rubs one's eyes. Denying that "the bankers or capitalists" had taken America into the war, it claimed the credit (no less word) for the intellectuals.

> The effective and decisive work on behalf of war has been accomplished by an entirely different class—a class which may be comprehensively described as the "intellectuals." . . . The American nation is entering the war under the influence of a moral verdict reached after the utmost deliberation of the more thoughtful members of the community.

Bourne was never again to write a really political article for the magazine. Two months later his answer to the editorial appeared in *Seven Arts:*

> A war made deliberately by intellectuals! A calm moral verdict, arrived at after penetrating study of the inexorable facts! . . . An intellectual class, gently guiding a nation through sheer force of ideas into what other nations had entered only through predatory craft or popular hysteria or military madness.

The pages burned with his scorn.

Bourne had found the theme that held together everything else he said: not simply the guilt of his own intellectual generation, but the betrayal by the "intellectual class"—which its representatives at *The New Republic* had so clearly and loftily identified—of its vocation and its responsibility to American society. He pursued the theme in a series of essays—which should be read together, and each in its entirety—in which the fierceness of the conviction still scorches. If they have an unyielding moral force, as is often said, it lies in an unyielding intellectual commitment. The criticisms that have been made in our own time of "the best and the brightest" for their responsibility for American involvement in the Vietnam War seem scarcely more than a form of the higher gossip when contrasted with Bourne's criticisms of the nature of the intellectuals' participation in World War I. We may still see through his prism. We must.

No one recognized more clearly at the time that something new had happened. For the technical organization and management of modern war, governments required the collaboration of the intellectual class. He saw the intellectuals—many of them his friends and colleagues—give this collaboration in 1917–1918. "It has been a bitter experience to see the unanimity with which the American intellectuals have thrown their support to the use of the war-technique." He wrote of "the coalescence of the intellectual classes in support of the military programme"; and one may recall in passing, for it is usually forgotten, that Eisenhower included the intellectual class in the military-industrial complex. When Bourne says of 1917 that "Our intellectuals consort with war-boards," we can count how many intellectuals today have launched their public careers from war boards. "War is the health of the state," he was later to proclaim. War had become the profit of the intellectual.

As he drove wider and deeper with his theme, his voice carries with it an edge to our own time. He warned that this intellectual collaboration must lead "toward the riveting of a semi-military state-Socialism on the country." He pointed to "the undemo-cratic nature of this war-liberalism." He said that

> the old radicalism has found a perfectly definite
> level, and there is no reason to think that it will not
> remain there. Its flowering appears in the technical
> organization of the war by an earnest group of
> young liberals, who direct their course by an oppor-
> tunist programme of State-socialism at home and a
> league of benevolently imperialistic nations abroad.

We may wish to qualify some of the harshness of his judgments, but we cannot deny that, writing in 1917 and not in 1968, he anticipated much of the course of American liberalism in this century, and many of the dangers, still not met, of a permanent war-state to the health of democracy. The size of today's defense budget is not just an economic but a political threat.

For he pushed yet deeper, wherever it took him. John Dewey had been his mentor since his days at Columbia. As late as March 1915 he had idolized him in *The New Republic*: " . . . the most significant thinker in America . . . , this intensely alive, futuristic philosophy . . . , some of the wisest words ever set to paper." In an essay in *Seven Arts* in October 1917, "Twilight of Idols," he expressed the depth of his disillusion. Again he reaches to our own time. For when he turned on Dewey for his support of American participation in the war, finding "a slack-ening in his thought for our guidance and stir, and the inade-quacy of his pragmatism as a philosophy of life in this emer-gency," he was anticipating the criticisms that must be made of the "pragmatic liberals" of our own time. He attacked the prag-matic intellectual liberal realists for believing that they could control events by giving their services to the very interests and forces that had created the events.

The realist thinks he at least can control events by linking himself to the forces that are moving. . . . But if it is a question of controlling war, it is difficult to see how the child on the back of a mad elephant is to be any more effective in stopping the beast than is the child who tries to stop him from the ground. If the war is too strong for you to prevent, how is it going to be weak enough for you to control . . . ?

In the nuclear age, that question is a hundred times more disquieting.

Almost half a century later this was my criticism, in *The Kennedy Promise*, of the liberal intellectuals who served John F. Kennedy:

The pragmatic liberal, acting within a "consensus" that he seeks both to foster and to manipulate, frees himself from political values, only to find that he has bound himself to react pragmatically to events as they occur, able to judge only their urgency, and not their importance.

(We now even have a phrase for it: crisis management.) The genius of Bourne was that he recognized this type as soon as he first arrived in Washington from the universities. In 1915 he praised Dewey because he said that "The mind is . . . a tool by which we adjust ourselves to the situations in which life puts us." But in 1917 he wrote of this instrumentalism:

To those of us who have taken Dewey's philosophy almost as our American religion, it never occurred that values could be subordinated to technique. . . . But there always was that unhappy ambiguity in his doctrine as to just how values were created. . . . It is now becoming plain that unless you start with the vividest kind of poetic vision, your instrumentalism is likely to land you just where it has landed this younger intelligentsia which is so happily and busily engaged in the national enterprise of war.

We are again brought sharply into our own time when he says that this younger intelligentsia has been trained to be

immensely ready for the executive ordering of events, pitifully unprepared for the intellectual interpretation or the idealistic focusing of ends. . . . They have absorbed the secret of scientific method as applied to political administration. They are liberal, enlightened, aware. They are touched with creative intelligence toward the solution of political and industrial problems. They are a wholly new force in American life, the product of the swing in the colleges from a training that emphasized classical studies to one that emphasized political and economic values. . . . Practically all this element, one would say, is lined up in the service of the war-technique.

He wonders "what scope they would have had for their intelligence without it." We know the answer each year in June when there come from the great universities to Washington, in their droves, those who have

no clear philosophy of life except that of intelligent service, the admirable adaptation of means to ends . . . , vague as to what kind of society they want, or what kind of society America needs, but . . . equipped with all the administrative attitudes and talents necessary to attain it.

The law schools now feed them to Washington, as interchangeable as disc jockeys. Every administration, liberal or conservative, must endure them.

> The war—or American promise; one must choose.
> One cannot be interested in both. . . . The conservation of American promise is the present task for this generation of malcontents and aloof men and women.

This was another note he struck—"the effect of the war will be to impoverish American promise"—and in it sounded his earlier writing. He did not change, he followed through. Herbert Croly, the first editor of *The New Republic*, had published *The Promise of American Life* in 1909, when Bourne went to Columbia. In looking to the fulfillment of the promise, Croly placed much of the emphasis on technical and organizational efficiency, a reflection of the time at which he wrote. Bourne uses the phrase, "the American promise," again and again, and surely deliberately, to give it his own meaning. He broke with the "new republicans," as he called them, on a deeper issue than the war.

Bourne's relations with *The New Republic* are of more than parochial interest. Croly and his fellow editors were sufficiently impressed by him to make him a contributing editor as soon as he returned from Europe. This was, as Max Lerner said, an ornamental role; as I am able to confirm, it is an ornamental title. (Most contributing editors of any magazine neither edit nor contribute very much.) Bourne was disappointed because his position did not give him any financial security. (Things have not changed.) His biographer says gently that this indicated a certain foresight on the part of the editors, "for though Bourne was a frequent visitor to the office during the years 1914–1916 . . .

his path led from that sanctum, rather than to it"; and this was "perhaps inevitable given his firm determination to be heard and his unwillingness to submerge himself into any of the movements of his time."

But there was more to it than the cussedness of by far the most independent and original voice that contributed to *The New Republic* in those years. The most famous of Croly's fellow editors, Walter Lippmann, wrote *Drift and Mastery* in 1914. It echoed the promise of which Croly had written five years before. Man's scientific knowledge now enabled man to escape from the "jungle of disordered growth." Man could now master himself and his environment; change had become "a matter of invention and deliberate experiment." The scientific spirit made possible "the discipline of democracy, the escape from drift, the outlook of a freeman." Simon Patten, in another key book of the period, had written: "The final victory of man's machinery over nature's is the next logical step in evolution." This was the intellectual credo of the Progressive era, and from the start Bourne would have none of it. When he spoke of "the American promise," he spoke of something that was still open, not closed and finishing: not a technique or system.

In July 1916 he wrote a remarkable article for *The Atlantic*. It was called "Trans-National America." Later that year he adapted it for *The Menorah Journal*, where it appeared as "The Jew and Trans-National America." Only those who know how fearful was the alarm and how fierce the dislike with which the mass immigration at the beginning of this century was met—even by cultivated men; one may almost say, especially by them—can have any idea of how unusual was the welcome that Bourne gave to this transformation of America and how unbounded the vision he had of its future.

America is a unique sociological fabric, and it bespeaks poverty of imagination not to be thrilled at the innumerable potentialities of so novel a union of men. . . . It is for the younger generation to accept this cosmopolitanism, and carry it along with self-conscious and fruitful purpose.

This was not only imaginative sympathy; it was also intellectual acuteness.

"We must perpetuate the paradox that our American cultural tradition lies in the future. It will be whatever we make out of this incomparable opportunity of attacking the future with a new key." He never wrote more remarkable sentences than these:

Just in so far as our American genius has expressed the pioneer spirit, the adventurous, forward-looking drive of a colonial empire, is it representative of the whole America of the many races and peoples, and not of any partial or traditional enthusiasm. And only as that pioneer note is sounded can we really speak of the American culture. As long as we thought of Americanism in terms of the "melting pot," our American culture lay in the past. It was something to which the new Americans were to be moulded.

He was "beyond the melting pot" almost half a century before Moynihan and Glazer. "The failure of the melting pot"—this in 1915, one must recall—"far from closing the great American democratic experiment, means that it has only just begun."

It has been said that Bourne was in this, as in so much else, the prophet of solutions only now being tried. The endurance of ethnicity even in the now unhyphenated American; the attempt to create or recover the intermediary associations by which people may more securely and even enthusiastically govern themselves; and above all, the unceasing effort to give to American nationality a particular meaning, then and now: again and again at the beginning of this century, he pointed the radicals of his generation to the truths, to the possibilities, which the liberals of this century then conceded to the conservatives. As he warned against the riveting of state-Socialism on America in the war, he was already far ahead of the flabby efforts of liberals now to reinvigorate their creed.

I have said that he was not really interested in the war itself. If we do not understand this, we will not understand his uniqueness. "For many of us, resentment against the war has meant a vivider consciousness of what we are seeking in American life," and he preserved the hope "that in the recoil from war we may find the treasures we are looking for." A malcontent? But how generous a one. Aloof? But how wedded to America. His biographer is not being cheaply sentimental when he says of Bourne's death that "America lost a son who loved her as much as any who had been in the trenches." He belonged to a generation of rebels and, from the publication of his undergraduate essays in *Youth and Life* in 1913, became its "clear-minded leader and critic." No other name of that rebellious youth has survived so strong and unstained. The rebellion had been celebrated by Van Wyck Brooks in *America's Coming-of-Age* in 1915. But it was Paul Rosenfeld, another of the rebels, who said in 1924 that, even as a young man, Brooks had "suffered from the third-ratedness, the sogginess, the impotence of American culture," and he went on: "The death of Randolph Bourne, for one thing alone, has deprived him of a powerful stimulus. The little soldier of liberty was the best of foils for the somewhat diffident scholar."

From where, in Bourne, did it come? Every subsequent writer on Bourne seems to find it necessary to deal first with the legend, the election to martyrdom, and even canonization by his generation after the war, as if to get them out of the way. But Bourne was one of those writers from whom, if we are to appreciate his work, we cannot strip either his life or the legend. We need a term of Christian theology to describe his example. Witness. To bear witness is to testify by words and deeds, or through the goodness of one's life and work, to a personal acceptance of the Christian faith. Bourne was not a Christian—he left open the question of whether there is a God—but we may use the term. Men may become martyrs by their deaths—and Bourne's early death left his generation stricken—but the witness of their lives also counts.

To this personal witness we may then add his sense of the role of the intellectual in public affairs. While he was deeply, even intensely, engaged in the social and political issues of the time— he touched on almost all of them, and almost always with the same clarity—he nonetheless believed that the intellectual should stand in his own realm and from there criticize the political or the economic realms. Thus, the growth of corporations in his day bothered him, and his criticisms of the corporate system are acute, but he did not waste his time thinking that one could bust the trusts, and he certainly placed little faith in regulating them under government supervision. This was why he saw no need to be a socialist or a conservative. If the rest of American society was kept vigorous and alert—including the intellectual realm—then it was a large and open enough society to contain, in the end, any overweening power. The struggle was unending —there was no complacency in him—but if the intellectual remained on his own ground, refusing to collaborate, he would play his role, and, however pitifully in his case, earn his keep.

One of Bourne's earliest essays—he was only twenty-five at the time, and still an undergraduate at Columbia—appeared in *The*

Atlantic in September 1911. It was called "The Handicapped— By One of Them." It has, as far as I can judge, one fault. He was both handicapped *and deformed.* He does not make it clear that he was writing as someone who was not only disabled, but also so facially deformed that a sensitive man could say that his appearance was without a redeeming feature. But this said, the piece is astonishing. For there comes a point in reading it when, as he talks of "the handicapped," one thinks not of him but of oneself. Who is not handicapped? Bourne's sympathy is almost imperceptibly translated to all of suffering humanity; and as he grows more explicit, one's own sympathies deepen.

> What one does get sensitive to is rather the inevitable way that people, acquaintances and strangers alike, have of discounting in advance what one does or says. The deformed man is always conscious that the world does not expect very much from him.

Where does that differ from the remark that a young leader of the Oglala Sioux once made to me as he talked of the policies of the Bureau for Indian Affairs: "We are not given the chance to fail"? Where does it differ from the small expectations that many liberals have of the blacks or conservatives of the poor? Where, indeed, does it differ from Antigone's flaming retort to her sister Ismene, who warns her that she may fail: "When I *have tried* and failed, I shall have failed"?

At the age of twenty-five, Bourne is pushing, from his own experience, to the social philosophy that sustained him:

> It makes me wince to hear a man spoken of as a failure, or to have it said of one that "he doesn't amount to much." Instantly I want to know why he has not succeeded, and what have been the forces that have been working against him. . . . My experience has

made my ideal of character militant rather than long-suffering. . . . The Stoics depress me. I do not want to look on my life as an eternal making of the best of a bad bargain. . . . Of one thing I am sure . . . : that life will have little for me except as I am able to contribute toward some such ideal of social betterment, if not in deed, then in word. . . . I want to give the young men whom I see . . . some touch of this philosophy . . . that will energize their lives, and save them from the disheartening effects of the poisonous counsel of timidity and distrust of human ideals.

Undergraduate writing? Well yes, some of it, undergraduate writing. But what does one say of a man who then goes on to live and write, suffer and fight, for it all under the severest of tests? I am not talking only of his opposition to the war, which cost not only the sacrifice of his career but the sacrifice of a magazine, but that second sacrifice is important. When *The New Republic* cravenly confined him to a few occasional pieces on literature and the arts, Bourne found the main outlet for his opposition to the war in *Seven Arts*. This magazine was founded in November 1916 by James Oppenheim, Waldo Frank, and Van Wyck Brooks, with money supplied by "a bored woman of means, Annette K. Raskin." It carried the work of many of the best writers and thinkers of the day. Bourne went to its office in the spring of 1917—when he saw, after the resumption of unrestricted submarine warfare by the Germans, which way things were going at *The New Republic*—and Oppenheim said later that he was the "real leader . . . of what brains and creativeness we had at the time." The editors of *Seven Arts* allowed Bourne to write what the editors of *The New Republic* would not take from him. As Frank said afterward: "We felt Bourne was our arm in the world of action." So it published what he wrote and, before

1917 was done, the bored woman had withdrawn her means, because the editors would not censor his protests against the war. Robert Frost, one of its contributors, had warned, at the beginning, that this would happen. When the magazine folded, he wrote a verse:

> In the Dawn of Creation that morning
> I remember I gave you fair warning
> The Arts are but Six!
> You add Politics
> And the Seven will all die a-Bourneing.

One cannot ignore the fact that, after writing as a professional journalist for only three years, Bourne had emerged by the age of thirty-one as the most independent, defiant, thoughtful, courageous exemplar of his profession. The writing cannot be separated from the example of the life. For he met even his easy allies with his criticism.

He was not only the leader but the *critic* of his generation. That is the testimony that we can read from the members of his generation. The early essay on "The Handicapped" had already included a criticism of youth, and it is perhaps here that we may discover why the "radical" youth of the 1960s did not adopt him. As he wrote of the feeling that his handicap and deformity, when he was young, made him "truly in the world, but not of the world," he went on to say: "The world of youth is a world of so many conventions, and the abnormal in any direction is so glaringly and hideously abnormal." As the editor of his most recent collection of essays puts it: "Bourne was at no time merely the prophet of a youth cult. . . . Youth does not guarantee a new beginning but merely its possibility." It was in two articles for *The Atlantic*—"The Two Generations" (1911), and "Youth" (1912)— that he made himself the leader of his generation. But not even in them did he concede any particular virtue to youth itself.

This is a rare discrimination in a writer of any age. Where was the censor within him? We have already seen that, in his opposition to the war, it was the intellectuals' betrayal of their vocation, more than the horror of the war, which really troubled him. (One can find in his writing barely a reference to the slaughter.) What he conceived to be the role of the intellectual is the key to his authority even now. He never called himself a "socialist." He was a "radical," an American radical. In a book review for *The New Republic* in 1916, he made himself clear, so clear that many middle-class radicals today may squirm.

> The real trouble with middle-class radicalism in this country today is that it is too easy. It is becoming too popular. . . . The ranks are full of the unfocused and the unthinking. . . . *The only way by which middle-class radicalism can serve is by being fiercely and concentratedly intellectual* [my italics]. . . . The labor movement in this country needs a philosophy, a literature, a constructive social analysis and criticism of industrial relations. . . . Labor will scarcely do this thinking by itself. Unless middle-class radicalism threshes out its categories and interpretations and undertakes this constructive thought, it will not be done.

There then comes this vital disassociation: "Intellectual radicalism should not mean repeating the stale dogmas of Marxism." He was to repeat this from the beginning to the end: " . . . much of Marxism is doctrinaire and static in its concepts"; he said that what he called "the old solution of State ownership and control" was not valid as an American solution. He said it then, and he said it again and again. He tested everything against his one touchstone, his vision of America and its possibilities. That is why they make a movie about John Reed and not about Randolph Bourne. Reed is not a threat, since he spoke no truth; the Bournes are threats.

Most people who write about him ask what he would have become if he had lived. It is a foolish question, not because we cannot know, but because he answered it. The timeliness which we find in his writing even today, seventy years later, tells us how little he would have had to shift his fundamental position in order to meet, one by one, all the alarms and excursions of this century. The man who so clearly rejected Marxism in 1917 would not have followed so many of the writers of the 1920s into the Communist camp in the 1930s. The man who was the critic of his own generation of rebellious youth, even as he was its leader, would have had no truck with the intellectual laxity and dishonesty of the New Left. Yet just as he did not have to reach to a political conservatism in his own times, so he would not have had to reach to it later. He would have had no need to become a neo-anything in order to make his position clear.

For *clear* is was. The words that Lewis Mumford used about him in *The New Republic* twelve years after his death merely echo the words that are always used by those who have studied him: "His view of life was maturing, deepening, not yet ready for rounded expression, it was still a promise; a cool luminous dawn was spreading across the skies." And what is astonishing is that even now it is like a cool luminous dawn that the freshness of his writing still touches us—almost, one may say, touches our cheeks. Mumford was writing of how, even then, Bourne seemed to have been set aside, and he protested: "It was the good fortune of American society to produce this man. We must not toss that luck away."

What is it, then, that stays in his writing? This was a radical who believed more in America than any Rotary speaker or sponger off the media. The man who had so clear a vision of transnational America was the same man who believed that the East Coast was still Europe and that only West of the Alleghenies did America begin. Yet he could believe all this without a page falling into the trap of a conservatism that is just one long grouch at the twentieth century. America must be kept open—no technique, no system, no ideology, must be allowed to close it down. There was his inspiration. He was—for try any other name against his—the last man who believed in America.

Tory Days

GEORGE F. WILL

The Morning After: American Successes and Excesses 1981– 1986
by George F. Will

With this new volume, which covers the years (so far) of the
Reagan presidency, George Will has given us three collections
of his newspaper columns in eight years. He has also published
one book whose title, *Statecraft and Soulcraft*, invites us to a work
of political philosophy. Given that he is taken to be a conservative, and announces that he is a Tory, we can look to him for a
clear statement of contemporary American conservatism, a definition of what an American conservative today should believe.
And since Will's career as a syndicated columnist has coincided
with the flamboyant rise to power of a cock-a-hoop conservatism of some stripe, this would seem to be a useful time to look,
and Will would seem to be well equipped to point the way.

He is not modest in his claims to be our guide. "My aim," he
writes in the preface to *Statecraft*, "is to recast conservatism in a
form compatible with the broad popular imperatives of the day,
but also to change somewhat the agenda and even vocabulary of
contemporary politics." He should charge more for the tour.
Will is "a lapsed professor of political philosophy," with "a continuing, even quickened interest in the state and standing of

The New Republic, November 10, 1986, originally titled "Tory Days."
Reprinted by permission from the Estate of Henry Fairlie.

political philosophy" since his lapsing. As a writer, he tells us in the manner of the Smith Barney commercial, "I write (of course) the old-fashioned way, in longhand, with a fountain pen"; and prominently displayed in the photograph on the cover of this book is a fancy fountain pen that Will is holding. If we are uncertain why this recommends him, he informs us elsewhere of his "firm conviction that the rushing typewriter, with its clackety-clack rhythm, is an enemy of well-crafted sentences," and that congressmen during the first 30 years of the Republic wrote a stately prose because they "dipped quill pens in inkwells."

Armed with the authority of statecraft, soulcraft, and sentencecraft, he tells us he is not like other journalists who are "too proudly 'factual' to pay attention to anything but the nuts and bolts," and so "miss the element of mind"; his subject is "not what is secret, but what is latent, the kernel of principle and other significance that exists, recognized or not, inside events, actions, policies and manners." (This last citation is from *The Pursuit of Happiness and Other Sobering Thoughts,* which appeared in 1978.) He assures us often that he will reveal "Conservatism properly understood. . . . Real conservatism. . . . The truly conservative critique"—the opening words of three successive paragraphs in a single column (reprinted in *The Pursuit of Virtue and Other Tory Notions,* in 1982).

Will's most beguiling credential, however, is his claim to be a Tory, a word (when used with the "t" in the upper case) hard to fix with any meaning on the American scene after 1783 (as *Webster's Third International,* by the way, would seem to confirm). This vaunt assumes its most outlandish form in the preface to *The Pursuit of Virtue.* Will begins with a mildly amusing quotation from Stephen Leacock about the writer's craft: "Just get paper and pencil, sit down, and write as it occurs to you. The writing is easy—it's the occurring that's hard." But not for Will.

"Actually," he at once says, "the 'occurring' is not hard for someone blessed with a Tory temperament."

The writer glides like a skater, and the reader can too easily glide with him. Will in his bow tie is an elegant Victorian skater on the pond, and the maiden on his arm feels blessed. "Ah!" she sighs, "a Tory temperament—you do like to sound old-fashioned, Mr. Will." Mr. Will pats her muff and skates on: " . . . and sentenced to live in this stimulating era." The maiden begins to flutter, "Oh, to be sentenced . . . " but realizes too late that they have been skating on not even thin ice, and she goes under, as the reader will many times, with no hand held out to rescue her.

But Will has jumped onto the op-ed bank to assert to the orchestra of his admirers that in his columns there are "continuities, and mine are conservative convictions. I call them 'Tory' because that is what they are. I trace the pedigree of my philosophy to Burke, Newman, Disraeli and others. . . . " Will tracks this lineage of his ideas many times, throwing in an assortment of "others," and still adding "and others." He even claims that their origin may be found in Aristotle, "a founder of conservatism, properly understood." The question is whether Aristotle has been properly understood. A liberal, after all, may as easily draw on his philosophy; to call Aristotle a "founder of conservatism" is an anachronism as facetious as it is perverse.

Still, the most bizarre genealogical claim for his ideas appears in *Statecraft*, a slim book that we are nonetheless entitled to take—since he so presents it—as his testament. "When a kind reader calls me unpredictable [not the drowning maiden's word for him], I am tempted to respond: to anyone sufficiently familiar with the minds of the Oxford Movement, circa 1842, all my conclusions are predictable." Of course few Americans, even if Will were among them, are "sufficiently familiar" with the Oxford Movement to know what he is talking about. We can only ponder, not to his credit, why the claim is made. There is no explanation. It is thrown in. Nothing follows from it.

Even if the whole sentence were not a giveaway, there is a giveaway at its core. According to the founders of the Oxford Movement in 1833, its purpose was to uphold "the doctrine of the Apostolical Succession and the integrity of the Prayer Book." Which of Will's conclusions is predictable from that? And what does it have to do with America, or with American conservatism, or for that matter with the price of eggs? The Oxford Movement reached a crisis in 1841, when John Henry Newman, one of the ancestors most frequently claimed by Will, published his *Tract 90*, demonstrating to his own satisfaction that the Thirty-Nine Articles of the Church of England were compatible with Roman Catholicism. In 1843 Newman gave up his living, and shortly thereafter he went over to Rome; but men such as Pusey and Keble held on in the Church of England. Thus, when Will tells us to look to the Oxford Movement, "circa 1842," he is pointing to the exact year in which it was riven in two by *Tract 90*. Before we can find his conclusions in "the minds of the Oxford Movement," we need to know whose minds Will is talking about. Those who followed Newman to Rome? Or those who stayed with Pusey in the Anglican Church?

His admirers may say this is picky, but it is not. Will's pretensions to a wider and deeper learning than is possessed by his audience, by other journalists, and by American conservatives in general (who he mockingly suggests at one point appeal to Burke without having read the essay on *The Sublime and Beautiful;* has he?)—these pretensions are not a mere trapping, an adornment to his writing or to his "recasting" of conservatism. They are not playful. They are the pillars and struts of such thought as there is. Moreover, since the ancestors to whom he appeals are rarely Americans, not even the Founding Fathers, but European and especially English thinkers and politicians, it is not unimportant to point out that no Englishman "sufficiently familiar with the minds of the Oxford Movement" could explain how this familiarity makes "all" Will's conclusions predictable. If he had said that *some* of his ideas were akin to, or drew nourishment from, *some* of the ideas of *some* of the minds of the Oxford Movement, we could let it pass. But as it stands, in so prominent a place at the beginning of his testament, it is a conceit (in both senses) and an ill-mannered use of what looks suspiciously like a little learning.

So Will has appealed to Toryism, a peculiarly English political tradition; to the names of three English conservatives, if we overlook the fact that Burke was Irish; and to an English movement that was concerned with the defense of the creed and liturgy of the Anglican Church. But then we are confounded near the end of *Statecraft* by another grandiose assertion: "The conservatism for which I argue is a 'European' conservatism." And he hastens to inform us that "it is the conservatism of Augustine and Aquinas, Shakespeare and Burke, Newman and T. S. Eliot and Thomas Mann." (What happened to Aristotle?) But hardly anything that matters is held in common between any English and (continental) European conservatism. As for the list of names—why doesn't he throw in Uranus, the first ruler of the universe; or Cato the Elder; or Virgil (*arma virumque cano:* he was clearly for a strong defense); or Jerome? And if he's going to rope in Shakespeare (what did he do to be card-filed as a European conservative?) why not Cervantes? (Of course, he can't have Rabelais. "Rabelais, the Hugh Hefner of his time," one can almost hear Will begin. . . .)

Weird lists of names recur; perhaps this is why the "occurring" is easy. But the list upon which one must gaze most fondly is in Will's defense of Solzhenitsyn against his critics. Solzhenitsyn's "ideas about the nature of man and the essential political problem are broadly congruent with [watch the skater glide] the ideas of Cicero and other ancients, and those of Augustine, Aquinas, Richard Hooker, Pascal, Thomas More, Burke, Hegel and others." Even if we keep our seats at the mention of Hooker, a mild commonsense skeptical Englishman, and of Pascal, surely we must jump to the ceiling at the inclusion of Hegel. There is nothing about the thought and writing of Solzhenitsyn, absolutely nothing, that can be deduced from such a roster.

With these lists, with the individual names he is always tossing out, in, and over his shoulder, we come to Will's famous use of quotations. His critics are usually satisfied to call it intellectual and cultural name-dropping. But Will's practice suggests a far more serious disorder. At times explicitly, but also implicitly in his whole posture, Will puts himself forward as an almost lone defender of our Western cultural heritage (but with support from William J. Bennett). And yet he rummages among its thought and literature like a bag lady. Commonly the quotations or references are introduced with parentheses that are leaden— "Arthur Koestler's *Darkness at Noon,* a classic of political literature"—but these seem designed to assure the reader of the author's familiarity with all of the culture. Or the parentheses are unforgivably tawdry: "Santayana and Plato, both of them clever fellows." "Dostoyevksy (who knew something about crime and punishment)"; "Willie Keeler, baseball's Plato"; elsewhere we are told that "baseball people are Pythagoreans."

Or take the beginnings of these consecutive sentences: "Like Moses, Humphrey was discovered early in his career. . . . Like Moses, Humphrey was a bundle of opinions. . . . " What discernible meaning could there possibly be in such an analogy? What discernible respect for either Moses or Humphrey? (Whatever Moses communicated, it was not "opinions.") Flaubert gets the same treatment as Moses: "Jim Wacker, professor of football at Texas Christian University, may have the finest sense of nuance in language since Flaubert." And again: Earl

Long "had Flaubert's flair for bons mots." Yeah, that's why we read Flaubert, for his bons mots. (Has Will confused the bon mot with the mot juste?) "*The Bill James Baseball Abstract*, the most important scientific treatise since Newton's *Principia*"; and "The Bible, which devout baseball fans consider the *Sporting News* of religion." This is the manner of a talk-show guest, or of an entertainer on the lecture circuit. Or, more to the point, of a new kind of columnist.

What is absent from Will's lists of names, from his entire papier-mâché model of Western culture, is a recognition of struggle—of the struggle of idea against idea in the civilization as a whole, of the strenuous and tormented struggle within the individual thinkers and artists he so lightly robs, like a pickpocket. One would not know from Will's appropriation of Augustine, for example, that the latter's certitudes were a recovery from the anguish of sin; or that Pascal placed faith above reason only after, and because of, tremendous doubt. There is a profound sense, after all, in which Western culture has been built on the admission of sin and doubt. But temptation, error, sin, pleasure—and the struggle with all of them—are absent from Will's smug defense of a placid cultural heritage. There is no evidence in his writing that he has ever fought with temptation or error. Civilization came to him gift-wrapped. It seems to have "occurred" to him, like the names. In this he reflects a persistent shallowness in American conservatism, not least in the alleged "revival" of conservative thought in recent years. There is no quest in it. It is quite remarkable that Will should quote with approval Jowett's question to D. G. Rossetti in Max Beerbohm's famous cartoon: "And what were they going to do with the Grail when they found it, Mr. Rossetti?" It is not any "true conservatism," but only the shallowest liberalism, that could ask that question.

In the new collection there are two essays extravagantly praising the columns of Miss Manners. Watch how he praises her: "Like Plato . . . Miss Manners knows . . . "; "Not since Edmund Burke's *Reflections on the French Revolution* has there been a counterrevolutionary trumpet call as ringing as Miss Manners's"; "Miss Manners is like Lincoln . . . "; "Miss Manners deals like Metternich with . . . "; "[Her prose] is compounded of . . . an adamancy never achieved by Pope Pius IX, whose Syllabus of Errors was, compared with Miss Manners's syllabus, halfhearted. . . . Actually, her book is the most formidable political book produced by an American since *The Federalist Papers*. . . . As Plato understood. . . . " All good clean fun, his admirers may say. But the fun is limp; and more important, it is an aping of any serious allusions to our cultural heritage, and so only belittles it. Will makes culture evaporate. In his hands it becomes a thing of no gravity. This columnist who so manfully shoulders the burden of upholding our culture is an Atlas bowed under a balloon.

There is in Will's attitude toward (and abuse of) culture a philistinism that is profoundly antithetical to any "true conservatism." It is a philistinism that can offer "Oscar Wilde . . . with the stiletto of his cynicism. . . . " A stiletto, Wilde's weapon? Wilde's purpose was not to draw blood. And anyone who can speak of Wilde's cynicism, who can think even for a second that Wilde was cynical, must either not have read a page he wrote, or read with such obtuseness that he might as well not have bothered. It is the same philistinism that calls John Buchan "an unsurpassed memoirist" (not surpassed—whom shall we pick?— by Cellini, or by Gibbon, or by the author of *The Education of Henry Adams*?); the same philistinism that pronounces that "Mallarmé should have been a columnist," a comment of colossal ignorance and vulgarity that cannot be based on anything Mallarmé wrote, or on anything Will has read, but merely on one of Auden's teasing clerihews, which Will quotes; the same philistinism that echoes a line from "Prufrock" so ineptly as to say that Nixon "measured out his life in forkfuls of chicken à la king"; the same philistinism that declares no less inappositely that Whittaker Chambers's *Witness* is "comparable in depth and power to the memoir of another American alienated from his time, *The Education of Henry Adams*"—adding even then that "Adams is less unsettling." Oh?

This philistinism that extends in so many ways through Will's writing is not a peccadillo we may overlook. It undermines his whole claim to speak in defense of our civilization and its cultural heritage, or more specifically in defense of any conservative tradition. But his fitness to be the conservative guardian of our culture, so ready to arm it to its teeth and engage it in rash military adventure, looks quite as questionable if we take our stand in the present, and not on what Will imagines to be our heritage from the past. For example, Will ends his embarrassing paean of praise to Oxford, where he spent a brief but much-advertised time, with: "What I am trying to say is that Henry James was wrong. He said that 'youth' is the loveliest word in the language. For those who favor 'old'—old ideas and institutions—this ancient community is the rainbow's end." ("Favor" is at least an honest word for the depth of his reverence for the past.)

But every "true conservative" knows that it is no service to the traditional culture to stand outside the contemporary culture, to separate himself so ostentatiously from its growing life that there is nothing to defend but a museum, a dictionary of quotations, and a conversation piece. If, as Will puts it, "2,500 years" of our civilization have brought us only to a wasteland, with the pitifully few blooms he finds in it, then there must have been something radically at fault with Western civilization's *past*, something so wrong that it is not even worth defending.

There is no need to show with more names and quotations

how little Will finds to interest him or to enjoy in modern literature, art, or music. His condemnations of modern art are facile and unilluminating. He fastens his attention on some of the works easiest to ridicule, and most of the time he is not looking at the painting or sculpture, but clipping some of the more unintelligible pronouncements of contemporary criticism. That there is babble in much contemporary criticism does not mean the work of an individual artist, or the whole effort and achievement of modern art, is babble. Again, it is not a quibble, but an essential criticism of Will's attitude toward contemporary culture, to point out that when he roundly condemns Jackson Pollock (in 1978, and again in 1985), he says not a word about any Pollock painting, not to mention the whole body of his work, except the old-hat criticism that they are "canvases covered with drips." On both occasions he bases his criticism on the same silly tribute to Pollock by an unidentified art critic. *Blue Poles*, to take but one Pollock painting, cannot be described as a canvas "covered with drips," and only an eye uneducated not only in modern painting, but in all painting, could say so. In fact, one doubts whether he knows what paint is, or for that matter what Raphael did with his "revolutionary" use of color.

It is an offense to the past, as well as to the present, to come down so clumsily on the experiment, the trial, the essay. But let us switch from "high" culture to "popular." Popular culture has always energized high culture in our civilization. In fact, that could be claimed as one of high culture's distinguishing merits: it has always kept itself open and receptive to what comes up from below. (This is not least true of our language, which Will's fountain pen affects to use and defend with a recovered stateliness denied to the rest of us.) And it is not rash to say that we live in a time, even a century, in which popular culture has energized high culture more consistently, and to greater benefit, than in any other. To Will, virtually the only emblem of that popular culture is (you guessed it) rock 'n' roll, and (you guessed it again) he condemns, rejects, and ejects it. Except for. . . .

Will's famous takeover bid for Bruce Springsteen in September 1984, which provoked Reagan's own takeover bid during the election campaign, was written after a friend took him to a Springsteen concert. It was simply very brave of him to go at all, since "I may be the only 43-year-old American so out of the swim that I do not even know what marijuana smoke smells like. . . . Many of his fans regarded me as exotic fauna . . . (a bow tie and doubled-breasted blazer is not the dress code)." But he is full of praise for Springsteen. "There is not a smidgen of androgyny in Springsteen, . . . rocketing around the stage in a T-shirt and headband." He is a "wholesome cultural portent," and "affirms the right values." And "if this is the class struggle, its anthem—its 'Internationale'—is the song that provides the title of his 18-month, worldwide tour, 'Born in the USA.'"

What is absent from the whole piece is any interest in or concern for the music, except to say, "This is rock for the United Steelworkers, accompanied by the opening barrage of the battle of the Somme. . . . I made it three beats into the first number before packing my ears" from a "pouch of cotton." Rock is now 30 years old. It has carried around the world, even penetrating the "evil empire" of the Soviet Union, crossed boundaries not only of nations and cultures but of classes and generations. It may be taken as a striking expression of the vitality of American culture. But it is the music that has done this. Will doesn't seem to know that what he is writing about is music, and not merely a "plague of messages about sexual promiscuity, bisexuality, incest, sadomasochism, satanism, drug use, alcohol abuse and, constantly, misogyny"—as if people go to rock for the lyrics and not the music. Will might do well to expose his prudishness to those rock stars of our venerated past, to the Goliard poets, the wandering scholars, the troubadour poets of the late Latin middle ages. He will discover the astonishing extent to which bawdiness gives to culture . . . life.

It was Disraeli, one of the English conservatives claimed by Will as an ancestor, who said in his rectorial address at the University of Glasgow that one must know the spirit of the times in which one lives, even if it is to resist it. One of the weaknesses of Will's conservatism is that he sets himself so vigorously and indiscriminately against the spirit of his times that he gives himself no chance to know it. Will's contempt for our culture, "high" or "popular," is evidence finally of an unexperiencing nature. Little in our culture seems to touch Will deeply, or often. Experience is hard, even the experience of reading; but the "occurring" not only comes easily in his writing, it seems to come as easily in his reading.

Does he read? If one goes back to one's "favorite" poem or painting or music in different moods, whether of exaltation, serenity, or gloom, there is always something more to find. Often such genuine reading leaves scars, marks of pain. Or, if you will, of sin. Before we go to God on proudly bended knee, as Will's writing suggests we should, we might at least acknowledge that he made us—once we were out of Eden, that "animal" place that Eve found as boring as Chevy Chase—the most revolting of his creatures. That is what Augustine, at least, should have taught Will: the strength of an experiencing nature. But it seems correct to say, on the evidence of Will's written work, that he has not *experienced* a feeling or thought, of guilt or of innocence, in his life.

In his self-appointed role of champion of our culture, Will naturally gives his attention to the parlous condition of American schools and education, not least as "transmitters" of our cultural heritage. Nobody will deny that there is cause for concern. But the slightly faddish alarm that is being voiced today—in Will's new book as well—carries its own danger. For if the

American academy is also such a desolation, people may begin to think, when the faddish interest dies down, that it is beyond recovery, except for some enclaves for the privileged that will turn out the elites in whom Will exhorts us from time to time to place our trust.

For one thing, if the "core curriculum" is such a shambles—William Bennett recently made the point again at Harvard—why do American universities continue year after year to turn out such fine scholars, not least in the disciplines of the humanities that the conservative wishes to keep strong? Barely noticed, American classical scholarship has been leading the world for decades; and I know no British historian who does not pay tribute to the work of American historians, and to the generally high standard of historical scholarship in America, even in the fields of English and European history. What is more, it is my observation that every profession in America has an abundance of good and well-educated minds. If all these are the exceptions, the survivors in the wasteland, one must ask how many such exceptions were produced by Oxford at whatever period Will imagines it to have been the noble institution he extols. As for the "transmission" of our cultural heritage, the great universities of Germany, Italy, and France did not produce a generation with enough understanding of, or care for, our culture to resist, for instance, its devastation by Hitler.

When the "brain drain" from Britain began in the 1950s, it included many graduate students. One of them, the writer Andrew Sinclair, later said that "America is today of course what the Grand Tour was to the 19th century." Another, the critic and novelist Malcolm Bradbury, declared that "America is intellectually attractive; not only as a sort of spell in the 'colonies' to get started, but as a real way of tuning in to advanced ideas, modern tendencies, intellectual excitements. So the pattern is likely to continue"—and of course it has. But it is precisely these *ad-*

vanced ideas, *modern* tendencies, intellectual *excitements,* that Will disdains, and encourages his readers to disdain.

Far too much of Will's conservatism merely adds one more voice to the long whine of 20th-century conservatives against modernity. But the "true conservative" does not wish only to "transmit" the cultural heritage, as Will keeps saying, as if it were finished and could be wrapped and mailed to the future. He wants to bring it forward and to understand it, so that it will help to energize the present, as it has indeed energized more of modern literature and art than Will appears to know. Will makes our precious heritage lifeless, a corpse, embalmed and carried before the people, with the ultimate and hardly disguised purpose of keeping them quiet, and the society quiet, and above all the culture quiet. It is not only the past he puts in a museum, as if there is nothing more left for the traditional culture to do. He puts the present in a museum, too.

Thus it is not surprising that he traces the "European conservatism" he says he loves to so few Americans, so few contemporaries. But one must ask: Which European conservatism, exactly? The English Toryism he also claims would find it very hard to go along, for example, with De Maistre.[1] But it is the absence of more than an occasional appeal to an American political tradition that is most damaging. There are only scant and usually dismissive references to the Founding Fathers, and even to *The Federalist Papers.* In all the lists of names and rivers of quotations, there is only one idle mention of Calhoun. Will's is a conservatism with the South left out, which makes no sense. There is no examination, for example, of the group of Southern writers who published a very conservative manifesto, *I'll Take*

1. Joseph de Maistre (1753–1821) was a fierce opponent of the French Revolution and the Enlightenment, advocating papal authority and a return to hereditary monarchy.

My Stand, against the way American society and its economy were going at the end of the 1920s—at the end of the administrations of Harding and of Coolidge (who is praised by Will because the "nation under his stewardship enjoyed a 45 percent increase in the production of ice cream") and of Hoover.

In fact, to an extent astonishing in a journalist, America itself is not very visible in Will's work. In all these volumes there is little sense of any region, city, town, or place in America; little of what its people actually do, feel, think, enjoy, and value, except going to baseball games, driving automobiles, and of course listening to obscene lyrics and reading pornographic magazines. ("[Hugh] Hefner, the tuning fork of American fantasies"!) And there is little of American history, either. We are entitled to ask Will to say, then, precisely on what things American his conservatism stands. "Cars and girls are American values" is not enough.

Still, Will has a difficulty with which one may sympathize. And unlike many American conservatives, he is at least honest enough to mention it, even if not quite to face it. His difficulty is with, well, America; and it is at this point that he most clearly resembles the Tory he claims to be. "Capitalism means the liberation and incessant inflaming of appetites," he acknowledges. "Capitalist dynamism" dissolves "cultural conservatism." Business should rise "above the morals of the marketplace." American conservatism "tends complacently to define the public good as whatever results from the unfettered pursuit of private ends. Hence it tends to treat laissez-faire economic theory as a substitute for political philosophy and to discount the importance of government." And from all this come "the somewhat barren and negative social prescriptions of American conservatism." These are genuine Tory sentiments, expressed by English Tories 200 years ago in voicing their early horror at the Industrial Revolution, and by Southern Agrarian writers 50 years ago. But it is hard to see where they can lead Will. This is the difficulty an English Tory feels in accommodating himself to American conservatism: the difficulty that there is in America itself so strong an attachment to, and presumption in favor of, "free enterprise" and the market and its values. One may almost say, deliberately leaning on the ambiguity in the word, that this capitalism is *constitutionally* part of the United States.

One may agree with Will in criticizing excessive individualism (libertarianism in its vulgar, contemporary form) and the opposition to strong government in American conservatism. But then there is another difficulty. Individualism is rooted in the culture, as well as in the political tradition, of the nation, even in its beginnings. Even if one does not question some of the purposes for which Will wishes to strengthen government—to "legislate morality," for example—an English Tory (or anybody else, for that matter) may still say he would not recognize an America in which there was not so strong a flavor of individualism in politics, in culture, in society.

In the end, it is not only American conservatism Will puts into question, dissociating himself from much of what most people understand it to mean. He rejects a great deal of America, too. When he argues not only against Thoreau, not only against Emerson and his transcendentalism, but (in this new collection) against Huckleberry Finn on his 100th birthday, one begins to wonder where his America may be found, now or in the past. One begins to understand why he sets himself on the shoulders of Augustine, Aquinas, the Oxford Movement, Oxford University, "and others," or at least borrows the support of their names. For what he discounts is nothing less than the liberation from political and theological oppression that has been the achievement of the United States and its inspiration to the world.

If I have not spoken of Will's columns on the topical issues of

American politics, it is because in these volumes, and not least in his new collection, he republishes relatively few of them, preferring to give his readers his lighter and easier reflections on such matters as baseball (a great deal of that in the new book), child-rearing, and what are today called the "social issues," mainly pornography, obscenity, rampant sexuality, abortion, and the withdrawals of life supports from the retarded and the handicapped. In the political columns that he has chosen to reprint, there is a running, rather awkward, and not terribly damaging criticism of "Reaganite conservatism," as one would expect from Will's own brand of "conservatism"; and surprisingly little, given his concerns about capitalism, on either current economic policies or more long-term developments that are profoundly altering the character of capitalism, and even the claims it has made in the past to encourage such virtues as thrift, hard work, and prudence.

For the rest, there are the columns exhorting the administration to create an armory to which Will seems to set no limits, or even to imagine any; to be ready to use those weapons; and at last to resist and even roll back the advance of the "evil empire"—an advance that always seems, when he lists the countries that have fallen since the division of Europe during the Second World War, to be far less menacing, or rather, far more carefully, quietly, and successfully resisted by America and its allies, than Will's rhetorical flourishes suggest.

What's more, just as Will offers few specific economic prescriptions, it is hard to see what he expects an American government to do when, for example, the Polish government with the Soviet Union behind it crushes an opposition movement—unless it is rashly to take up arms. On the 25th anniversary of the building of the Berlin Wall, Will asked, "What if the blockade begun in 1947 had been smashed by force? What if the Allies had used force to unseal East Berlin at dawn, August 13, 1961?" But those "what ifs" are too lightly asked and answered. What if war had resulted? The Soviet Union in 1947 was indeed a "shattered nation"; but Western Europe was a shattered half-continent, over which Soviet tanks would have swarmed with little resistance. And if one is going to count the Berlin blockade a terrible defeat for America, when in fact that blockade was broken and West Berlin was saved, why not count the Marshall Plan in 1947 a far greater American victory? Because it was peaceful?

When Challenger Fell from the Sky

With an immediate concern for the feelings of the pupils in his charge, Mr. Charles Foley, the principal of Concord High School, asked the students to return to their classrooms and the reporters and cameramen to leave the building. In that local and exact response, he distinguished himself from the hollow emotions that television tried to arouse in the American people from the moment Challenger exploded and fell from the sky. For a nation, rightly, a president speaks. Like presidents before him at such moments, President Reagan was adequate to the occasion and humble in his address. But as if that was not enough, all day the network anchormen assumed the duty of telling us what to feel. The event, the disaster, the tragedy, the grief: one by one they were transformed, beyond their measure, beyond their place, and above all, beyond the point where we could recognize ourselves.

Again and again the comparison was made to Dallas in 1963 and Memphis in 1968. But the explosion in the sky bore little resemblance to those tragedies. In Dallas and Memphis there were assassinations, and the acts were deliberate. Above Cape Canaveral there was an accident, a mechanical failure, or at worst (we may never know) a human error. In Dallas and Memphis the nation lost two unusual and significant leaders; in Challenger we lost five American men and two American women who might live next door. There was, perhaps, a common sense of loss uniting all three: in each case, a nation's hope for its future was dimmed.

But what the assassinations and the explosion truly had in common was the presence of the camera and the swarm of anchormen. They must spend a day inviting us to the titillation of watching a toy explode in the sky. That is what it became: television had launched a toy and made it explode—before our very eyes. The comparison to Dallas was made, in some cases explicitly, to exalt television as the legitimate creator of a common national emotion. Everything led to Koppel, and once he told us what to feel, we could go to bed secure in our emotions.

HEROES OF THE HEAVENS screamed the *New York Post* the next morning. Television had already spent a day making heroes out of five men and a woman doing their job, at a risk they knew and accepted, and one schoolteacher who had eagerly sought to join them in a mission she understood, again knowing and accepting the risk. It is brave to travel into space, and it is daring; and it is still something like a human miracle that we are up and out there at all. The bravery, the daring, the endeavor benefit us when we are reminded of them. But they do not, singly or together, make heroes. A soldier is brave and daring to go into battle; he is not by that reason a hero. He becomes a hero when by some conspicuous act he takes a risk that, more likely than not, will demand the sacrifice of his life.

It was not heroism that was at issue this time; it was symbolism. Challenger carried with it a human hope and yearning that is as old as the ages. After 25 shuttles we have been reminded, and some may have discovered for the first time, that what may have come to seem routine, scientific, technological in the astronauts is exactly what gives them their meaning in our place and time. That was what sending an ordinary citizen up into space was meant to recapture. And that excitement and wonder were precisely what Christa McAuliffe conveyed; those qualities came through not because of the press hype, but in spite of it.

The more obsessively the media watched the shuttle explode and the faces crumble, the less they saw. The world may be transfixed by disaster, but as Auden explained, it is not transformed.

> In Brueghel's *Icarus*, for instance: how everything
>> turns away
> Quite leisurely from the disaster; the ploughman
>> may
> Have heard a splash, the forsaken cry,
> But for him it was not an important failure; the sun
>> shone
> As it had to on the white legs disappearing into the
>> green
> Water; and the amazing delicate ship that must
>> have seen
> Something amazing, a boy falling out of the sky,
> Had somewhere to get to and sailed calmly on.

In that, which might almost be about Challenger, Auden (and Brueghel) had the perspective right: he described the suffering, and he enabled us to recognize ourselves. The media once again got it wrong.

Acknowledgments

The early stages of this project took place several years ago, when I was on the staff of the *New Republic*. From original conception to finished form, it could not have progressed without the encouragement and support of Leon Wieseltier and Martin Peretz. I am also in debted to the skilled and dedicated staff of Yale University Press, especially John Donatich, William Frucht, Ann-Marie Imbornoni, Keith Condon, Dan Heaton, Joseph Calamia, and Liz Casey.

Many of Henry Fairlie's friends and colleagues graciously shared stories, correspondence, and tips on how to dig deeper into his life and work. The account of Fairlie's days and nights on Fleet Street owes a great deal to published memoirs of, and lunchtime conversations with, Sir Peregrine Worsthorne and Alan Watkins; details of his American sojourn came from too many editors, friends, and colleagues to list here. I owe particular thanks to people who took the time to talk to me about Fairlie, then took even more time to read a draft of the book's introductory essay: Anthony Howard, Dorothy Wickenden, Peter Pringle, Leon Wieseltier, Alan Watkins, and Charlotte Fairlie. (Responsibility for any errors, however, remains mine.)

Librarians at the New York Public Library, the Brooklyn Public Library, and the Library of Congress offered crucial help in hunting down autobiographies and obscure periodicals. The angel hovering above this project, though, is Kris McCusker, who, with her colleagues at the University of Colorado, went to astounding lengths to make the archive of Fairlie's papers in Boulder accessible. I'm grateful to Michael Braham for supplying information about Fairlie's brief but memorable career as a Liberal politician, and to friends in the United States and the United Kingdom for their hospitality on research trips: James Carmichael, Ben Weeden, Diane Mastromarino, Hillary Rosner and Philip Higgs, and Ben Soskis and Rebecca Deutsch. Jennifer Joel at International Creative Management and Jeff Beals supplied vital feedback and even more vital boosts in morale.

Above all, I thank Lisette Fairlie and her children. This book would not exist without their candor, support, and willingness to share so many memories of their husband and father. This book is dedicated to them with gratitude and affection, and to my grandfather, John Patrick Campbell, in loving memory.

Index

Brogan, Sir Denis William, 74 and *n*3

Brooks, Van Wyck, 305, 317, 320

Bryce, Lord, 13, 174

Buchwald, Art, 300

Buckley, William F., 26, 181

Burgess, Guy, 8, 68–71, 74

Burke, Edmund, 327–28, 329, 332

Burns, Rabbie, 246, 248

Bush, George H. W., 30, 227–31, 242–44

Butler, David, 46 and *n*2

Butler, R. A., 15, 48–49*n*7

Butskellism, 7, 48 and *n*7

Byron, Lord, 266 and *n*5

Carter, Jimmy, 18, 28, 152, 199, 242, 268–79

Castlereagh, Viscount, 266 and *n*5

Chamberlain, Neville, 152–53

Chambers, Whittaker, *Witness*, 333

Chandler, Otis, 292

Chicago, 90, 138–39, 154, 247

China, 117, 123, 124

Christianity, 11, 77, 80, 318

Churchill, Clementine, 110, 235–36

Churchill, Randolph, 72–73 and *n*2, 74–75, 76, 110

Churchill, Winston, 5–8, 41, 53*n*2, 72*n*2, 99–111, 152–53, 158, 183, 184, 235–36, 266; speeches, 41–42, 103–5

Church of England, 78, 80, 82, 83, 94, 328

Claudel, Paul, 43 and *n*4

Cobbett, William, 79 and *n*6

Cohen, Richard, 297

Coke, Edward, 77

Coleridge, Samuel, 93, 183

Commentary, 181*n*1, 186

communism, 66, 99, 117, 150, 323; Soviet, 102–4, 108–9

Congress, 16, 131, 171, 177, 219, 303

Connolly, Cyril, 170

Conservatism, 7, 11, 43, 64, 77–78, 90–91, 101, 147–50, 180–92, 265, 270–72, 283, 296, 302, 325–42

Croly, Herbert, 314, 315

Cromwell, Oliver, 264 and *n*2

Cronkite, Walter, 268–69, 278

Crosland, Anthony, 91

Crossman, R. H. S., 43 and *n*6, 77, 104

Daily Express, 22, 282–84

Daily Mail, 11–12, 22, 281 and *n*1, 285 and *n*2, 286, 290

Daily Mirror, 26, 263 and *n*1, 266

Daily Telegraph, 1, 35

Daley, Richard, 90, 139

Dalton, Hugh, 44 and *n*9

Darwin, Charles, 80

"Dead Men," 32

"The Death of Politics," 30

Defoe, Daniel, *The Shortest Way with Dissenters*, 264 and *n*2

De Gaulle, Charles, 12, 262 and *n*1

de Maistre, Joseph, 338 and *n*1

Democratic Party, 21, 22, 127–40, 160, 180, 184, 202, 228, 231, 268–79

Dewey, John, 311–13

Dewey, Thomas, 104

Dial, The, 307, 308

Disraeli, Benjamin, 140, 183, 184, 211, 327, 336

Donat, Robert, 95–98

Dos Passos, John, *1919*, 305

Dowd, Maureen, 245

Dukakis, Michael, 227, 229, 230

London, 3, 9, 92–95, 144, 148, 208, 254, 304
Long, Huey, 139
Luther, Martin, 64, 65 and n4

Maclean, Donald, 8, 68–70, 71, 74
Macmillan, Harold, 7, 11, 12, 75, 78, 285–86
MacNeice, Louis, 166
Mais, S. P. B., 169
Mandela, Nelson, 245
Mankiewicz, Frank, 276 and n9
Marías, Julián, 176, 237; *America in the Fifties and Sixties,* 237
Marples, Ernest, 66 and n5
Marshall, George C., 106, 178
Marshall Plan, 106, 155, 161, 342
Marxism, 92, 322, 323
Massigli, Rene, 42 and n3
Massingham, Hugh, 6
McGovern, George, 139, 231
McGrory, Mary, 272 and n3
McKenzie, Robert, 46 and n2
McNamara, Robert, 117–18, 302
media, 26–31, 231–32, 293–304; coverage of Challenger disaster, 343–45. *See also* press; radio; television
Mencken, H. L., 26, 146–47
Mendès-France, Pierre, 49 and n9
Midgeley, John, 37
Mill, John Stuart, 140
Milton, John, 264 and n2
Modern Maturity, 217–18
movies, 94–98, 164
Moynihan, Daniel Patrick, 178, 180, 222, 224
Mrs. Dale's Diary, 47 and n5, 48
Muggeridge, Malcolm, 47 and n4, 64, 65, 74, 76, 266n4

Murdoch, Rupert, 20, 288–92
Mussolini, Benito, 127, 152

Nation, The, 308
National Review, 26, 133
neo-conservatism, 32, 148–50, 180–92, 296
New Deal, 155 and n1, 156–58, 200
Newman, John Henry, 328, 329
New Republic, 2, 3, 21–28, 33, 34, 92, 99, 126, 151, 162, 193, 197, 203, 212, 217, 226, 240, 245, 261, 268, 291, 298, 300, 305, 325, 343; Randolph Bourne and, 305–24
New Statesman, 7, 47 and n3, 79, 81, 126
Newsweek, 26, 127
New York, 148, 153, 154, 177, 194, 195, 204, 207, 215, 304
New Yorker, 9, 68
New York Times, 89, 115, 117, 195, 215, 227, 245, 291
Nixon, Richard, 17, 18, 47n3, 149, 197, 199, 231, 241, 242
Northcliffe, Lord, 285 and n2
Novak, Robert, 271 and n2, 297

Oakeshott, Michael, 16, 33, 187, 191
Observer, The, 5, 6, 69, 71, 72, 164, 265, 290, 291
O'Donovan, Patrick, 164–65
oratory, 29, 41, 197–202, 226–33
Ortega y Gasset, José, 149, 176, 237
Osborne, John, 64–65 and n4
Oxford, 4, 71, 160, 161, 333, 337
Oxford Movement, 327–29, 340

Palestine, 5, 108
Paris, 148, 294, 304

Parliament, 4, 5, 7, 41, 46, 51–54,
101–2, 183, 263, 264*nn*2–3
Parties, The, 22
Pascal, 330, 331
Patten, Simon, 315
Pearson, Hesketh, 79–81
Pepper, Claude, 219
Peretz, Martin, 21, 24, 25
Perrier, 245–48
Pitt the Elder, William, 44 and *n*8
Plato, 330, 332
Podhoretz, Norman, 200
Pollock, Jackson, 334
Poujade, Pierre, 49 and *n*9, 50*n*9
press, 2, 24–28, 89, 195–96, 261–345;
American, 24–28, 195–96, 231–32,
268–79, 288–92, 293–304, 325–45;
barons, 280–92; Randolph
Bourne, 305–24; British, 263–67,
280–92; freelancing, 6, 34, 37;
wealth of journalists, 293–304;
George Will, 325–42. *See also spe-
cific publications and journalists*
Proust, Marcel, 142
Pryce-Jones, Alan, 69 and *n*1
Pulitzer, Joseph, 287
Punch, 47*n*4, 76, 266 and *n*4

radio, 151–54, 295
Raven, Simon, 63 and *n*3
Rayburn, Sam, 139, 197
Raymond, John, 76 and *n*4, 77
Reagan, Ronald, 17, 18, 21, 28–30,
147–50, 180–92, 196, 197, 199,
222, 232, 242, 269, 270, 301, 335,
341, 343
Reporter, The, 164
Republican Party, 21, 22, 128, 130,
136, 137, 146–50, 181–92, 229, 270
Reston, James, 273 and *n*6

Roberts, R. Ellis, 81
Rockwell, Norman, 147–48
Rome, 121, 124, 126, 141, 169, 200, 294
Roosevelt, Franklin D., 16, 22, 106,
127, 138–39, 151–61, 197, 244;
radio and, 152–54, 158
Roosevelt, Theodore, 228–30
Rosenfeld, Paul, 317
Rothermere, Lord, 12, 281 and *n*1,
282–86
Rowan, Carl, 297
Rusk, Dean, 120

Safire, William, 300
Salisbury, Lord, 101
Sampson, Anthony, *Anatomy of
Britain,* 63 and *n*3
Schlesinger, Arthur, Jr., 16, 119
Scotland, 3, 34, 92
Sedgwick, Ellery, 306
Seven Acts, 307–9, 311, 320–21
Seven Deadly Sins Today, The, 34
Shakespeare, William, 79, 329
Shinwell, Emanuel, 41, 42 and *n*1
Sinclair, Upton, 169
Singer, Isaac Bashevis, 194
Sitwell, Osbert, *The Four Conti-
nents,* 166
Solzhenitsyn, Aleksandr, 329, 330
Sorensen, Theodore, 198
South Africa, 12, 245
Soviet Union, 8, 41, 100, 108–10,
120, 123, 124, 335, 341, 342; com-
munism, 102–4, 108, 109
Sparrow, John, 71, 72
Spectator, The, 6, 7, 8, 11, 18, 41, 46,
48, 51, 60, 70–76, 113, 263, 266,
300, 302
*Spoiled Children of the Western
World, The,* 22